RUMOR HAS IT

RUMOR HAS IT

A Curio of Lies,
Hoaxes, and Hearsay

Bob Tamarkin

Prentice Hall General Reference
New York   London   Toronto   Sydney   Tokyo   Singapore

Acknowledgment: The author wishes to thank the following for their respective contributions to this book: *Contributing Writers:* Charley Custer, Jim McCormick, Mark Mravic, Maya Sahafi, Prahbha Raja, Jordan Wankoff; *Research Director:* Scott Althaus; *Researchers:* Dave Arnold, Suzanne Rollier

PRENTICE HALL GENERAL REFERENCE
15 Columbus Circle
New York, New York, 10023

Library of Congress Cataloging-in-Publication Data

Tamarkin, Bob
Rumor has it ; a curio of lies, hoaxes, and hearsay / Bob Tamarkin
p. cm.
Includes index.
ISBN 0-671-85033-4
    1. Folklore—United States, 2. Rumor—United States—Miscellanea, 3. Disinformation—United States—Folklore. I. Title.
GR105. T33 1993   92-40864
398' .0973—dc20   CIP
                    AC

Designed and produced by Les Krantz
Manufactured in the United States of America
10 9 8 7 6 5 4 3 2 1
First Edition

To Michael, Michele,
Meridith, and Elisa
who know the truth
when they see it

Contents

INTRODUCTION

Everyone, it seems, loves a good rumor, as long it's not about them. From grade school days when the kid next to you whispers, "There's no Santa Claus" (a vicious rumor to a true believer) to the resurrection of Elvis (a wistful rumor to the hard-core fan) Americans grow up on a steady diet of rumors, ingesting them like fast-food burgers in both speed and quantity.

Rumors are woven into the tapestry of our society. They shape our lives as much as our schools and churches. As you read the pages that follow, you will see just how strong a wagging tongue can be.

Is our government really covering up the UFO phenomenon? Have you heard that Procter & Gamble gives a large portion of its earnings to the Church of Satan? How about the Jewish shop-keeper running a white slavery ring from his basement? Or a certain soft drink bottler intentionally adding a chemical to render black men sterile? Did you know that a small town in Texas has an AIDS epidemic that dwarfs New York's and San Francisco's, and that the Russians are selling Lenin's body to the highest bidder? Have you heard that Paul Mc-Cartney is dead? That Elvis is alive?

Are these and other outrageous stories simply the latest rumors, or are they outright lies, carefully planned hoaxes or just the latest hearsay? Whatever they are, these various forms of misinformation represent opportunities: manna for the speculator, an edge for the competitor, hope for the loser, a dirty trick for the sneaky politician, or frivolous gossip for the chronically bored. They're juicy, savory, served up in every manner — hot, cold — and appeal to the what-if part of the brain, often defying logic.

Misinformation has caused runs on banks, long gasoline lines, hoarding of food, and even wars. Gossip, hearsay, unconfirmed reports — they circulate in society like a contagious virus.

Sometimes rumors come in clusters. On April 18, 1984, gold and silver prices rose sharply, while interest rate and stock index futures fell. The reason? A rumor-plagued day that had President Reagan being shot, Federal Reserve Board Chairman Paul Volcker resigning, a big bank taking a large loss on a Government National Mortgage Association securities position, and Iraq sinking an oil tanker in the Persian Gulf. All those rumors, in just one day, and all of them reported in the most hallowed financial publication of all, the *Wall Street Journal*.

The information mill seems to churn even faster these days, and with little regard to the validity of the "facts," which, whether true or false, can sometimes have devastating effects. For example, a politician's off-hand comments about an opponent can be transmitted via television to tens of millions of homes within hours, thus creating a serious campaign issue; a stock rumor heard in New York can reach Tokyo in seconds over the phone or fax, perhaps sending markets there plunging or soaring.

Rumors can be laughed at, jeered at, taken seriously, proved wrong, or confirmed. They've been around since creation and are a part of history and man's perception toward reality. Some rumors never die — and some die hard. Did you hear that the dinosaurs were done in by a gigantic meteorite? Or that a big bang got us going? Rumors can be a blend of fact and fiction, ironically not to be taken lightly nor summarily dismissed. After all, the notion that the world wasn't flat was once a rumor.

Rumor Has It provides a wide-ranging and entertaining look at the pervasive and highly influential phenomenon of misinformation. As you read the many rumors, hoaxes, and hoodwinks the author has assembled, you are likely to be amazed at the profound impact of things that never actually happened.

ARTFUL DODGERS

Milli Vanilli Fools Record Industry and Public

"**A**nd the Grammy Award for best new artist goes to . . . Milli Vanilli!!!"

The crowd went wild as the two handsome, corn-rowed singers walked on stage to accept their award. "This is for all the artists out there," one of them said in a faintly German accent. "Never give up on your dreams."

Dreams must have been the world Rob Pilatus and Fab Morvan were living in when they accepted that Grammy. Though they were at the time one of the most celebrated new singing groups in the world, they neither sang nor played on "Girl You Know It's True," the multimillion-selling single and album that put them on the top of the pop charts in 1988.

"Girl You Know It's True" was part of an elaborate hoax conceived and executed by German record producer Frank Farian. The hoax left the music industry with egg on its face and has engendered a continuing controversy about lip-syncing.

Farian and three studio musicians had already recorded "Girl You Know It's True" when Morvan and Pilatus approached him looking for a recording. Farian sensed that the looks of these unemployed male models were more promising than their voices, so he pledged to give them a contract after they lip-synced "Girl You Know It's True" in a promotional video. When the video, which showed Pilatus and Morvan with $750 hair extensions and waxed bodies, became an unexpected smash, Farian convinced Morvan and Pilatus to do more videos and even to lip-sync on tour.

Farian reaped most of the financial rewards from the album, but Pilatus and Morvan got swept up in the allure of stardom. They began to believe their own hype and started acting like spoiled rock stars, even demanding that Farian use their voices in the follow-up record.

This final demand was too much for Farian, who called a press conference on November 14, 1990 and spilled the beans. The press and the recording industry were outraged, though the tactic of lip-syncing was long-established. The music industry stripped Milli Vanilli of its Grammy, and Arista, the group's record company, denied prior knowledge. As for Pilatus and Morvan, all they could feel was relief. "We were afraid for two years that this day would come," Pilatus said later. "We've cried about it sometimes, that the secret might come out."

Eventually state's attorneys around the country filed class action suits against Arista, forcing the record company to refund the record's wholesale price to consumers. At the time of this writing, Pilatus and Morvan have appeared in commercials but have not released their promised album, "with our own voices on it, which will prove our talent."

Poland's Nationalist Copyright

The copyright on Poland's hymn of praise and loyalty, its national anthem "Mazurek Dabrowskiego," was reported as up for sale early in 1992, as the nation faced the prospect of turning capitalist. The copyright was said to have been bought by Jerzy Urban, editor of the popular weekly newspaper *Nie*, meaning "no," which delights in raising Polish ire with its alternative slant on things. All these commercial goings-on were somewhat uncharacteristically reported in the pages of *Nie* itself.

The selling price for the anthem, which in translation is simply titled "Dabrowskiego's Mazurka," was said to be $1.46 million. This didn't surprise one Polish woman, obviously wise to the ways of the West, who said, "You can buy anything for money."

Late in March, Urban shocked the nation from the Baltic Sea to the Carpathian Mountains by announcing that he would charge anyone who performed the national anthem 10,000 zlotys (about seventy-five cents) each time it was played. An army unit soon contacted him and asked where to send the money.

Elsewhere, consternation, dismay, and anger followed his somber announcement, which was made by an editor widely despised in Poland. Urban's had a unique career: He was originally despised as the contentious official spokesman of the now-defunct Polish Communist Party. His satiric paper, with a circulation of seven hundred thousand is, like most alternative press, lively and colorful; it ridicules the powerful Catholic church and strews sexual drawings, which many stern Polish people feel are obscene, throughout its pages.

Urban revealed just before April 1, 1992, something that the lamenters ought to have considered, since it is a national law: "The truth is the copyright runs out twenty-five years after the death of the author, so it would be impossible [to sell the anthem]," he said. Dabrowskiego wrote his mazurka in the seventeenth century, and Urban has given it spice.

Mozart Was No Starving Genius, Just a Genius

Romantic tales of the lives of artists are popular and numerous. Stories of poverty, isolation, and despair seem to increase the value of an artist's work. If these qualities make a genius, Mozart was indeed among the most brilliant. Stories of Mozart's life are full of these themes, but the tale of his death is an even better example.

The young musical genius Wolfgang Amadeus Mozart has long been the subject of reverence and fascination: reverence for his wonderful musical compositions, including a Mass for the Dead which he wrote on his own deathbed; and fascination with his remarkably odd personality and life—if you believe all the stories.

December 5, 1991, marked the 200th anniversary of Mozart's death, which along with his burial has been the subject of many rumors and half-truths. The movie *Amadeus* popularized one such misconception, that Mozart was buried in a mass grave with no mourners or ceremony, with his recent composition left unfinished and unperformed. This version of Mozart's burial complemented the theory that Mozart lived his last years financially deprived and isolated from friends, audiences, and benefactors.

Recent research by two Mozart scholars, however, disproves these legends. Volkmar Braunbehrens and Walther Brauneis have battled against the common tales of an outcast Mozart. They have documented a burial that followed the customs of the day, and sets aside all romantic rumors. A funeral procession was held on December 6 from Mozart's apartment to St. Stephen's Cathedral. It consisted of a crossbearer, four pallbearers, and four choirboys. The followers of the procession included family, students, colleagues, and friends. Baron Gottfried van Swieten, one of Mozart's greatest benefactors and supporters, paid for the funeral. A Requiem Mass for Mozart was also held on December 10 at St. Michael's Chapel. This mass was organized by Vienna's court and theater musicians. At the mass, Mozart's deathbed composition was performed.

The stories of a poverty-stricken artist unceremoniously tossed into a mass grave are complete fiction. Mozart not only received the traditional Viennese burial ceremonies, but they were organized and attended by friends, benefactors, supporters, colleagues, and family. The mourners concluded a fitting ceremony by playing his most recent, apposite composition, his great *Mass for the Dead.* Luckily for posterity, eliminating Mozart's apocryphal starving-artist compositions diminishes his genius not a whit.

Scuffed Sculptures Made Modiglianis — Life and Art in Italy

Italy is one vast underground and underwater museum of old ruins and artifacts. Everybody who swims, dives, who excavates a house foundation, or builds a well, comes up with treasured fragments of the nation's brilliant past.

So citywide anticipation greeted the day in 1984 when dredging started in the "royal ditch," a junk-strewn canal in Livorno, Italy, where it was rumored the perennially drunk painter and sculptor Amedeo Modigliani had tossed some sculpted heads seventy-five years before, after a friend criticized his work.

The city council had finally, after years of badgering by Livorno art curator Vera Durbe, set aside $35,000 to sift through seven feet of mud in the canal to see what was in it. Given the Italian penchant for burying fake art pieces in land and water, then discovering them for prompt sale in the world's art markets, the city fathers might have smelled a canal rat on the loose.

As the digging proceeded, the workmen found plenty of objects—some guns, fittings for a complete bathroom, and bicycles. After a week of work the first carving was discovered, eight hours later a second and two weeks later a third. The art world rejoiced; happy Durbe wept.

Art critic Cesare Brandi pronounced the heads "certainly Modiglianis" and very important finds. Jean Leymarie of the French Academy in Rome called them "a resurrection." The sculptures, named Modi 1, 2, and 3, were disinfected and cleaned. The three works were insured for $1.5 million, and the city went wild.

For six weeks.

Killjoy Italian weekly *Panorama* then called them fakes, with Modi 2 being made by three eagerly gloating university students who had carved it in two afternoons using a screwdriver, a chisel, and a Black & Decker electric drill, and thrown it into the canal for a lark. "Just wanted to help them find something," the students said. "It's not our fault so many people made a mistake."

Modis 1 and 3 were fakes as well, made by the more militant ex-art student Angelo Froglia who said he did it "to reveal the false values of art critics and the mass media." He even offered to show how to make a fake Modigliani: Find an old paving stone, chip it up a bit, marinate it in Livorno mud, scouring powder, and hydrochloric acid, and cook it on a hot grill.

Durbe, now crying real tears, blamed the Mafia. Critics supported her. The boys were featured in a three-hour television special where they created another fake masterpiece.

It's all in a day in the art world.

Kiss Drummer Isn't on Skid Row, But Someone Is

Who would feel sorry for a zillionaire glam-rock drummer who landed on skid row? Lots of people, it turns out. Who would feel sorry for a homeless alcoholic panhandler who conned all those people by claiming to be someone he never knew? Many of the very same people.

The confusing questions began with a headline in the supermarket tabloid the *Star*, which screamed "Kiss Star Hits the Skids." The accompanying story told how ex-Kiss drummer Peter Criss had become a street bum, panhandling tourists, drinking rotgut, and sleeping on the men's room floor of the Santa Monica pier. But there were two strange twists to this fairly ordinary tabloid tale of how-low-fall-the-mighty. First, people cared. Tom Arnold, the comic husband of comedienne Roseanne Barr and a recovering substance abuser, went out with ex-Crosby, Stills, and Nash drummer Dallas Taylor and another friend to look for the fallen drummer. They found him. Three old Kiss fans from nearby Ontario, California, offered him a place to stay. And an aspiring actress-model in Boston who said she used to go out with the Kiss drummer bought him a first-class plane ticket to come stay with her in Boston.

Then another strange twist began to unravel: When he arrived in Boston, the actress knew at once that he was an impostor. "I really almost threw up," she said. "I wanted to run out of there as fast as I could." But she was moved to help the man anyway, because "anyone who'd come that far knowing that I was going to find out had to be desperate."

And then there was the actual ex-Kiss drummer Peter Criss, who is in fact well-housed in Redondo Beach, California with his wife and daughter. Criss learned of the story while he was in New York City visiting his dying mother. She was concerned about the news. Criss was furious. And as for the exposed impostor, he was still confused. The Santa Monica street person turned out to have used Criss's name in local hospitals. "It just got to be well-known around Santa Monica that that's who I was," he explained later. "I had gotten my real ID stolen. Why I said it, I really don't know . . . I was just very confused, very mixed up from alcohol."

Criss—who, by the way, denies knowing the Boston actress—soon hired an attorney to get the *Star*. "A hundred reporters called Peter's house after the story broke," said the lawyer. "So how come the *Star* couldn't call?" But Criss was easier on everyone else, especially the recovering show-biz folks who rescued his Doppelganger from the gutter. "I want to thank them," Criss said. "I hope they keep helping this poor guy, whoever he may be."

Arnold and Taylor are also forgiving. "I was resentful we were made fools of," said Taylor, "but fraud or no fraud, the guy is a very sick man who deserves a chance." And the actress invited the impostor to stay with her and her mother until he got his feet on the ground, so all in all it seems the fraud business has it all over honest panhandling for at least one ex-derelict. "I'm trying to get healthy," he said. "Being around normal people is doing wonders for me." As for what the *Star* did, he has only praise: "They gave me $500 dollars, and it came in real handy. I'm just happy to be off the streets."

The Great Poet Who Wasn't Either

The editor of *Angry Penguins* was thrilled by his morning mail. His little literary magazine in Adelaide, South Australia, was known—where it was known at all that day in 1944—for its state-of-the-avant-garde tastes in modern writing. In the editor's hands were sixteen feverishly modern poems, written by a reclusive, unlettered mechanic who had just died at age twenty-six of an exotic thyroid disease. The poet's sister wrote in a cover letter that she had found the poems among his effects, and sent them to *Angry Penguins* to ask whether the editor, Max Harris, thought they were any good.

Harris thought they were good. He ran the poems in the next issue of his magazine, and trumpeted Ern Malley, the dead youth, as one of Australia's greatest writers. Shortly after, Malley's posthumous renown skyrocketed, and his reputation sank, when it came out that the poems were actually written in one afternoon by two authentic Australian poets, James McAuley and Harold Stewart, who were sick of the trendy gibberish that passed for art on the cutting edge. They felt that Australian aesthetes had lost all discrimination, and proved it with lines like these:

> You have hawked in your throat and spat
>
> Outrage upon the velocipede of thriftless
>
> Mechanical men posting themselves that
>
> Built you a gibbet in the vile morass
>
> Which now you must dangle on, alas.

Unfortunately for editor Harris, the hoaxters had misleading poet wits about them. Amid all the overwrought honking and tooting of Ern Malley's verse, near-genuine glimmers of poetry could be seen. A verse about poetic imagery says, "All must be synchronized, the jagged/Quartz of vision with the asphalt of human speech." There were some nifty sexual innuendoes, too.

Australians love to lay low the mighty—especially poms and fops—so the hoax was hugely appreciated by the unversed public. The police, however, begged to differ, and promptly brought suit against *Angry Penguins* on obscenity charges. A policeman at the trial offered this unexquisite though candid commentary on a poem about a park at night: "I have found that people who go into parks at night go there for immoral purposes. My experience as a police officer might, under certain circumstances, tinge my appreciation of poetry."

The judge dutifully piled injury upon insult, and fined the still-smarting editor $16. According to Australian tastes, that makes it an even better yarn, and Ern Malley has ever since held a proud, even mythical place in literary history Down Under. What's more, even at the risk of being respected by Brits for it, Australians seem to be good sports: The newest of several editions of "Ern Malley's" poems was recently published, accompanied with lengthy commentary, under the co-authorship of the older, and perhaps wiser, avant-garde literary editor, Max Harris.

Backwards Masking Doesn't Do Much Evil

One of the most persistent rumors in the entertainment industry concerns the use of a technique called "backwards masking," to encode heavy metal songs with subliminal backwards messages of evil intent. If one listens closely to the records of bands such as Led Zeppelin and Black Sabbath, it is rumored, one can tap into a conspiracy to turn a whole generation on to the powers of evil. In particular, Led Zeppelin's "Stairway to Heaven" is rumored to contain a paean to the Dark One: When played backwards, some say, singer Robert Plant can be heard incanting, among other devilish things, "Here's to my sweet Satan." Few have taken such rumors seriously — that is, until an event in Nevada and its aftermath brought the issue to national attention.

On December 23, 1985, Raymond Belknap and James Vance of Reno listened to the song "Better for You, Better by Me" on the Judas Priest album *Stained Class* for hours on end, pounding beers and smoking joints all the while. They had also dropped acid that day. After tearing up Belknap's room, they went off to a local playground with a sawed-off shotgun. "I really fucked up my life," Belknap reportedly said. "Do it," Vance responded. Belknap put the gun to his throat and blew his head off, killing himself instantly. Then Vance's turn came, but he succeeded only in blowing away the lower portion of his face. He lived three years before dying of complications from his wounds.

Five years after the incident, in August 1990, the members of Judas Priest found themselves in a Nevada courtroom, on trial in a $6.2 million product liability suit implicating them in

16

the deaths of the two young men. Prosecutors claimed the band used backwards masking to produce subliminal messages imploring listeners, among other things, to "try suicide" and "do it." Lawyers for the parents maintained that the masked messages could be unscrambled by the unconscious mind, no matter which direction the record is played. Members of the band denied they had placed any such messages on the album. Eventually, the judge rejected the suit. Those who heard "do it" in the song, he said, were perceiving merely "a chance combination of sounds" — a juxtaposition of Halford's exhaling and a guitar playing on another track. Though the ill-fated Belknap and Vance may indeed have thought they perceived some subliminal message, the judge ruled, other factors prompted their grisly suicide pact.

Musicians have experimented with backwards music ever since the technology to do so became available — the Beatles' song "Rain" contains extensive use of both backwards vocals and instrumentation. It was only after the release of *The Exorcist* (in which Linda Blair evinces her demonic possession by speaking backwards) that paranoid anti-rockers began rumoring of dark messages in certain songs. In response, some bands have had fun mocking the idea of hidden demonic messages in their works. Listeners who play one of Cheap Trick's songs at a very slow speed will hear the Lord's Prayer. And a Chicago band ·called I.D. Under has a sound-bite on their album that, played backwards, says simply, "This is a satanic message."

Paul's Alive!

Though the rumor that Elvis was alive was generally regarded as tabloid journalism at its junky best, millions of Beatle fans genuinely believed that Paul McCartney was dead. The evidence, after all, was "in."

In October of 1969, Paul McCartney, exhausted from the relentless media scrutiny that accompanied the release of *Abbey Road*, the Beatles' most commercially successful album, gathered his wife, child, stepchild, and sheepdog and quietly retreated to High Park, a remote Scottish farm. On October 12, Russ Gibb, a Detroit disc jockey, announced that he had received an anonymous phone call alleging that McCartney had undertaken a rest of a far more permanent nature — that he was, in fact, dead. The proof of this assertion, the caller supposedly claimed, lay in the final moments of the Beatles' song "Strawberry Fields." If one listened closely, through the weird flute music with which the song ends, John Lennon (McCartney's by-then estranged bandmate) could be heard maliciously chanting, "I buried Paul."

Within hours of Gibbs' broadcast, Apple Records' London switchboard was deluged with queries from reporters and fans. Company spokesmen, finding no humor in these morose speculations, curtly informed callers that Paul was in fine health, but refused to give any indication of his whereabouts. Cagey Beatlemaniacs, well aware that snippy, blanket denials invariably accompany "establishment" cover-ups, steeled themselves for the worst.

The specificity of information that circulated over the next few days about the death of the beleaguered Beatle was incredible, or, more accurately, unbelievable. Paul, it was widely said, had been killed in a car accident — a tragedy that the "surviving" Beatles had cathartically retold in their song "A Day in the Life." The accident occurred in November of 1966 (the "stupid bloody Tuesday" of "I Am the Walrus"); McCartney "blew his mind out in a car" because he "hadn't noticed that the light had changed." His funeral, it was further claimed, was depicted in the byzantine cover illustrations for the *Sgt. Pepper* album. Although a current photograph of McCartney appeared on that cover, those "in the know" revealed that the likeness was actually that of an actor named William Campbell, who had been paid handsomely to undergo comprehensive reconstructive surgery and impersonate Paul, in order that the other Beatles might continue their lucrative careers.

Sleuths soon began seeing all sorts of McCartney death clues in Beatles paraphernalia. The *Abbey Road* cover was said to be particularly replete with cryptic signs: "Paul" is depicted barefoot in the cover photograph (the way a corpse is buried in England); he is also out of step with the other members of the band as they cross the road; an automobile license plate in the background that read "28 IF" supposedly indicates Paul's age "if" he were still alive (in fact, he would have been twenty-seven). A story even circulated that musicologists could detect distinct differences between Paul's voice in pre-1966 recordings and "Paul's" voice in recordings made after his presumed death.

After a week of hysteria, McCartney's publicists, appalled by the hundreds of interwoven rumors at play on the international grapevine, prepared a press release revealing the secret but innocuous details of his vacation. Even this, however, was not enough to convince many. Only after an incorrigible team of *Life* magazine employees trekked miles through the Scottish countryside to photograph the irate former mophead did the flap begin to quiet down in earnest.

Lennon, himself the victim of a *real* tragedy a decade later, always claimed that what he had really said was not "I buried Paul" but "cranberry sauce."

Negativland Confesses

The San Francisco band Negativland recently found a second calling in satirizing the gullibility and incestuousness of popular news media. In the winter of 1987, the group released their fourth album, which featured a song called "Christianity is Stupid" (centering around a "found" a cappella sermon by the Reverend Estus Pirkle, recorded in 1968). In February of the next year, a *New York Times* article chronicled the arrest of sixteen-year-old David Brom for the axe murders of his entire immediate family in Rochester, New York. The confrontation between David and his father, a devout Roman Catholic, the article speculated, may have evolved from an argument about the youth's penchant for rock and roll music.

The following month, Negativland members, incensed by uncritical and sensational coverage of evangelical censorship of popular music in the national media, composed a bogus press release attributing the cancellation of an upcoming concert tour to pressures from a fictitious federal agent, Dick Jordon, who had purportedly advised the band "not to leave town" pending a full investigation of their role in the Brom killings (the real, mundane motivation behind the cancellation of the tour was insolvency). The release went on to imply, in a transparently hyperbolic and ridiculous manner, that Brom and his parents had been arguing about the song "Christianity is Stupid" just prior to the murders.

In the weeks that followed, Negativland received dozens of press inquiries. The group, citing federal "gag" restraints, demurred to elaborate on the infamous press release, but hinted darkly of the existence of a "bloody tape." By mid-May, unquestioning accounts of the made-up link between Negativland's music and the Rochester crimes had appeared in over a hundred publications, including the *Village Voice* and *Penthouse* magazine, despite the fact that no one had been able to verify the existence of the shadowy agent Dick Jordon, or that the real investigators had never even *heard* of Negativland. In June, the media's cannibalistic feeding frenzy reached full force, with Negativland interviews and coverage dominating the San Francisco evening news on two successive days. On June 19, a Negativland spokesman informed the *San Francisco Chronicle* that the band would no longer offer any statements about the Brom case, explaining that every previous utterance had been distorted beyond even their jaded expectations. "Sensationalism," he said, "reigns."

Fix or Fluke? Liston's Reputation Down for the Count

When Sonny Liston went down for the count in the first round of his rematch with Cassius Clay in May 1965, boxing writers joined the screaming fans in shouting "fix" and "fake," with the fans adding, "We want our money back!"

But this was big money, big enough to send righteous politicians flying to the TV stations demanding some action be taken ranging from an investigation to ending the sport of boxing altogether.

Fifteen months earlier the two boxers had met in their first bout at the Miami Beach Convention Center. There the thirty-three-year-old, previously indomitable Liston called it quits from his corner after the sixth round, claiming an injured shoulder. This was shocking, but, well, it could happen. The heavyweight championship of the world went into the hands of the twenty-three-year-old Clay, who the next day joined the Muslim faith and took a new name, Muhammad Ali.

As ever, the former champion was still worth money. How about a rematch? One was set at a high school hockey rink in Lewiston, Maine. The "Shame in Maine," as it still is called, followed.

What laid Liston low was described as a harmless-looking right-hand punch thrown by the 13-10 underdog to his face. To many it looked like a slap, and some jokesters made famous the line "I've spanked my kid harder."

Columnist Jim Murray of the *Los Angeles Times* said, "I saw the punch, and it was a good one. But the point is, Sonny was old and out of shape. I don't think he could've beaten a ten-count if he'd tripped over his shoelaces."

Melvin Durstag, then writing for the *Los Angeles Herald Examiner*, demurred. He said, "I've covered a lot of championship fights, and that was the only one I didn't think was sanitary. In my opinion, Liston either took money to go down, or the Muslims had him scared to death."

In the days before the fight, a rumor had surfaced that Muslim followers of Malcolm X, who had been assassinated, now planned to avenge themselves by killing Ali, who had stayed loyal to Elijah Mohammed through the bitter infighting and schisms that had led to Malcolm X's death. The Lewiston auditorium and training regimen was subjected to security unprecedented in boxing history.

Durslag remembered, "We heard all kinds of things at Lewiston. One theory was that the Muslims were very anxious to keep the title, and told Sonny, 'Be a good boy and take the money.' Then we heard that Sonny was scared to death that he'd be hit by stray gunfire [meant for Ali] during the fight."

The great fight was over before it had properly begun, and it went into the sports annals as one of the biggest and most controversial shocks in boxing history. Will the truth ever be known? Maybe not. But it should be emphasized that many observers and reporters believed that Liston was honestly KOed. He died in Las Vegas under mysterious circumstances five years after the "Shame in Maine," having won each of his next fourteen fights, thirteen by knockouts. Ali developed a form of Parkinson's disease and retired to his eighty-eight-acre farm at Berrien Springs, Michigan.

Jackson Defection Hoax Gets Hollywood Reporter Scribe Fired

The Jackson family is one of the highest paid clans in show business. Michael signed a multimillion-dollar deal (including incentives) with Sony, Janet Jackson is nearly as big, and even younger sister LaToya, who twice appeared nude on the pages of *Playboy*, is raking in big bucks. Other members of the family have also had hits, as members of the Jackson Five and as solo acts.

So it was definitely news — maybe not front-page news, but still news — when in February of 1990, the *Hollywood Reporter* received a fax claiming that the Jackson family was planning to begin its own entertainment company and record label, and that it was preparing to make an initial public offering of stock.

The release, typed on Walt Disney Company letterhead, also mentioned that superstar singer Michael Jackson would leave CBS Records to join a new record label formed by Walt Disney Company. Jackson's deal with Disney would, according to the fax, also include a commitment to do several films and to have Jackson design several theme-park rides.

Reasoning that a relationship between Disney and Jackson — who had already made a film with Steven Spielberg for Disney World's Epcot Center — was not unlikely, *Hollywood Reporter* music columnist Jeffrey Jolson-Colburn jumped on the story and printed it in his daily column. Unfortunately for Jolson-Colburn, Michael Jackson was not about to defect from CBS records. The fax was a hoax. Within two hours of the *Hollywood Reporter*'s appearance on the newsstands, everyone he named had denied the story's truth.

"It's a forgery," fumed Walter Yetnikoff, president and chief executive officer of CBS Records. "It's not even worth ten seconds of your time. The *Hollywood Reporter* has lost its rocker." At Disney, a spokesman said the company was investigating the incident and was planning to "take action" against the prankster.

The editors of the *Hollywood Reporter* were even more upset than Yetnikoff; they fired Jolson-Colburn despite his being the victim of an anonymous hoax. Jolson-Colburn protested the firing as being too severe a punishment but *Hollywood Reporter* editor Terry Ritzer had little sympathy. "We have no comment," Ritzer told the *Wall Street Journal*, "Disciplinary action has been taken, and it was proper."

Perhaps Jolson-Colburn should have been more skeptical of the fax. An identical fax had been sent to Claudia Eller at the redoubtable show-biz sheet *Variety*. Eller, who days previously had received an anonymous fax accusing a Disney secretary of "lying, cheating, and misappropriation of funds," became suspicious of the Jackson fax when she noticed that the same secretary's name was listed in connection with Jackson's defection to Disney. So the *Hollywood Reporter* got the big scoop, and the deep poop, all to itself.

Nice Guy Rock Hudson, Gets 30-year Pass from Tabloids and Muckrakers

Tragedy is sometimes the force that reveals the hidden part of the picture. In the case of Rock Hudson, that tragedy was AIDS. When Hudson revealed to the world he had AIDS on July 25, 1985, it became apparent that he—perhaps the last of Hollywood's square-jawed leading men—was gay and that his public persona was a charade.

Hudson's sexual preferences had long been an "open secret" in Hollywood where tolerance, good relations with the press, and a little strategic acting allowed him to live as he wished within certain bounds. He entertained friends at his ten-room house and made frequent trips to San Francisco where he could go unrecognized to clubs and discos. Even in Hollywood he rarely made much of an effort to fool people. "When we used to go out to eat or to the movies," a friend told *People*, "he never said anything like, 'Maybe I should go out with a woman sometimes.'"

Hudson was born in Winnetka, Illinois. His father, an auto mechanic, left when he was a child, and he grew up with a mother he loved and a stepfather he did not. Friends at New Trier High School thought of him as quiet with a good sense of humor.

After high school he joined the navy and in 1946, at the age of twenty-one, he went to Hollywood. In Hollywood there was no question he was gay. "One thing I can tell you," a close associate told *People*, "is that Rock has always been gay—at least as far as his adult life goes. Anybody who tells you different is lying."

Though Hudson never tried to hide his sexual preferences from his friends, he went along with his studio, Universal, which was intent on protecting its star's image. He went on dates with actress Mamie Van Doren and participated in a 1955 *Life* magazine cover story, "The Simple Life of a Busy Bachelor." His movies portrayed him as a steamy romancer, and when *Confidential* magazine threatened to expose him as gay he married his agent's secretary, Phyllis Gates. The ceremony and the honeymoon were choreographed by the studio but no amount of prodding could get Hudson really interested in the marriage, which ended after three years.

Of all celebrity AIDS cases, Hudson's was perhaps the most important since it awakened powerful political and media forces to the dangers of the disease. Then-President Reagan, who had previously never publicly mentioned the disease, called Hudson in his Paris hospital room, and Nancy Reagan telephoned French President Francois Mitterrand to ensure that Hudson received the best possible care.

Before Hudson died, his spokesman, Dale Olson, said: "It has been his desire that if he can do anything at all to help the rest of humanity by acknowledging that he has this disease, he will be happy to do that."

BROTHERLY LOVE

Stroh's Denies Link to Rainbow Coalition

Though there were many people proud to stand up in support of Jesse Jackson, the man who might have become the United States' first African-American president, there were many other politicians and businessmen who avoided supporting Jackson for fear of alienating economically and politically significant anti-Jackson forces.

Their fear was that links between businesses or politicians and Jackson would lead racists in America to vote against the politicians who endorsed him or to boycott the products of companies whose executives contributed to his campaign.

One company expended tremendous amounts of time and energy fighting an economically damaging rumor that linked it to the Jackson campaign. According to the rumor, Stroh's, then the nation's third largest brewer with $2 billion in sales, was contributing to the Jackson campaign a percentage from the sale of every case of beer.

The rumor was on its way to having a devastating effect on business when the company became aware of it in November of 1983. In December of that year, local Stroh's distributor Gene Seivers, of K & E Distributing Company in Kankakee, Illinois, told United Press International that the rumors were costing him an estimated 6 percent of his business. He told UPI he had first heard the rumor from his truck drivers who in turn had talked to bar owners. "People refused to drink

[Stroh's] because of that rumor," Sievers told UPI. "It's a racial thing, I would say, for some of the people."

Stroh's for its part vigorously denied any connection to the Jackson campaign in full-page advertisements in eight Illinois and Indiana newspapers and two trade publications. It also took steps to find the rumor's source. It hired the Investigative Research Agency of Chicago and offered a $25,000 reward to the first person who identified those responsible where such identification led to successful legal action.

The Jackson campaign was predictably depressed by the seriousness with which the rumor had been greeted both by beer drinkers and by Stroh's itself. Jackson campaign spokesman Frank Watkins told UPI the rumors were "preposterous," and added that a corporation cannot, by law, contribute to a candidate's campaign. "We know there are going to be attempts to smear the campaign," he told UPI. "If Stroh's wasn't taking it so seriously the whole thing would be unbelievably laughable."

KKK Not in Bottling Business

"Our soda was becoming the number one soda in Mom and Pop stores," Brooklyn Bottling Company owner Eric Miller told *Newsweek* in April of 1991. Becoming king of the corner grocery would have been a nice step for Mr. Miller, but a vicious leaflet and rumor campaign claiming that "Tropical Fantasy" was produced by the Ku Klux Klan stopped him in his tracks and destroyed the beverage's reputation in the African-American communities where it was sold.

Tropical Fantasy was introduced by the Brooklyn Bottling Company in September of 1990. Aimed at small stores throughout the northeast, at forty-nine cents for a twenty-ounce bottle, it was significantly cheaper than national brands, which often sold for seventy-five cents for a sixteen-ounce can. Sales were strong initially, grew quickly, and by the end of 1990, according to Miller, seemed likely to edge out Coke, Pepsi, and the other beverage big boys in the corner store market.

The brand was well on its way to reaching $15 million in 1991 sales, when anti-Tropical Fantasy fliers began appearing throughout the northeast. These fliers claimed that the Ku Klux Klan produced the beverage and that Tropical Fantasy contained stimulants that would sterilize black men.

The Food and Drug Administration investigated the claims and called them outlandish. At the same time KKK Imperial Wizard James Farrands of Sanford, North Carolina, insisted that "the KKK is not in the bottling business."

Despite reassurances, and the bizarre quality of the claims, reaction to the rumors and fliers in the African-American community was extreme, perhaps reflecting a distrust of the government's commitment to looking out for African-American interests—especially in matters of health. Anxious blacks struggling to protect their communities went so far as to threaten Tropical Fantasy distributors with baseball bats, and pelted delivery trucks with gravel.

Sales of Tropical Fantasy fell rapidly. Some stores refused to take delivery of the product. Whether they believed the fliers or not, many customers who previously enjoyed the product were not now taking any chances with their fertility.

No one has speculated on the source of the rumors, though the fact that leaflets were found throughout the northeast suggests that whoever or whatever was propagating the story was some kind of organization rather than an individual. Obviously, local and national competitors have to be considered as do any of Mr. Miller's enemies.

Bottling company owner Miller passed out fliers meant to reassure nervous Tropical Fantasy drinkers. Ironically, if the rumors continue, their ultimate victims will be the black,

Hispanic, and Asian employees of the Brooklyn Bottling Company, since the failure of the Tropical Fantasy brand would cost them their jobs.

KKK An Equal Opportunity Employer

Who's to say, after a cross burning party, that white supremacists don't pull off their sheets and head on to the symphony? Certainly not the Florida musicians who went through serious soul searching to decide if they would join the KKK Symphony, supposedly the Klan's latest effort to promote "a kinder, gentler attitude" toward itself as a "historic American institution."

The call for musicians went out to various unions in the South early in 1990: The Ku Klux Klan was organizing a symphony orchestra—all were encouraged to apply. According to a widely distributed press release, the KKK Symphony would tour the country, bring culture to various underprivileged areas, and work to modify mainstream attitudes toward the white supremacist organization. The call offered generous terms: $1,500 a week and $60 per diem. Principals would be paid more, and everyone would be covered by Blue Cross health insurance. *De rigueur* orchestral attire would, of course, be the Klan's traditional white sheet.

Among musicians, the offer provoked some difficult decisions. The early 1990s weren't exactly boom times in the American economy, and since musical entertainment is usually one of the first things cut from people's budgets, there would have been no dearth of classically trained musicians in need of work.

Would some violinists be willing to forsake a moral stand in favor of a lucrative contract? Would black and Jewish musicians, lured by the promise of "equal opportunity," be willing to apply? Would some hope that behind the white sheets they could conceal what they did for purely monetary reasons? How many might see nothing wrong with joining the Triple K's orchestra?

It's probably lucky for those caught in the moral quandary that the KKK Symphony turned out to be a hoax. Both the Center for Democratic Renewal, a Klan-watch group in Atlanta, and Richard Ford, the National Wizard of the Fraternal White Knights of the Ku Klux Klan agreed that whoever sent out the call for musicians was not acting in an official Klan capacity.

"I wouldn't be surprised if [an individual] Klansman was behind this, we're jokesters," Ford told *Esquire*. Generally speaking, Ford said, "Klansman don't appreciate classical. And about that equal-opportunity thing. Well, there wouldn't be much point to being in the Klan if there was equal opportunity, would there?"

Rat-Poison Rumor Recalls Beef

Milwaukee was embroiled in a battle during the summer of 1990 over naming a street after Dr. Martin Luther King, Jr. Some merchants on the street approved of the idea and changed their part of the street to honor the slain civil rights leader. Dissident merchants complained that the name change would inconvenience them and kept the old name for their part of the street.

Among the recalcitrant along now-divided North Third Street was Usinger's Famous Sausage, Inc., a century-old family business in Milwaukee that had a fortune tied up in labels and business stationery that would have to be changed.

In the course of the debate, a rumor was spread that Usinger sausages contained rat poison. The company was forced to recall eighty thousand pounds of meat from 150 stores and examine it. Usinger said no tainted meat was found.

The source of the rumor was a black alderman, Michael McGee, whom the mayor, John O. Norquist, bluntly called "demented." Other city council members suggested McGee fabricated the warning to call attention to Usinger's stand on the street-renaming fight.

McGee, in his defense, said he had received an anonymous phone call alerting him to the fact that an organization called the Militant African Underground Squared had injected the poison in Usinger's products. He called it an underground group, which indeed it was. The militants had no listing in the city's telephone directory, nor did they make any statement regarding the well-publicized incident.

Norquist and other council members called McGee a liar. Why, they wondered, did McGee take the story to the media instead of reporting it immediately to the cops? For their part, the police said they had received no reports of food tampering and didn't expect to file criminal charges against McGee.

Race and Eleanor Roosevelt

Minority groups have often been victims of rumors, with many stories playing on age-old stereotypes or on society's fears about a particular group's hidden agenda.

One such instance was the "Eleanor Clubs" rumor that flourished in the southern states in 1943. It said that masses of black women, especially servants, had banded together under the spiritual leadership of First Lady Eleanor Roosevelt to foment rebellion against the existing social order. Fueled by those who hated New Deal liberalism and President Roosevelt, the tales traveled wildly.

The clubs were variously called "Daughters of Eleanor," "Eleanor Angel Clubs," "Sisters of Eleanor," or the "Royal House of Eleanor." Spread with the rumors was the alleged motto of these clubs: "A white woman in every kitchen in a year."

Typical stories about these clubs mainly involved reversals of traditional servant/mistress (which often were synonymous with black/white) roles. These included alleged instances in which a white woman left her home for a while and returned to find her black maid sitting at her dresser combing her hair with her comb; or a white woman found her black maid bathing in her bathtub or entertaining friends in her parlor.

In one rumor, an "Eleanor Club" cook was called by a white woman to come and make dinner for her company. The cook replied that if she obeyed, her mistress must get up by eight o'clock Sunday morning to fix breakfast for the cook's guests. In another, a black servant offered to pay a white woman to wash her clothes. Almost inevitably, the magnitude of the supposed trespasses grew to include violent rumors of black club women saving ice picks and butcher knives for a rebellion.

These rumors were current in the last years of Franklin Roosevelt's presidency. They were only squelched—to take new forms—by Roosevelt's sudden death.

"Little Tree" Author: Klansman, Terrorist

The gentle novel you might read to your school-age child was written under an assumed name by a Ku Klux Klan terrorist with a thirty-year career of racist right wing politics. Despite his story's heartwarming details and positive treatment of its Native American protagonist, it has a disturbing subtext that suggests we have no responsibilities beyond blood kin and a close circle of comrades.

Asa (Ace) Earl Carter, who under the name of Forrest Carter authored the best-selling *Education of Little Tree*, benefited greatly from a de facto amnesty given to many Ku Klux Klan terrorists. Between 1946 and 1973, the Alabama native carved out a violent career in Southern politics as a Ku Klux Klan terrorist, right-wing radio announcer, home-grown American fascist and anti-Semite, rabble-rousing demagogue, and secret author of the infamous 1963 speech by Alabama's then-governor George Wallace that included the lines, "Segregation now . . . segregation tomorrow . . . segregation forever."

Carter organized the 100-member Original Ku Klux Klan of the Confederacy, a Birmingham group that assaulted Nat King Cole during a 1956 concert and castrated a Birmingham black as a warning to "uppity niggers."

He was cruel and ruthless, a man not to be toyed with. In 1957, he critically wounded two fellow Klansmen in an argument over finances. Though he was indicted for assault with intent to murder, the Jefferson County district attorney, influenced by the highly charged racial climate in Alabama at the time, ultimately decided to drop the charges.

Yet despite a thirty-year career as a professional racist, Carter was able to move into the mainstream of 1970s America with two best-selling books.

He took the name Forrest Carter — taking "Forrest" from Nathan Bedford Forrest, who founded the Klan in 1866 — and posed as a Cherokee cowboy, self-taught writer, and spokesman for Native Americans.

In this guise, his familiar themes and persuasions were disseminated to a wide audience. His first publishing success was *The Rebel Outlaw: Josey Wales*, a novel that eventually became a motion picture starring Clint Eastwood. In the story, Wales tries to find common ground with Comanche chief Ten Bears: "What ye and me cares about has been butchered . . . raped. It's been done by them lyin', double-tongued snakes that run guv-mits. Guv-mits lie . . . promise . . . back-stab . . .

eat in your lodge and rape your women and kill when ye sleep on their promises."

The Education of Little Tree, Carter's final book, was a gentle memoir of his supposed Native American childhood. First published in 1976 by Delacorte Press, and reprinted in 1986 by the University of New Mexico Press, the book, which bore no relation to the facts of Carter's life, was in first or second place on the *New York Times* paperback best-seller list for fourteen weeks, until a disgusted scholar and distant relative, Dan Carter, publicized Asa Carter's actual biography. Despite its heartwarming details, the book, like its author, was not what it appeared to be.

Rodney King Verdict Spawns Riots, Real and Rumored

Some rumors have the power to do great damage. They incite people to fear, anger, and action. Racial rumors are among these potent stories because of the strong feelings of divisiveness and discrimination they play upon. The damaging riots in Los Angeles of May 1992 were the result of white officers beating a black man, and being found not guilty of the crime. Anger was heightened by a videotape of the beating that was broadcast around the country. The events in Los Angeles spread anger around the country, and potent rumors sprang up to take advantage of it.

Here's what happened in the normally calm and quiet city of Minneapolis. Allegedly, a fourteen-year-old black boy was shot and seriously injured as he was riding his bicycle. White police had done this to the black boy, touching off rage and violence. Fliers were distributed in the area saying, "Earlier this evening, cops shot a fourteen-year old boy. Protest is happening. Join us." The slogan on the bulletin was, "No Justice, No Peace." People flocked to the streets. A news reporter was hit with a brick and suffered a concussion. Another media worker was knocked unconscious. A house in the neighborhood was firebombed. Some University of Minnesota students blocked an intersection in a related protest, and took out their anger at police by pelting their cars with garbage and stones.

Police enlisted the help of neighborhood black leaders to calm the situation. These leaders expanded the pool of sanity by asking others with a voice to help out, including gang members. They roamed the streets calling for peace and calm.

The rumor that caused such violence in the middle of America was unfounded. A fourteen-year old boy was shot and did lie injured, but he was not shot by the police. Rather he was injured by an elderly black man who had often warned teenagers to stay out of his front yard or he would shoot them. This boy chanced to be there when the man made good his threats. The boy was taken to a nearby medical center and underwent treatment for buckshot wounds in his chest and stomach.

Numerous rumors also floated around the much larger and more active city of New York. New Yorkers, like Americans all over the country, had watched the videotape of the beating and heard the verdict of the trial. They also watched the blazing riots in Los Angeles. But before any of these images had spurred New Yorkers to violence, rumors were taking over the city. They said the Abraham & Straus store in Brooklyn had been set afire, the Port Authority Bus Terminal was forced to close because of rioting, the bridges were blocked, and Brooklyn and Manhattan were cut off from each other. Rumors flew through the city, and City Hall attempted to debunk them. The director of public information put in many hours on the phone clearing up misinformation about rioting and violence.

The rumors that wracked cities like Minneapolis and New York in the aftermath of the Los Angeles riots seemed plausible and consequently believable. They are further proof that police conduct in the Rodney King affair was a dangerous business indeed, serving to confirm stories that ought to be wild fantasies, not challenges to justice.

Rumors Take Down a Chain Store

In 1989, rumors began to circulate about a chain of sporting goods stores called Troop Fashions. The store had branches in Atlanta, Chicago, New York, and Detroit, among other cities, and specialized in athletic footwear that was more stylish than functional. A large percentage of the store's customers were black. The details of the rumor varied from city to city but the message was the same—Troop Fashions was owned by the KKK. The Atlanta version of the Troop rumor maintained that the soles of the tennis shoes have the words "Thank you nigger for making us rich" stamped on them. Chicago's version centers around a Chicago-based TV talk show, the "Oprah Winfrey Show." It relates how Oprah had famous rap singer L.L. Cool J as a guest on her show. During his appearance he tore off his Troop jacket and declared that the Troop company hated blacks. Memphis rumor mills spread stories about the name itself, which was said to stand for "To Rule Over Our Oppressed People."

The rumors mightily damaged the company. The firm had made $10 million in the first five months of 1988. In the same time period in 1989, after the rumors began, the company made half that figure. The parent company of Troop Fashions filed for bankruptcy in 1989, and shut down all its retail stores across the country.

Was there any truth to the damaging rumors? An inspection of a pair of Troop shoes by the *Atlanta Journal and Constitution* revealed only rubber soles, no words. Nix the Atlanta rumor. A spokeswoman for the "Oprah Winfrey Show" said that L.L. Cool J was never a guest on the show. Nix the Chicago rumor. And Troop officials claim that their name is not an acronym. Nix the Memphis rumor. On top of these facts, both Troop and the KKK strongly deny any association. But the rumor lives on despite all refutation of rumors, and denials by all parties.

Many stores that carried Troop merchandise experienced hostility by blacks who believed the KKK was in their midst. An Oakland, California store received bomb threats because they carried Troop shoes. In Detroit, vandals smashed windows of stores that carried Troop. A store owner in Atlanta slept in his store, behind the cash register for twenty days, after repeatedly being hit by vandals. Troop tried to fight back and keep its business. It spent hundreds of thousands of dollars to hire blacks to promote Troop and dispel rumors. It managed to get the help of Operation PUSH, the National Association of Colored People, rap singers, and black athletes. The company distributed scholarships in Detroit, held church rallies, and printed posters and fliers against the Klan to be placed in stores. The massive publicity didn't help much — when rumors start flying, they are hard to stop. Troop continued to be seen to be in white sheets, until the only cover that fit the company was a death shroud.

White Slavers Have Submarines Now!

Sometimes idle gossip from giggling teens can gradually grow to achieve the stature of full-fledged rumor. Witness the strange events in the quiet French town of Orleans, population eighty-eight thousand, some seventy miles south of Paris. In May of 1969, several Orleans high-school girls made up a story about a Jewish dress-boutique owner, and began spreading the story among friends. As the tale went, two girls had disappeared while shopping for dresses in the store; they had, according to the gossip-mongers, been drugged by the owner, carried into the boutique's cellar and kept there awaiting sale into the white slave trade.

As the story circulated among the teenage population, and then to the adults of the town, it gained details that added to its "authenticity" — now the police had reportedly found the two drugged women in the store's cellar and brought them to the hospital. In addition, sources were claimed to be reliable — "the wife of one of the police told her neighbor . . . " and so on, although, as with most such rumors, no reports appeared in the press and police knew nothing of the incident.

Soon the story grew in complexity and insidiousness. Now not just two, but as many as sixty girls had disappeared, not just from the shop but from an entire network of stores, specifically named in the rumor, all of which were Jewish-owned. One shoe store was said to have drugged its girls by means of a hypodermic syringe in the heel of a shoe.

The town began to worry seriously. Several schoolteachers admonished their students to avoid these "dangerous shops" and beware of unwanted advances from strangers. Such unwarranted warnings simply spread the rumor and its concomitant fear. Town authorities, including the police and the town leaders, were inclined to treat the tale as a practical joke, and did nothing to quell the rumor. The shopkeeler himself did not take the story seriously at first.

In the absence of opposition, the rumor grew wildly. Now an entire system of subterranean tunnels linked the various shops together; these tunnels led into the town sewer system, which fed the Loire river; the abducted girls were being whisked through this netherworld to boats or submarines waiting in the Loire to take them to North Africa, South America, or other locales. The newspapers' failure to report the abductions, and the police's failure to make any arrests, tied into the giant plot: they had all been bribed.

The climax came on the last day of May. An unruly mob of housewives and other townspeople descended upon the shops, threatening customers who went inside. Owners expected chaos until the mob finally dwindled toward the end of the day.

Finally, the town's authorities began to take the matter seriously. Papers printed articles and editorials attacking the rumor as utter fabrication and condemning its anti-Semitic nature. Local associations issued formal protests against the rumor-mongering, and police threatened to begin investigating those propagating the tale.

There the story died, as rumors often do in the face of strong, active opposition. The people of Orleans sheepishly began to realize the preposterousness of their belief: that a group of Jewish white slavers controlled everything in the town, from the newspapers to the police and political offices. Many, of course, claimed they never believed the story in the first place.

DON'T PANIC

Hatchet Woman Spotted in Yorkshire

Everyone always moans about our modern society—people don't help each other anymore, people don't do each other favors, there is no common courtesy. The complaints are endless. But are they valid? What happens when people do help each other, do favors, and show courtesy to strangers? The story of "the hatchet in the handbag" is enough to stop all that complaining.

A story in the editorial page of the *Yorkshire Evening Post* on November 11, 1977, described the "hatchet in the handbag" tale, which it described as a story running through the gossip mill of the town. A young girl was walking out to her car during a power outage one night. She was approached by an old woman who said she was frightened in the dark, had missed the last bus, and could not find her way home in the dark. She pitifully asked the young girl for a ride to her house. The girl, being a compassionate person, agreed. The old woman entered the car and reached into the back seat to place her shopping bag down. The girl noticed that the woman's hand was large and hairy, and became suspicious and frightened. Thinking on her feet, the girl asked the old woman to leave the car to make sure that the car's back lights were on. When the "woman" got out of the car, the girl sped off leaving the "woman" in the dust. When the girl reached a safe place, she looked into the "woman's" shopping bag. Inside she found a hatchet. The author of the editorial did not know whether the story was true or not, but wanted the victim to respond so they could find out.

A similar story that had been roaming town told of a nurse who was driving, and an old woman who asked for a lift to the phone to call her husband for a ride home. She had missed the last bus — none were running now because there were no working traffic lights in the city, due to an electricity workers strike that had just eliminated the city's power. These details aside, the end of this story was the same as the published one.

These two versions of the hatchet tale spread to cities neighboring Leeds, England. They spawned other published versions. The first, in the *Bradford Telegraph and Argus* was published on November 17, 1977. The second was in a university paper, the *Leeds Student*, on the 18th of November. These articles also requested verification of the articles — everyone wanted to know the truth. Then the story exploded — by the 22nd of November, seventeen instances of the hatchet incident had been reported to police stations in the area. It began to be associated with a criminal of the time, the Yorkshire Ripper, who had assaulted eight women and murdered seven at the time of the story. The search was on for the woman driver of the car to get a description of the "woman." No one ever turned up, but the story kept running through the rumor mill.

True or not, the story serves as a reminder of modern times — things are not as they seem, women can be men, and no one is to be trusted. A good rumor for a moment makes paranoia justifiable — until reality intervenes and the world is predictable again.

Mall Slasher Makes Shopping More Exciting

"The Mall Slasher" may sound like a bad horror flick, but many believe that such a film would be a case of life imitating art. Malls try to feature carefree shopping and roaming crowds, but a recurring story has turned these bastions of placid capitalism into places of panic for many women around the United States. Female visitors to many malls are taking quick peeks under their cars after they park, and bringing along escorts to protect them from mall maniacs.

Rumors warn of young men who hide under cars at the mall parking lots. When a woman passes by, they slash her ankle tendons, and after she falls, sexually assault her. The story has it that these men are involved in a gang initiation rite.

Variations of this story have spread across the United States since it first appeared in Fargo, North Dakota, in 1978. An actual victim has never been found. The accounts, of course, revolve around the testimony of a friend's friend, or a neighbor's Great-Aunt Bertha. They are real enough to the listener but cannot be proven true. Often the rumor attributes police inaction to a conspiracy. Police and media are said to be hiding the story in order to protect the mall's business.

The tale has permeated Columbus, Ohio, Phoenix, Tacoma, Washington, and other cities. A recent example of its panic pattern occurred in 1991 in Joliet, Illinois. A caller to a radio talk show told the story of the mall slashers. His source was as reliable as the neighbor's Great-Aunt Bertha: In this case it was his sister's girlfriend's husband who worked in the local police department. His call was immediately followed by many others who had heard the same story. No direct victims called. The radio station investigated the story with the police and aired the police denial of the story.

Nevertheless, the rumor caught fire in the town. The police station had to create a special hotline exclusively for slasher stories. The station received over six hundred calls about slashers in less than a week. Each caller was told that the story was false, only a rumor. Still, the manager of a store in a local mall was frequently warned of slasher incidents by her customers. The slasher story even touched the most sacred of institutions—the church. A local pastor was about to include a warning about the mall menace in his Sunday service, but refrained in order to allow the police more time to resolve the situation. Of course, the police had already resolved the situation as entirely unfounded, and continued to debunk the rumor and defuse the panic as best they could. Meanwhile, women all over Joliet were checking under their cars, carrying Mace, and calling malling escorts.

Just as the rumor has attacked cities such as Fargo and Joliet since 1978, it will no doubt continue on to others. You'll know better when it comes to your town, won't you? . . . unless of course, your mother's best friend's daughter's boyfriend's second cousin had it happen to her!

"Mental Epidemic" Hits Mattoon

It's a truism of modern psychology that neurotic symptoms can't be so transparent that even the neurotic sees through them. Society's common symptoms of mental distress are constantly evolving, always just beyond the pale of pop psychology's explanations for them.

Think, for example, of the hysterical symptoms first popularly explained by Freud—symptoms like compulsive hand-washing, uncontrollable blushing, and fainting fits. These behaviors are far less common today than they were a century ago, because their meaning would be embarrassingly clear even to the hysterical person enacting them. Mass hysteria, too, can be embarrassingly clear—only with retrospective eyes. With this in mind, we can focus our retro-spectacles on the town of Mattoon, Illinois, near the end of World War II. Here's how one of the more sensational Chicago papers, the *Herald-American* began its coverage of Mattoon's phantom anesthetist:

> Groggy as Londoners under protracted aerial blitzing, this town's bewildered citizens reeled today under the

repeated attacks of a mad anesthetist who has sprayed a deadly nerve gas into thirteen homes and has knocked out twenty-seven victims . . .

All skepticism has vanished and Mattoon grimly concedes it must fight haphazardly against a demented phantom adversary who has been seen only fleetingly and so far has evaded traps laid by city and state police and posses of townsmen.

The story had begun a week earlier, around midnight, when a distraught woman had a friend call the police to report that she and her daughter had been mysteriously gassed. Police found nothing. Two hours later the woman's husband came home, and told police he saw a man running from the house. Mattoon's local newspaper the next evening featured a front-page story headlined "Anesthetic Prowler on Loose."

The next night, two more families reported gas attacks. The next night, two more. Over the next week and a half, nineteen more gas attacks were reported, causing symptoms such as vomiting, nausea, palpitations, and leg paralysis, from which all of the victims quickly recovered. The four cases that went before doctors were all diagnosed as hysterical, not physical, in origin. Three weeks after its first report on the Phantom Anesthetist, the local Mattoon newspaper editorialized that, though much of the recent fuss might be attributed to hysteria, there *was* a funny smell in town—blowing up from neighboring Decatur, where their newspaper had made merry over Mattoon's excitable citizens.

Donald M. Johnson, a social psychologist who studied the Mattoon "mental epidemic," noted that calls to police concerning neighborhood prowlers had skyrocketed during the great gas scare and plunged to unprecedented low counts afterwards. He theorized that free-floating anxiety in some citizens eagerly glommed onto the terrifying reports, and as quickly censored itself when skepticism increased.

Johnson wrote in 1945 that "mental epidemics" had virtually died out as a social phenomenon. Just a few years after his words were published, the great American "Red Scare" erupted, and endured for more than a generation. Amidst the changing symptoms of mass hysteria, have things changed? Today's epidemic fears—of phantom child-snatchers and molesters, for example—suggest that, far from dying out, mental epidemics have evolved into larger, national pandemics, spread to the susceptible by media eager to "report" but reluctant, or embarrassed, to retract.

Trippy Tattoos Don't Wash

The Mother's Day Out Preschool in suburban Maryland near Washington, DC, had another scare in 1990. Two years earlier, the administration had confiscated dinosaur candies in the school after a lab report wrongly found the candy to be coated with strychnine. This time, they posted a notice warning that paper tattoos called "blue stars" were soaked with LSD, which can enter the bloodstream through the skin. Police were summoned, and they promptly called off the scare.

It turned out that a teacher had received the posted flier from a friend in another city. The flier was titled "A Warning to Parents," and expostulated on the danger that children touching the blue stars could take a "fatal trip."

On the other hand, "They don't exist," according to a Fairfax County officer Bill Coulter. "Some well-intentioned individual sees [the flier] and takes it upon himself to post this thing in preschools and churches and what have you, and creates a panic among families."

Such scares over "blue star" tattoos have come up regularly for the last ten years. Police have never tracked down the source of the stories, nor defused them. "It's a phantom, it's a ghost," said Montgomery County police sergeant Harry Geehreng. "It's the most ridiculous thing I've ever seen and it just won't go away . . . It has a life of its own. You can't kill it. I wish we could find all the copies of it so we could burn them."

Part of the problem seems to be that a common form of LSD, familiar to teenage drug-users since the 1960s, can look vaguely like the washable tattoos that much younger children play with. "Blotter" LSD is soaked into paper, which is often printed with cartoons or designs on each "hit" torn off of a larger, perforated sheet. The anonymous flier warns parents that stamp-sized paper tabs — actual LSD tabs are much smaller than stamps — may have pictures of Superman, clowns, butterflies, and even Mickey Mouse, as well as the once-ubiquitous acid-laced microdots familiar to drug folklorists. Whoever is whipping up the LSD tattoo scare, it seems, can't tell the difference between teenagers and tots — and hasn't much sense of proportion.

"It's so ridiculous, it's hilarious the way this thing seems to slither across the country," said Coulter. "If it were up to me, I'd even tow a banner behind a helicopter telling people, 'Blue Star Does Not Exist!'"

But the director of the preschool, Jean Stanley, had already exercised caution, she says, by not sending copies of the flier home to parents until she had looked into it. "You don't want to scare parents, but on the other hand you want to make sure," she said. "We do seem to get this a lot, and it's hard to sift through."

K mart Kidnappers Strike

In the mid-1980s, a rumor swept through St. Bernard Parish in Louisiana that fed on parents' worst child-abduction fears — fears no doubt fanned by an increased fervor over the epidemic of missing-children reports in the news media.

According to the rumor, a woman was shopping in a suburban K mart with her young daughter when, perhaps distracted by some blue-light special, the mother suddenly realized that her little girl had disappeared. Upon being notified, the manager of the store immediately locked all the doors and searched the store thoroughly. There in the ladies' room they found the girl — with another woman who had cut the youngster's hair and dressed her as a boy, intent on smuggling her out of the store after the quick gender change.

The Sheriff's office, when contacted by reporters, insisted that the rumor was untrue, that no such incident had ever occurred in the parish, either at K mart or any other store. Nevertheless, the story persisted, spreading throughout areas of Louisiana and Texas. K mart officials were understandably vexed. They investigated the reports and interviewed store employees who had heard it told, but no one could pinpoint the source.

Eventually, the story traveled across the country, making it to both coasts. Citings in suburban Boston towns prompted the *Boston Globe* to print a piece debunking the tale. And a writer to Ann Landers, to whom many a modern Chicken Little turns, issued a "West Coast Warning," pinpointing the attempted abduction in time as "last week," and embellishing the account by saying that the poor tyke had been given a sedative before her sex-change. Landers, normally one to quash such stories, instead offered the "warning" as "a sober reminder of what can happen if a child is allowed to wander off for even a moment."

Persistent rumors can maintain an overall shape while the details change to feed off of prevalent fears. A rumor similar to the K mart kidnapping tale gripped Detroit in the winter of 1967-68, playing on the racial tensions that had plunged the city into riot the previous summer. In the rumor, a young boy had been attacked and castrated in the lavatory of a Detroit department store. The races of the victim and of the assailants were always opposed, depending on whose fears and which stereotypes the rumor was being played to; the victim normally assumed the race of the storyteller. The rumor keeps its general outline — harm to a child in a department store rest room, with sexual overtones — while exploiting whatever fear seems to be most readily at hand.

"Bloodsport" Exposé Exposed

"Bloodsport," on Denver's Channel 4 KCNC News, was ace reporter Wendy Bergen's exposé of a vicious and outlawed gambling underground. Each evening between April 29 and May 2, 1991, she took her audiences on a guided tour of suburban and urban basements where dogs drew blood and humans exchanged money.

But there was something troubling about the pictures. Where were the crowds of bloodthirsty gamblers? And why did it seem like the same dogs were doing all the fighting?

Dusty Saunders, broadcasting columnist for the *Denver Rocky Mountain News*, also noticed something wrong. On the morning of May 2, 1991, Saunders reported Bergen's main video source — the so called "anonymous tape" she claimed to have received in the mail — was actually a dogfight staged for the benefit of KCNC.

Bergen and her cameramen denied Saunders' charge, but within days of the broadcast Denver police had identified the dogs in question, and Bergen's main outside collaborator had agreed to cooperate in exchange for immunity.

What the police eventually found was that in her desperation for the story, Bergen had taken step after step away from journalistic integrity until she found herself, almost unwittingly, in the realm of pure fabrication.

Bergen's primary source for the story was Mark Labriola, a twenty-eight-year-old telemarketer who claimed to have connections in the dogfight world. After a small exchange of money, Labriola introduced her to a man named Phil Walker, who arranged a dogfight for September 21, 1990. Bergen brought a camera crew but didn't seem to notice that there were no other spectators. "I just thought they didn't want to be on camera," she told the *Washington Journalism Review*. "Once we got what we got no one really questioned it."

At the station, executives wanted footage of training and sparring. Unable to convince Walker to let her do further filming, Bergen staged these scenes with the help of her cameramen. One sequence even showed dogs working out on cameraman Scott Wright's personal treadmill.

Finally, after finding that attending a dogfight was a felony punishable by up to four years in prison, Bergen re-edited the tape to make it look like a home video. She sent it to herself and told executives that it had arrived anonymously. During the trial, these executives claimed not to have noticed the similarity between the two tapes.

"It was just one small, bad decision after another," Bergen told the *Washington Journalism Review*. "I knew it was wrong, but no one ever believed it would go to this level."

Bergen and her cameramen lost their jobs and were indicted on a total of eleven felony charges, ranging from perjury to conspiracy to commit dogfighting. After a two-week trial, the judge threw out the perjury charges and found Bergen, who did not testify at her trial, guilty of conspiracy, being an accessory, and one count of dogfighting. She was fined $20,000. Her lawyer said the sentence will be appealed.

Dobermans Prefer Finger Food

In June of 1981, the *New Times* of Phoenix ran a story about an unusual incident that had recently occurred in Las Vegas. A woman came home from work to find her Doberman collapsed on the floor, struggling for breath. Alarmed at her pet's condition, she carried the large dog out to her car and sped him to a local animal hospital. The veterinarian at the hospital quickly examined the dog and announced he would have to perform a tracheotomy on the animal so that it could breath normally. As the procedure was not for the faint hearted, he advised her to go home and leave the dog for overnight observation.

Returning home, the woman found her telephone ringing incessantly. She picked up the receiver and was surprised to hear the veterinarian's voice. Get out of the house immediately! he urged. Go to the neighbor's and call the police!

His hasty phone call had been prompted by the unusual obstruction he removed from the dog's throat—three human fingers. When the police arrived they found a man hiding in the woman's bedroom closet, unconscious from loss of blood, missing three fingers from one hand.

The *New Times* reporter had gotten the story from a local industrial worker, who had learned it from another employee, who had in turn heard it from a woman whose relatives in Las Vegas were friends of the dog's owner. It seems that the *Las Vegas Sun* had also been chasing the story, but neither it nor the local police department was able to find any proof that the incident ever took place.

Very quickly the "choking Doberman" rumor took on a life of its own. Four days after the *New Times* article, the story appeared in a column in the *Atlanta Journal*; on July 4th it was featured in a Nebraska newspaper which cited the Paul Harvey radio show as its source. August found the story titillating homeowners in Florida, and in early November the tabloid

Globe published a version of the choking Doberman story (in this case, involving a sleek black sheep dog called Tiger) that was supposedly written by a neighbor of the victimized woman. By this time the story was so widespread that an investigative journalist decided to check the authenticity of this "eyewitness" story. He eventually discovered that it had been written by a Lansing, Michigan woman who had intercepted the story in a crowded beauty parlor.

As the tale gained momentum, there grew variations in the number of fingers lost, the breed of dog, and the race and location of the intruder. By early December the story had spread as far north as Ontario, Canada. Soon afterward it jumped the Atlantic, and in March of 1982 a choking Alsatian tale was making the rounds in Sheffield and West Sussex, England. In May of that year the *London Times* picked it up, and by December of 1983 a choking dog was the talk of Australia. In all of these stories the incident was reported to have occurred locally.

Despite its rapid proliferation in the early 1980s, it turns out that the choking Doberman story dates back much further than 1981. Folklorist Jan Brunvand believes the tale grew out of several European rumors that have been circulating since before the Middle Ages. The faithful dog theme comes from a Welsh legend called "Llewellyn and Gellert" about a pooch who saves his master's baby boy from a wolf. When the master returns home and sees the dog's bloody mouth, he kills the dog, thinking that the animal has eaten his son. Only when it is too late does he find the dead wolf and realize the misdeed he has done. "Llewellyn and Gellert" was passed around Wales for hundreds of years and dates back to the 16th century, when it was imported to Wales from an even older Middle Eastern tradition.

Severed fingers are added to the story by an English rumor of the early 1960s, in which a man was said to have been attacked while driving home in his car. As the story goes, a band of youths attempts to overturn the car, but the driver guns his engine and manages to speed away. Next morning he finds four fingers that have been severed by a fan in the engine compartment. Stories like this circulated throughout the U.S., Scandinavia, and Germany in the late 1960s and early 1970s.

But even this tale had its predecessors. A similar story was collected in a book of French fables published in 1579. This one involved a sword-wielding horseman who, while returning home in the darkness, slashed out blindly at a highway robber who tried to gain control of his horse. The rider hit the spurs and got away, and in the morning found a severed hand holding his horses reigns.

As we know it today, the choking Doberman story probably started in England in September, 1973. It was then that a repairman mentioned to a professor of sociology that he had a friend with a boxer dog who came home one night to find a human finger lying behind his front door. The boxer was thought to have surprised a burglar and nipped off his finger, but no trace of the intruder remained.

From England the tale jumped to America, where it quietly acquired its most recent details — the dog became a Doberman who got the severed fingers lodged in his throat while keeping the intruder at bay inside the house — until it suddenly hit the presses in mid-1981.

And the moral of this story? The taller the tale, the longer the wag.

The Driver's Not Wearing the Pants — Is His Wife?

In the 1960s, a Midwestern couple decided to take a long, well-deserved vacation. The husband, a dentist, wanted to go all out. He bought a brand new, comfortable house trailer as well as a new car. The couple took the scenic route out to

Colorado and had a relaxing vacation. The driving, however, was beginning to tire the man. He had done all the driving because he didn't trust his wife with the strange routes and new car.

As he got back to the Midwest, he was beginning to get very exhausted. They didn't want to take the time to stop and spend the night on the road. The man decided that the only option was to let his wife drive the remaining portion of the trip — about thirty-five miles. Exhausted, and having made the decision to trust his wife, the dentist climbed into the trailer, stripped to his boxers and lay down to sleep. His wife was driving quite well when she came to a stop at a light near their home. The husband was jarred out of his slumber, and curious to see where they were, opened the trailer door. Just as he did this, the light changed and the car took off.

The distrustful husband was jerked out of his trailer and landed in the middle of the intersection, in his underwear. His wife was completely oblivious, and continued homeward. The husband ran to the nearest gas station, enlisted the aid of a gas station attendant, and was escorted home. He told the attendant of a short-cut, and they beat his wife home. Unfortunately, he did not have his house keys. He took a seat on a lawn chair and tried to continue his nap. Just as he dozed off, his wife pulled up the driveway — safe and sound. The shock of seeing her husband, whom she thought was asleep in back, ruined her perfect driving. She pressed the accelerator instead of the brakes and drove the new car and new trailer through the garage.

It sounds possible, but it probably never happened. The story has made its way through many cities, many couples, and a few books, all claiming that it was true. These stories have minor revisions but the basic story of a scantily clad husband stranded in the street remains the same. One other version describes the husband wearing striped pajamas, and when he is propelled out of the trailer he is mistaken for an escaped convict. Another version had the distinction of being carried by the Associated Press wire service. In this version, the couple are American tourists in Canada. The husband steps out to see what the problem is when his wife stops driving. She keeps driving. The police have to chase his wife to return the husband. Many newspapers picked up this story from the wire service, but it was mere myth.

This urban legend probably darkly relates to women's changing roles and authority in middle-class life. But it's also attached to stereotypical cautions against letting women behind the wheel.

What Do Rumors Really Mean? Experts Explain

In the winter, 1947 issue of the influential quarterly *Public Opinion*, Gordon W. Allport and Leo Postman, who were intrigued by the challenges experienced in controlling rumors during World War II, examined incidents that set off widespread rumors. Following the great San Francisco earthquake of 1908, they wrote, "the wildest rumors were afloat in the city." Here are four choice ones, as reported by Jo Chamberlain in the *Baltimore Sunday Sun* in 1946, and interpreted by Allport and Postman:

A tidal wave engulfed New York City at the same time as the San Francisco quake. (This illustrates the fecundity of rumor, the authors said. One big city has been destroyed, the rumor-logic goes, so why not others? "The fecundity makes for sharpening through a multiplication of catastrophes.")

Chicago slid into Lake Michigan. (As well as being fecund, this rumor also illustrates how, having lost so much—homes, photographs, often everything—San Franciscans conveyed their desolation metaphorically with a vision of total disaster.)

The quake loosed wild animals in the city's zoo, and the animals were eating people who fled to the zoo for safety. (This was interpreted as an effort at making meaning through syllogism and condensation: Wild animals were in the zoo, some may have escaped; people had taken refuge in the zoo; therefore the wild animals ate the refugees in the zoo. "Imagination," the authors noted, "often unifies discrete events, drawing simplicity and a specious order out of confusion.")

Men had been found with the cut-off fingers of women in their pockets, women's rings still on the fingers. These ghoulish men were summarily strung up on the nearest lamp post. (These hangings, the authors said, represented a "moralized closure and a fantasized revenge." The greedy men were scapegoats for a devastating act of God, Who was not at hand to take the blame.)

But we needn't take these passing terrors too seriously, the authors caution: "The fact that some of the samples seem out-of-date is itself a demonstration of the *ephemeral* quality of rumor. 'Propositions for belief' are likely to be short-lived simply because the panorama of human interest changes rapidly."

What's rather more thought-provoking is that Allport and Postman's rather dated definitions of a rumor can still quite accurately describe much of the stuff we call news.

Mandatory Reporting of AIDS Test
Spooks High Risk Groups

When people began taking AIDS seriously in the late 1980s, some public officials felt that the names of people who tested positive for the human immuno-deficiency virus (HIV) should be reported to public health agencies, in order that their sexual partners could be traced, notified, and tested.

Politicians, playing to the fears of their constituents, picked up the idea of mandatory reporting and made an issue of it.

In Illinois, state legislators proposed a bill requiring that cases of HIV infection be disclosed to the health department. In the hysteria surrounding the AIDS crisis, the bill passed the state legislature but was eventually vetoed by then-governor Jim Thompson.

The bill's passage sparked rumors about the confidentiality of AIDS tests, and the rumors wreaked havoc with Chicago's AIDS testing programs, especially during the period between the bill's passage in the spring of 1987 and Thompson's veto the following September.

More and more people called city and private clinics for appointments, saying they wanted to be tested while anonymity was still guaranteed. At the same time, "no show" rates at clinics climbed steeply: People skipped their appointments in the erroneous belief that the proposed bills were law, and that their names would be reported if they underwent tests.

In May and June of 1987, the number of appointments scheduled at the city's two test sites rose by 20 percent. No-show rates rose from 34 percent in April to 41 percent in May, then to 46 percent in June. At the Howard Brown Memorial Clinic, a private facility dealing with sexually transmitted diseases, cancellation rates rose from 28 percent in June to 39.4 percent in July, and to 56 percent in early August.

"It depends on what rumor is going around at the time," Patrick Lanahan, spokesman for the Chicago Health Department, told the *Chicago Tribune*. "If people hear the bill will become law, they try to beat the deadline. If the word goes out that somehow their names are already being reported, they fail to show up."

Why was anonymity so important? Because people who test positive for HIV are often stigmatized and discriminated against. If a person tests positive for HIV, insurance companies may cancel coverage. Employers, fearing debilitating health costs, may find reasons to terminate employment. Business associates and personal acquaintances may assume the infected person is a drug addict or homosexual, and make other assumptions as well. Practically speaking, people admitting to testing positive for HIV have a well-grounded fear of being discriminated against.

After Governor Thompson vetoed the bill, no-show and cancellation rates fell. But fear about the social impact of the disease remains and discriminatory practices toward AIDS patients change slowly.

Mass Murderer Not Such a Bad Guy

By his own count, former roofer and drifter Henry Lee Lucas committed about four thousand murders. More than two hundred and fifty cases were closed in twenty-six states as authorities rushed to wipe their slates clean of unsolved homicides. Texas Rangers escorted Lucas around the state as he lucidly, calmly pinpointed the sites of his confessed murders, which he described in detail.

Later he would recall this as the best time of his life — traveling around Texas, devouring all the burgers and shakes he wanted, and glorying in national attention.

Then the roof fell in on the overzealous authorities. Lucas recanted. He now said the only murder he ever committed was that of his mother in 1960, and he had already served fifteen years for that.

Lucas' story began in 1983 when, during an investigation into the death of Kate Rich in Montague County, Texas, he confessed to murdering her. He followed that outburst with the statement, "And I got at least one hundred more out there." Then he began confessing to murders that had occurred throughout the country, and the authorities swarmed in to hear it.

In 1985 he was convicted and sentenced to death for killing a woman known only as "Orange Socks," the only items she was wearing when her body was found in Georgetown, Texas. He received seventy-five years for the Rich murder and sixty years for killing his fifteen-year-old girlfriend, after he led police to her body.

Did Lucas kill all the people he said he had? Former Dallas reporter Hugh Aynesworth thought he had not. He wrote in the Dallas *Times Herald* in 1985 that, after a fifteen-month investigation, he believed the confessions were a hoax except for the three murders for which Lucas was convicted.

The confessions were sometimes prompted by the police, he wrote, and the Rangers had information that would have disproved some of them, but those leads were ignored or in some cases altered to match Lucas's confessions.

What was Lucas' motive? His obsessive drive to gain revenge on law enforcement by making fools out of them, which Aynesworth's investigation did. "I'm gonna show them," Lucas told Aynesworth during the investigation. "They think I'm stupid, but before this is all over everyone will know who's really stupid."

Lucas was never executed for killing "Orange socks." His sentence was commuted twice, largely due to Aynesworth, who said witnesses had seen Lucas in Florida the day of the murder. A grocer in Florida actually cashed a paycheck for Lucas that day, but the grocer said no police ever questioned him about it. Lucas nonetheless is in prison for the rest of his life.

Mock Hijacking Frightens Lebanese Immigrants

Governments and airlines around the world spent millions upon millions of dollars during the 1970s and 1980s to prevent skyjackings, the forcible wresting of a commercial aircraft from control of the crew to the control of outlaws.

A sinister pattern quickly emerged: Most of the skyjackings were prompted by terrorists from Arab countries who thought they could influence the national policies of major Western nations by kidnapping and sometimes slaughtering innocent passengers on the world's aircraft. They reasoned that the West's humanitarian ethic, which puts transcendent value on human life, would force Western nations to give in to the skyjackers' demands.

Throughout those decades world governments and the airlines made a few grudging concessions to the fanatics. But for the most part the terrorists either lost their lives or went to jail. Gradually the horror faded away.

So, asked newlyweds Joe and Sarah Fawaz of Dearborn, Michigan, who in January 1991 were on their way from Pittsburgh to a honeymoon vacation in Palm Beach, Fla., how did they find themselves on a USAir flight where two men in Arab headdresses and black shades were suddenly pushing stewardesses around and waving guns? Sarah Fawaz had just come from Lebanon to enjoy the societal peace of America with her new husband. She was terrified by the scuffling that occured in the aisle of their Florida-bound flight, and not greatly mollified to learn soon after the uproar that it was a hoax, a mock hijacking put on by playful crew members pulling each others' legs. The Fawazes cut short their Florida honeymoon as a result of the incident.

Describing what happened to the *Detroit News*, Mr. Fawaz said he tried to calm his wife telling her it was a joke. "She looks around and it's like everybody's laughing at us. We were the only Lebanese on the plane. It wasn't a joke."

USAir was repentant but unsure of what actually happened. "If something was offensive to even two of our passengers, we will not condone it, and the people involved will be disciplined," USAir spokesman David Shipley told the *New York*

Times. "We have a firm policy against any kind of ethnic slurs. But what we have discovered so far suggests that the initial allegations seem to be somewhat overstated."

At least in these turbulent times it's nice to know the airline business hasn't lost its sense of humor.

Students Have Nothing to Fear but the Same Old Rumors

If you're a student at a northeastern university that boasts a pond and a building named after John F. Kennedy, you're in trouble. If your school's key feature is an L-shaped dorm or a domed stadium or a dorm near a cemetery, you're in the same trouble. What's up? At any of those institutions you can expect a disaster, a massacre, or a murder that will occur around Halloween.

Students believed a psychic made these predictions on the "Oprah Winfrey Show," or on Cable News Network or "A Current Affair"—the source changed with the schools that heard the rumor.

At the University of Massachusetts at Amherst, one hundred women who had heard the Winfrey version called for a meeting with campus police chief John Luippold. "I think there was definitely some concern because the rumor was so widespread," he said charitably as he tried to calm the students. No such psychic had appeared on the Winfrey show, he soon learned.

One administrator, who had spent the day on the phone with worried parents, called the rumor an urban legend appearing every five years or so, usually around Halloween. Grace McNamara, who heads the communications department at Franklin Pierce College in Rindge, New Hampshire, wondered if she was getting across to her students the message of her classes. She said that when the rumor broke on campus it spread like wildfire, with some students "very upset."

Despite denials to all who called from Linda Simon, director of media and corporate communications for the Oprah Winfrey show, who said the show never featured such a psychic, the rumor struck a nerve throughout New England.

"Quite a few people were between nervous and very nervous," said Donald Stewart, an official at Wheaton College in Norfolk, Mass. "And I'm having people look at me straight in the eye and tell me they saw such a show."

DOWN THE HATCH

Pop Rocks Cause Kids to Explode

Did you know that after a kid on the other side of town ate three bags of Pop Rocks and drank a Coke, his stomach exploded and he died?

The Pop Rocks rumor was one of the most virulent of the 1970s. It started soon after General Foods introduced the product in California early in 1974 and it followed Pop Rocks as they were introduced into new markets around the country. Sometimes the rumor named an attending doctor or a school where officials supposedly searched lockers and confiscated the candy. At other times it claimed the product contained an illegal drug, was declared illegal by the government, or was reformulated by the company so that it wouldn't pop anymore. Whatever its variants, the result was always the same — abdominal explosion and death.

Pop Rocks was a phenomenally successful product. Described by *People* magazine as "carbonated candy crystals that crackle on the tongue," they were invented in 1956 by William A. Mitchell. After their introduction in 1974 the candies sold more than 500 million packages in their first five years, despite limited market access. In 1978, *Time* reported that "Kids are like junkies — hungry for the stuff," and that in New York City the street price could double or quadruple over what was recommended by the manufacturer.

To guard the runaway sales of its product, the company took massive steps to combat the rumors. It sent public-relations experts to local newspapers and brought chemists and food technologists to radio and television stations. In February of 1979, it took out advertisements in more than thirty news-papers. One of these ads, a full-page spread in the Sunday *New York Times*, cost $18,240. The ads took the form of an open letter to parents signed by "Bill Mitchell, Pop Rocks Inventor."

This virulent rumor continued into the early 1980s, years after General Foods had stopped manufacturing the product. According to urban legends expert Jan Brunvand, the rumor eventually attached itself to little Mikey, the boy who ate Life cereal by the bowlful in television commercials. Brunvand found that kids were saying that Mikey had died from the lethal combination of Pop Rocks and soda pop. Incited by General Foods' reassuring advertisements, which asked parents with doubts about the product to write to inventor Mitchell, he wrote to General Foods. The company responded, "We're sorry to tell you that the product you asked about is no longer being produced." Life manufacturer Quaker Oats, meanwhile, reassured Brunvand that little "Mikey" was still alive.

Rumor Threatens Beer's Appeal to Gun-owning Public

Pickup drivers with shotguns and rifles, urbanites with protection pistols, suburbanites who collect attack weapons as a hobby—these may not make up a majority of beer drinkers, but gun owners definitely drink a bit of brew, and they are serious about their right to bear arms.

Aware of the economic importance of this group, officials at Anheuser-Busch—makers of Budweiser and Busch beers, and the nation's largest brewer—were concerned when, in the late 1970s, rumors began circulating that the Busch family supported gun control. After all, offended gun-owning beer drinkers could easily switch to Miller, Coors, or a myriad of other low-priced beers.

To combat the rumor, Anheuser-Busch bought full-page ads in outdoor magazines. These ads disclaimed support for gun control, and in fact emphasized the company's support for the right to bear arms. When anti-gun control forces called the company to inquire about the rumor, operators asked them to identify their source so the company could take legal action. These efforts were largely successful and by 1979, Anheuser-Busch was receiving few, if any, inquiries about the matter.

Unfortunately for another beer manufacturer, the rumor did not disappear in the late 1970s. It just migrated. In 1978, the Adolph Coors Company suddenly became the focus of gun-control rumors. Like Anheuser-Busch, Coors wasn't about to alienate the gun-owning public. It battled the rumor with news interviews, provided denial notices for retail stores, and sponsored local gun clubs and trap shoots. It even helped produce a pro-hunting documentary film. People who inquired about the rumor received an emotional letter from W. K. Coors, who was then chairman and chief executive.

"It would be an outrageous disregard for my own personal safety to support gun-control legislation," Coors' letter read in part. "Ever since my brother was murdered nineteen years ago in an abortive kidnap attempt, I have always had a gun close by for my own personal protection. I am well prepared to use it and to use it effectively if need be. My personal arsenal comprises of two shotguns, a hunting rifle, and two handguns, and I am proficient in the use of all of them."

Beyond the pros and cons of gun control, and whether or not anyone at either company has an opinion on the subject, the rumors about Anheuser-Busch and Coors demonstrate the essential neutrality of capitalists on these issues.

Our Psychic Dark Continent
Illumined by Archetypal Bananas

Ever hear the one about the snake that crawled out of a banana and bit and killed a child? It's older than the United Fruit Company and ranks in popularity, even today, with such perennial rumor-legends as tooth fillings operating as radio receivers, pets exploding in microwave ovens, and spiders buried in beehive hairdos.

But why are bananas always killer cobra-carriers, and not peaches or plums, which also may come from the tropics? The banana-snake connection has been around a long time, say folklorists, the Union of Banana Exporting Countries (UBEC, the OPEC of bananas), and Cubans, who began exporting them to the U.S. in 1804. But unlike most rumors, the snake in the banana bunch story varies little as it travels. The rumor always involves a banana, always a snake, and always a person who is bitten and dies.

In Sweden, land of banana eaters, people panicked when they first heard the story about what happened in the town of Boras: A mother bought a bunch of bananas and gave one to her little boy, telling him to sit in the kitchen while she did housework. Soon she heard him shout, "Mum, something is moving inside my banana." "Sure," she said, "ha, ha, ha." Then she found him dead, the half-eaten banana clutched in his hand. He had been bitten by a miniature cobra.

The story moved west to Gothenburg, then to Stockholm, across the Baltic to Finland, and on over the Atlantic, back to the Americas. Nowhere in all the rumor's travels had there been a report of anybody being bitten and killed by a snake in a banana.

As a matter of fact, according to a curator at the Museum of Natural History in Gothenburg, snakes and spiders have indeed been found in cargo spaces carrying the delectable fruit around the world, but that was before bananas were gassed and dipped in preservatives before they left the exporting countries. Snakes hiding inside bananas simply could not exist, he said.

Which brings us to the reason that this rumor always involves bananas, and not peaches or plums. A Swedish sociologist, Bengt af Klintberg, thinks he has the answer. He says the myth "tells about a poisonous . . . snake from a distant, exotic country. Dangerous insects and reptiles do not belong to our modern Western milieu . . . The legends [about snakes and spiders] point out the difference between our civilized world and a primitive world where poisonous spiders and snakes are prevalent. They are smuggled into our everyday world hidden in bananas and potted plants, undermining our security. One may see them as symbols of the wildness and potential danger of the Third World."

Weigh that thought the next time you bite a banana.

Mexican Beer Sales Suffer

The ingredients in most beers are similar: It's the way the beer is brewed that makes most of the difference in taste. A story circulating about Corona Extra beer, however, claimed that it had a unique ingredient. The added twist was urine. The story was false, but had spread around the country and eaten into the profits of this popular import beer.

The story that Corona was contaminated with urine spread from Reno, Nevada, to Los Angeles and Orange County, northern California, Phoenix, Seattle, Boise, Aspen, Minneapolis, and Milwaukee. In fact, it pretty much roamed the country. The story caught on quickly because of the popularity of the beer, the popularity of rumors, and, perhaps, the popularity of each when under the influence of the other.

The company that imports Corona into the United States, Barton Beers, allegedly traced the rumor to its origins and filed a $3 million law suit. They contended that the urine story was initiated by a rival importing company, Luce & Son, which imports the most popular foreign beer, Heineken, and several others. It was alleged that the rumor had been initiated to try to cut into the spectacular and sudden success of Corona Extra in the import beer market. Barton Beers took action against Luce & Son and settled out of court. The settlement? Luce & Son had to publicly declare that Corona was not contaminated with urine. The company charged with testing the ingredients of beers has never found that Corona was contaminated with urine. The president of the testing company stated that Corona was "a pure product with no contamination." These reports had virtually no effect on the rumor, however, and other companies jumped on the bandwagon, continuing to spread the urine story in hopes of ruining their competition.

Corona sales suffered. The beer had enjoyed major success in a short time, having entered American markets in 1981 and quickly becoming the favorite of California surfers. The tastes of the surfer dudes rubbed off on others, and Corona jumped to the position of second-highest-selling import beer. All this changed after the urine-word flooded the markets. Areas subject to the tale experienced sales drops as much as 80 percent in only a few weeks.

Rather than sit on the story, Corona importers have decided to fight back and face the rumor, openly addressing the fact that people around the country hesitate to drink their beer because they don't want to drink urine. Considering that the pet name for domestic American beers among premium beer drinkers is "piss- water," the beer-ad biz just may get more interesting.

Watch Out for Swedish Rat Food

A group of students were eating together at a restaurant in Stockholm, in September of 1973. They had chosen an Italian pizza restaurant, and were having a wonderful time when one girl suddenly found that she had something hard stuck in her tooth, and she could not remove it. The evening passed, and the girl still had the painful object stuck in her mouth. She did not know what it was or how to get it out. The next day she went to a dentist to have the object extracted. When the dentist managed to remove it, he told her what it was—a rat's tooth.

Disgusted, the girl went to the National Health Board to report the Italian restaurant as unsanitary. The National Health Board investigated the restaurant, and discovered a freezer full of flayed, deep-frozen rats. Does this story sound like enough to make you stop eating pizza in Stockholm, or anywhere for that matter? The rumor spread around the city, leaving in its wake a mass of disgusted pizza eaters. A Swedish paper, *Dagens Nyheter*, published a similar version of this tale in its popular morning edition.

Another story was circulated within a month of the pizza rat story. The concepts were the same, but the setting had changed. Now a group of Swedish tourists were enjoying Greek food on the island of Rhodes, when one of them almost choked while eating his chicken salad. The man had choked on a rat bone. An inspection was carried out and once again deep-frozen rats were found in the kitchen of the restaurant. This story found its way into a provincial paper. From there it spread to the front page of the famed *Dagens Nyheter*, as well as a large number of other Scandinavian papers—all within a week of the first published account. A twist was added to this rat story—a diplomatic move made by the Swedish superintendent of the Food Office. He mentioned, in an interview carried by many newspapers, that rat flesh is entirely safe if well cooked, and that Swedes did not have anything against Greeks if Greeks should happen to be habitual rat eaters.

It is doubtful, however, that either story is true, despite the fact that it was well reported by many newspapers. The stories resemble each other too strongly—rat remnants in foreign food. The fact that the foreign restaurant is crucial to the story adds to the idea that it is just a long-lived rumor. People have long been wary of eating foreign food—many shy away from delicacies such as frog legs, alligator, and snails. Many have a deep suspicion of foreigners and strange things. Stories that show distrust of foreign foods are very old. These two incidents are seemingly based on older myths. In other Scandinavian cities, the offending restaurant was said to be Chinese, the remnant was a rat bone, and the delicacy was a spring roll. This story had been reported by a Danish paper in 1973, but was reported as a rumor without factual basis. The story also traveled to France where a Chinese restaurant was also the purveyor of a rat's tooth in 1971. But England takes the prize for the earliest pseudo-episode. A 1960s story had Chinese restaurants fully stocked with flayed cats.

So our friend in the Italian pizza restaurant in Stockholm most likely never existed. She was just the latest version of a tale that started years earlier and preys upon a fear of the foreign. Remember the many variations the next time you hear of rat or dog or cat remains at funny little foreign restaurants.

Manna from Heaven, Burgers from Hell

On August 25, 1977, public relations officers for fast-food visionary and multinational burger meister Ray Kroc, received three separate inquiries about contributions made by the McDonald's founder to the distinctly unsavory Church of

Satan. By Christmas, thirteen such queries had been noted, ten of which were postmarked from Ohio or Indiana. By January, rumors of the Big Mac/Big Black connection had jumped the borders of the Ohio Valley and were spreading through Texas, Arkansas, and Oklahoma.

Details recounted in say-it-ain't-so letters from clergymen, customers, and McDonald's owner-operators were remarkably consistent. The correspondents related, almost invariably, that a friend, co-worker, or relative had heard Kroc boast that he gave 35 percent of his income to the Church of Satan on the "Tonight Show," "60 Minutes," "Phil Donahue," "Merv Griffin," "Tom Snyder," or the "Today" show.

By mid-1978, news of Kroc's supposed pact with the Dark One had found its way into dozens of church-based newsletters, despite the chain's panicky mailings to thousands of religious groups (which included disclaimers and actual episode transcripts from the producers of every suspect television show, as well as letters of support from Billy Graham, Jerry Falwell, and other national religious leaders). Ironically, however, just as the crisis reached its apogee in the summer of '78, with boycotts planned nationwide, public attention was drawn away by an even more pernicious and silly rumor that fellow burger giant Wendy's had admitted to fortifying their hamburger meat with red worms. So the worm turns.

Orange Terrorists Strike

The war between Israel and the Palestinians has been fierce for many years, and has often taken untraditional forms. In January 1978, a story began to circulate that threatened Israel's economy. On a routine trip to the supermarket, a housewife in Holland bought three and a half kilograms of Jaffa oranges, imported from Israel. A member of her family bit into an orange, noticed an odd taste, and saw a silver liquid in the fruit. The housewife took the fruit to the authorities to have it examined. Four oranges in the bunch contained liquid mercury. Dutch newspapers, being effective media hounds, reported the story to the public the very next day. Within a few days the newspaper received a letter regarding the poisoned oranges from a Palestinian organization that claimed responsibility. The news spread around Europe and some poisoned oranges were found in other countries, with other newspapers also receiving letters of responsibility from Palestinian groups. Sales of Jaffa oranges dropped drastically.

It is unclear whether Palestinians actually poisoned the fruit or simply took advantage of the situation. The newspaper stories may well have served as an opportune instruction guide for Palestinian sympathizers who bought Israeli oranges, injected them with thermometer mercury, and returned them to the store. It is doubtful that the rumor of Israeli mercury oranges is fully true, because many of the poisoned oranges were from countries other than Israel.

The mercury oranges did not cause harm to any one, nor were they a good terrorist threat because the combination of mercury and oranges is very visible. Still, the story spread quickly enough to have an impact on the Israeli economy. Clearly, rumors can be a continuation of war by other means.

The Leaflet of Villejuif: Vitamin C Causes Cancer

Chemicals like disodium inosinate, disodium guanylate, calcium carbonate, and trisodium phosphate are unfamiliar to most people . . . for all the general public knows, these chemicals could be carcinogens. They could cause bizarre, irreversible, crippling conditions. Or they could be perfectly harmless food additives which is, in fact, what they are.

Rumors about these obscure chemicals are imaginable enough, but in France there has been a persistent rumor about a substance most people know is safe—citric acid, the chemical found in citrus fruits.

In the spring of 1976, simple typewritten leaflets began appearing in France referring to research conducted at "a hospital in Paris." The leaflets urged French consumers to boycott products containing certain food additives, which it claimed were carcinogens.

The leaflet—which was later modified to claim its research had been conducted at the Hospital of Villejuif, an internationally famous cancer research center—asserted that E330 was the most carcinogenic food additive. Under the European system, which uses coded ingredients to overcome language differences, E330 refers to citric acid. Since few people knew the code, many took the leaflet seriously.

France's major food companies picked up on the rumor almost immediately. But though Coke, Schweppes, Martini, Amora Mustard, Banga Orange Juice, and other products were named explicitly, Coca-Cola, Cadbury-Schweppes, Martini, BSN, and Gervais-Danone were not able to formulate a common response to stop the rumor's spread.

Concerned citizens, unaware of the leaflet's falsity, photocopied it and distributed it to their friends and neighbors. People handed it out at school or at the entrances of banks, supermarkets, factories, and offices. Nurses gave it to patients, and doctors posted it in offices. Probably the worst offender in spreading the mass poisoning rumor was the press. Not the national press, but rather local, specialized, in-house association bulletins and magazines were responsible for spreading the panic. The leaflet was even reprinted in a textbook on natural science for primary school pupils.

Eventually, the leaflets reached at least half of France's general population. Among people who had read the leaflet, reaction was mixed. Of a group tested by a French public opinion research organization, 12 percent posted it in their homes; 20 percent used it when shopping; 40 percent talked about it with others; 3 percent photocopied it for distribution; 2 percent gave it to somebody else; and 39 percent did nothing.

While the leaflet continues to appeal to the country's doubts about the industrialization of the food industry, and some people obviously believe its claims, it is difficult to pinpoint effects. According to J. N. Dapferer, writing in *Public Opinion Quarterly*, sorting out the variables that affect a product's sales is quite difficult; no sharp drop in consumer sales clearly attributable to a boycott was ever noticed.

MEDIA MADNESS

HIV Counselor Tries Scam

In tiny Bogota, Texas, people panicked when Dona Kay Spence, an AIDS/HIV case manager for the Texarkana-based Ark-Tex Council of Governments, revealed she was counseling six HIV-positive students at Bogota's Rivercrest High School.

Six cases in a population of 197 students at Rivercrest gave the area an HIV rate six times the national average. News of the outbreak spread through Texas and eventually reached the national media. Soon members of some opposing sports teams refused to play Rivercrest or to shake their hands if they did compete.

This outbreak of AIDS-related hysteria seemed even more extreme once the Texas Department of Health concluded that Spence's report was a hoax.

Spence first revealed the "situation" to the nearby *Mount Pleasant Daily Tribune*. Just before Christmas in 1991, a stunned Bogota school board called Spence into a closed session where—citing state and federal law—she refused to divulge the names of the students in question. None of the cases involved drug use, she told the board, and only two were the result of homosexual activity. Instead, she blamed rampant heterosexual sex. "We knew we had sexually active college kids," she later told *People* magazine. "But all this business on the high school level will surprise some people."

The controversy grew quickly, and soon some began looking suspiciously at Spence herself. She was planning to open an AIDS center on April 1, 1992, and critics wondered if she was using the HIV epidemic to help raise funds. U.S. Attorney Bob Wortham of Beaumont, Texas launched an investigation, as did the Texas Department of Health.

As reports of the outbreak began reaching the national media, newspapers and magazines also began investigating Spence. She claimed she held a nursing degree from the City College of San Francisco and had served two tours of duty as a nurse in Vietnam. In fact she had attended, but never graduated from, the City College of San Francisco and had never been to Vietnam, though she had served in both the army and the air force.

Given these claims and the fact that in August of 1992, the Texas Department of Health reported it could find no evidence to support Spence's claims of six infected students at Rivercrest, nor of any of Spence's other claims about school-age children, most observers have discounted her reports. Nevertheless, Dr. Charles Bell of the Texas Department of Health told the *New York Times* the existence of these cases is indeed possible if "all . . . these people gave her made-up names and birth dates."

Hughes Hoax Tops Everything

Watching the normally conservative publishing industry eagerly pay whopping sums for "authentic" pieces by or about famous people is a spectacle all by itself. But it is nothing compared to the spectacular squirming of editors and their financial backers, when they find they've been bilked of millions of dollars.

One of the greatest of literary hoaxes is the "authorized" biography of Howard Hughes, the reclusive billionaire. Hughes had long fascinated the media. His activities were the subject of intense interest: his rise as an industrialist, his experimental airplanes, his Hollywood directorial adventures, his liaisons with starlets, and his final retreat into a Las Vegas penthouse, where it was whispered, he kept a germ-free environment and never cut his nails.

In 1971, a little-known author named Clifford Irving contacted New York publisher McGraw-Hill with the claim he could provide an "authorized" biography of Hughes. McGraw-Hill's normally skeptical and conservative management realized the hot property such a book would be and began negotiating with Irving, eventually agreeing to pay him, along with his German wife Edith and their collaborator Richard Suskind, a $750,000 advance.

McGraw-Hill executives had to trust Irving and his associates because the reclusive Hughes could not be expected to confirm or deny any relationship with Irving and his associates. Moreover, to cover its own costs, McGraw went on to sell worldwide syndication and magazine rights to *Life* magazine.

For a year Irving and his collaborators lived high off the hog — and themselves became celebrity figures on the literary circuit.

In 1972, the scam came crashing down. A variety of circumstances — including Irving's own marital indiscretions in Mexico, where he was supposed to be interviewing Hughes — led McGraw-Hill and law enforcement officials to discover that Irving and his collaborators were selling a fake.

Imprisoned and forced to return the money, the experience destroyed Irving's marriage and left him close to $1 million dollars in debt. After being released from prison he eked out a living in Long Island as a travel writer, published a few books, and eventually moved to Mexico with longtime girlfriend Valdi Sherwood. Despite modest publishing success, he told *People* magazine he felt the publishing industry was still trying to punish him for his hoax. "There's a boycott of my work among many publishers. To me it's the depths of pettiness and vindictiveness," he complained.

Edith Irving got a divorce from Clifford and married Long Island lawyer Bill Maloney. She, her husband, and the two sons she had with Clifford eventually moved to the Spanish island of Ibiza.

Wedding Photo Hoax Angers Duped Newspapers

There's someone for everyone, or so the saying goes.

That saying must not have been far from the collective minds of the *Seattle Times* and the *Austin American-Statesman* when each received prank paid wedding announcements.

On July 16, 1991, the two papers were victims of separate but similar pranks by morning radio disc jockeys.

In Austin, KLBJ-FM morning disc jockey Dale Duddley dressed up in a formal white wedding gown and had his picture taken with his co-host, Clark Ryan, who wore a tuxedo. The photograph of "Delana Marie Epstein" and "Larry Nack" was sent to the *American-Statesman*, which printed it that Sunday. The following Monday, the station held a contest about the bogus announcement. One of six listeners who spotted the phony photo was awarded $94.

American-Statesman publisher Roger Kintzel, already victim of an earlier KLBJ hoax, was not amused. He canceled an advertising agreement between the paper and the radio station and announced that the paper would no longer participate in promotional activities with the radio station. "After they pulled the first stunt," he told *Editor & Publisher* magazine, "I wrote the manager that that sort of thing was unacceptable at the paper . . . I made it clear we can't accept false advertising, and I told them what the risks were."

At KLBJ, disc jockey Duddley thought Kintzel was getting hot under the collar for nothing. "I don't know why he got so mad," Duddley told the *Austin Business Journal*. "We probably sold more Sunday papers than they've sold in years."

In fact, KLBJ station manager Ted Smith claimed that since KLBJ had an advertising agreement with the *Statesman*, the *Statesman*'s advertising department must have known that the photograph came from the radio station.

The hoax in Seattle was similar to the one in Austin. Morning disc jockeys Alan Budwill and Kent Phillips posed in a gown and tuxedo and sent their picture to the *Seattle Times*. But to beat the *Times*' more stringent verification process, they had to convince their parents and even a church pastor to lie when *Times* fact checkers called.

The *Times*, which seems to appreciate a good practical joke, was nevertheless unappreciative of being made to publish false information. "Looking at the picture," assistant managing editor for features Patricia Foote told the Associated Press, "I have to recall what my mom used to tell me about strangely matched couples: 'There's someone for everyone.' Fortunately, Kent and Alan seem to have each other."

Are Bloodmobiles Delivering AIDS?

Rumors and misconceptions about AIDS and HIV seem to spread with speed and virulence that puts the actual virus to shame. The employer sanctions and social stigma that are the common lot of HIV-positive people make public dread, and whispered fears, all the more virulent. According to one recent rumor, even being tested is dangerous. The whisper mill maintained that Red Cross Bloodmobiles were infecting people with the very thing they were desperate to avoid.

It was students at high schools in Charlotte and Winston-Salem, North Carolina, who heard the word, in May 1992, that students donating blood in the mobile labs later tested positive for the AIDS virus. In Raleigh, North Carolina, twenty-two of 185 students were said to have tested positive.

Red Cross officials were quick to point out that nobody has ever gotten HIV by giving blood. They said similar rumors were spreading through high schools nationwide, after starting at black colleges in Tennessee and North Carolina in November 1991, when basketball star Magic Johnson announced that he had the AIDS virus.

The Red Cross immediately undertook media campaigns in the three North Carolina cities stung by the rumor. The campaigns undercut the bloodmobile rumors, but no doubt many more such stories will come.

Nonexistent Skinheads Attack
Shock Talk Show Host

Remember Morton Downey, Jr.? He was a master at whipping up controversy, and his syndicated "talk" show often seemed on the edge of violence.

Racial and anti-homosexual epithets flew freely, and fists were always tensed. It was not uncommon to see belligerent gay-bashers, racists, or Nazis lunge at often equally belligerent homosexuals, Jews, and blacks. Unlike most talk show hosts, Downey was not a conciliator or mediator. He posed questions in the most inflammatory, even hurtful, way he could.

His most common guests by far were skinheads — the youthful racists who were offshoots of the 1980s punk subculture. With shaved heads and combat attire, their almost clean-cut looks belied a radically violent, racist agenda. Often skinheads would appear with selected Jewish and black leaders. Critics have suggested that Downey sometimes orchestrated the show so that for moments the skinheads and blacks would actually ally against Jews.

Downey's exploitive exploration of the dark side of American race relations became very popular television fare during the latter half of Reagan's second term. But by 1989 his formula was becoming his downfall. Besieged by protests from community leaders and discouraged by sagging ratings, station managers pushed the show later and later into late-night oblivion.

In April of 1989, Downey left his New York base and went to San Francisco to do some shows on the West Coast. His flight went as scheduled but before he could leave the airport, Downey claimed, he was grabbed by three skinheads who dragged him into a rest room, cut off a clump of his hair, and drew swastikas on his face and clothing. Such an attack would have been a shame, but in this case there's reason to believe it never happened.

"We can't say for certain this is a hoax," Ron Wilson, director of community affairs at San Francisco Airport, told the *Boston Globe*, "However, after completing our investigation, we've found not one shred of evidence to substantiate any of Mr. Downey's claims."

In the rest room in question, investigators found the scissors and pen used in the incident. Outside there were no skinheads in sight and a witness who'd recognized Downey heading into the men's room swore there had been none then, either.

"The rest room sits in the middle of the terminal." Wilson explained. "It's extremely visible. The witness says Mr. Downey spent about fifteen minutes in there and came out with his daughter and a member of his staff."

Former "Downey Show" producer Jim Langan was probably right when he characterized the stunt as the "act of a desperate man."

Californians Attack Mickey Mouse

As the date of *Fantasia*'s San Francisco showing approached, members of the Coalition Against *Fantasia*'s Exhibition increased their activities. The group—an association of Bay area organizations and activists who opposed the Disney animated film's showing because they found certain of its themes unacceptable—sent out press releases, held rallies, and spoke of their concerns to various news organizations.

Dieters United claimed the film's hippos in tutus were offensive to overweight people. Another group, SPASM (Sensitive Parents Against Scary Movies), argued that some scenes were too frightening for children. Anti-drug groups claimed that dancing mushrooms and animated poppies glamorized the use of opium and hallucinogenic drugs, while BADRAP (Bay Area Drought Relief Alliance Party) contended that Mickey Mouse's waste of water in the "Sorcerer's Apprentice" segment sent the wrong message to northern Californians who badly needed to conserve what water they had.

Newspaper editors felt these were all legitimate concerns that right-thinking people might very well have. The local media, including the *San Francisco Examiner*, were quick to cover the protest. On a national level, *Time* mentioned the group in a cover story on our new nation of whiners and crybabies. Soon, *Washington Post* reporter Henry Allen picked up on the *Time* story and used it in his own article, "The Politics of Tuna and Tutus," which was reprinted in other newspapers.

The protests and the media's reaction to them was an exhibition of sensitivity and understanding that showed just how far newspapers and magazines had come in understanding the feelings of diverse minorities and interest groups. No one could have felt more satisfied by this coverage than the pranksters who organized the protests.

In late March, 1992, the Coalition Against *Fantasia*'s Exhibition announced that it and its subgroups' existence was an April Fool's joke. It was, said Peter Doty, an assistant janitor for an acting company, "a way to show that within the media there are those who will buy almost anything. Few media people bothered to check up on us to see if we were real." The prank was, he added "a challenge. We were taking ridiculous arguments and making them appear legitimate."

Media people with the greatest of ease deconstructed their authority in the aftermath of the hoax. *Time* correspondent Edwin Reingold said "It was a perfect anecdote for that story . . . . Nothing surprises you anymore." The *Post*'s Allen said "All I know is what I read in *Time*." Rob Morse, who mentioned the protests in the *San Francisco Examiner* said, "I've been in San Francisco so long, I tend to believe anything . . . You've got to go pretty far in San Francisco to make something look like a joke."

To CNN Senior Staffers:
Please Double-Check All Hoaxes

An off-camera supervisor's shout of "Stop!" saved Cable News Network from broadcasting a false report of President Bush's death at a Japanese banquet. The harrowing incident caused the Atlanta-based news network to pull out all stops in its continuing efforts to make certain that unconfirmed rumors never hit the airwaves.

A seventy-one year old Idahoan, James Edward Smith, posing as the President's doctor, called the station on January 8, 1992, three hours after Bush collapsed at a Japanese state dinner from stomach flu, and said that Bush had died. He left his phone number. Tracked down later, the masquerader was hustled to a private mental facility in Garden City, Idaho, for observation.

CNN Headline News anchor Don Harrison began to report "tragic news" at 9:45 a.m. EST, but before he could say another word, the shout came. Harrison nimbly shifted gears and read another report stating merely that the President was ill. Unconfirmed information, given by an unidentified caller, was slipped into a computer by a typist and nearly made it over the air. The station immediately reinforced requirements that senior staff members must be notified when important bulletins hit the centralized computer. That computer is also used by CNN's subsidiary operation, the Headline News Service, which edits down longer CNN news stories for people on the run. It was not revealed whether any staff members were reprimanded.

Maury Green, a retired Los Angeles newscaster, observed, "It's a perennial hazard on TV these days when instantaneous news is reported as it is happening. A newspaper has a little more time to check, but a TV network is just more susceptible to a hoax than other media."

But, Green pointed out, drawing on his experience many years ago as a reporter for the *Chicago Tribune*, preventing suspect reports from making headlines can also leave the media with egg on its face.

"In 1939, at the *Tribune* we hired a Berlin correspondent named Sigrid Schultz,'" Green recalled. She was told to warm up to the Nazi big shots and learn when and where war would break out. There followed detailed reports to the paper on tanks thundering into Poland, but the shirts and ties in the newsroom at the time refused to replate the front page of the morning editions until the story was confirmed by the Associated Press, which of course swiftly blanketed the country with the grim news.

"We could have scooped every newspaper in the nation by four hours if we had believed our own correspondent," Green said.

There's Gold in Them Thar Gallerias

The brash *New Times,* Phoenix's alternative to the two stodgy newspapers owned by Vice President Dan Quayles' family, the *Arizona Republic* and the *Phoenix Gazette,* started the gold rush in the Galleria, a shopping mall in affluent Scottsdale. In its December 4-10, 1991 issue, the *New Times* reported that a gold mine had been discovered below the Galleria's men's room. By December 19 more than one thousand people had swarmed over the mall in what can only be termed an idiotic "rush," bearing out the truth underlying a joke told by former Arizona Senator Barry Goldwater that the desert sun produces "right-wing politics and gold fever."

Of course the paper, with its reputation for serious investigative reporting, backed up its hoax with real journalistic elan. It quoted an assayer as saying the ore tested richer than that of a fabled Arizona mine called the Lost Dutchman (which has never been found). It also quoted business and government officials, including the head of the Arizona office of the U.S. Geophysical Service, who said test drillings had followed the underground vein back to Camelback Road, under posh golf clubs and million-dollar homes.

According to the story, the mall had been built on federal land, leased on terms that did not divest mineral rights. Therefore the president of "Homestake Gold Mining Company" planned to demolish the Galleria once he had consolidated all claims made by prospectors. A quaint touch was added at this point: The article advised prospective gold seekers to pin on their sleeves a drawing of a miner's shovel, using a ball-point pen and a magic marker.

Prospectors came in droves, fluttering their little drawings. One such disappointed gold seeker was native Nick Benson, who said he had wandered over to stake out a claim and ended up in an expensive cappuccino-and-beanery back in town drinking regular ninety-five-cent coffee with an angry crowd of other disappointed Arizonans. Asked about the drawing on his arm, he replied that the paper said "it was a government rule that those seeking a claim should wear something to identify them as miners instead of shoppers."

Benson went on, "I didn't go at first. But when I checked the *Republic* and saw that it didn't have a follow-up story, I figured they were trying to cover things up. So I came down anyway, even though it was a day late."

How late it was, Benson demonstrated in the men's room. There, standing on the rim of a toilet seat in his timeworn jeans, he said, "Listen to this," and jumped to the floor. A hollow sound came from the clean tile floor. He said, "Do you know what's below this floor? The parking garage is under this floor." "I didn't find any gold," he said on leaving. " But maybe my lawyer can get me some when I sue somebody."

Advice from a Pro Hoaxter

Alan Abel went into the professional hoax biz in the late 1950s, when he campaigned to put pants on animals ("A nude horse is a rude horse"). He made national headlines in 1988, at the age of sixty-two, by engaging in a talk show shouting match that featured Chicago sex therapist Dean C. Dauw.

That program, shown on Los Angeles' Sally Jessy Raphael TV show, involved two part-time performers, Tani Freiwald and Wes Bailey, who previously had fooled the station when they appeared on the show to discuss sexual problems they made up. The two had been invited back on the show by producer Burt Dubrow to clear the air.

Abel had been blamed for the Raphael show fiasco, and for similar capers on the Geraldo Rivera and Oprah Winfrey shows, to which charges Abel said in September 1988, "I'm clean."

Not so clean, however, was his record in other hoax endeavors. Like a World War I flying ace, he has painted TV cameras and press symbols in rows commemorating his adventures with Cable News Network, the *Miami Herald, New York* magazine, *Newsday*, the shouting, rough-and-tumble "Morton Downey, Jr. Show," and the *New York Times*, which ran his fake obituary in 1980.

A CNN spokesman confirmed that it was hoodwinked when Abel appeared on a program with host Sonya Friedman as spokesman for "Omar's School for Beggars," a school Abel says has been listed in the Manhattan phone book for twelve years.

Why did he do it? "To shake people up," he said. And to add a little levity to life and contribute to the well-being of the republic. But it's also noteworthy that hoaxing became a living for Abel. He lectured and wrote about his gambols and performed them for pay at corporate functions.

Spokespersons at all the outlets he has hoaxed insist that they verify everything and double-check their verifications. But Abel said there are ways to get around that.

After studying a given show and learning its style, he explained, "you come up with a concept that fits a certain niche, one that's off-the-wall, funny, educational, and has all the elements of a good story.

"You have stationery printed . . . then you get a telephone answering service. Use that service as your headquarters, because what [show producers] do is interview you on the phone. And if you pass their interview . . . you're on the air."

The Bigger, Better Miracle
Machine: Your New Free Press

A human interest news story flashed around the world from Moscow in January 1989, excitedly reporting a "miracle."

It seemed that six men had been found alive in the basement of a nine-story building that collapsed during an earthquake in Armenia the month before. Their survival story earned press notice around the world, and confronted Soviet press organizations with novel difficulties. Formerly, Soviet newspapers had been forbidden to report immediately and in detail concerning disasters or their related events. But then-president Mikhail Gorbachev's policy of *glasnost* suddenly opened the arena to negative and positive news stories alike. Unfortunately, Soviet newspapers were swept up in their freedom to report and neglected to fact-check thoroughly before they printed the story.

Television had fallen for the story, too, and even interviewed one of the "trapped" men, Aikaz Akopyan, who had told the story to Tass.

The day after the world rejoiced that six men had been saved from the rubble of a collapsed building in Leninakan, Armenia, Tass announced that it now had serious apprehensions about the validity of the story. Upon closer inspection, it said, Mr. Akopyan's story "had holes in it."

"Regrettably, we are unable to confirm with full certainty," the story said—marching gallantly into a pitfall of journalistic freedom—"the authenticity of the reports made by our Armenian colleagues about the 'Leninakan Miracle,' nor can we categorically deny them."

That left it up to the Armenian news agency, Armenpress, on whose shoulders Tass had nimbly shifted responsibility for misinforming the world.

Armenpress admitted that it could not find any witnesses in Leninakan who could back up Akopyan's story. The electrician's family and the other five men involved had disappeared, it said.

The Soviet government newspaper *Izvestia* reported that its reporters saw the demolished building the day the six men were said to have been pulled out. "It was two in the afternoon," the story read, "and the six were found in the morning. But where had they gone? Who saved them after all?"

Akopyan, suffering from pneumonia, stuck by his story. He maintained that the five missing men had probably gone to a village where their relatives live.

It was noted that, the week before, Soviet television had reported on seventeen other men who were said to have been found alive in a devastated grain silo, also in Leninakan. That report was dropped without explanation, and denied by town officials. The town mayor, however, was quoted as saying that the last survivor had been found and rescued only nineteen days after the terrible earthquake. That wasn't quite miraculous enough for international television, though perhaps it should have been.

Aphrodisiacs Have Their Down Side

There's been a lot said and thought about aphrodisiacs through the centuries. About apricots, for example, marinated in crushed garlic with zinc, vitamin E, and olive oil, plus one raw egg.

Then there are oysters, the root yohimbe (said to work in fifteen minutes), Korean ginseng, ground rhinoceros horn, and on and on to the eighty-seven or so herbs and spices that East Indians say make them better lovers than the French.

The late movie star Errol Flynn, world traveler and lover of a score of film stars, once said he had tried every aphrodisiac known to man. And the best thing he'd found to stimulate and intensify sexual desire is "the embrace of a woman you love."

Perhaps next in repute and common use as an aphrodisiac in Western countries is Spanish fly, a preparation made from the European blister beetle. These little creatures, besides reputedly speeding up the libido, also secrete a substance capable of blistering the skin, and some species also damage crops. Like many other well-known aphrodisiacs, it is banned for sale in the United States by the Food and Drug Administration — many aphrodisiacs, whatever their primary benefits, have been implicated in damage to secondary organs such as the brain, heart, and stomach.

In the fall of 1991 the FDA took off after blister beetles with renewed vigor, announcing that illegal importers of Spanish fly had better watch out — it could contain strychnine. Strychnine is a poison for rats and other pests, but is also used by doctors in treating central nervous system disorders.

The tainted capsules came from a California distributor who labeled the boxes: "Spanish Fly Pills. Legendary Sex Exciter." A man who bought a six-capsule box in Oshkosh, Wisconsin in midsummer and swallowed one tablet, the agency said, was stricken with seizures and hospitalized. The man recovered, and the FDA did not disclose if the seizures came before, during, or after the pill had done its work.

So, fading lovers, the FDA seems to be warning, forget about the blister beetle, and go back to apricots.

DJ Drains Lake

Fishing enthusiasts around Lake Lanier in Atlanta angrily leaped at the hook one day in February 1988 when they heard

97

on a radio broadcast that the lake was to be drained. The reason given was to clean up the lake's pollution; it would be dry for two years, beginning in April.

Their howls of protest were immediately joined by complaints from marine dealers, officials at Lake Lanier Islands, real estate agents, and the Army Corps of Engineers.

Loudest of all, understandably, were buyers of boats at a recent Atlanta Boat Show. To emphasize their displeasure, many canceled contracts for boats they'd just signed to buy.

Then the broadcaster, Steve Sutton of station WAPW-FM, admitted over the air that it had just been a joke. "Basically, I lied," he said of his broadcast, which features a "rumor a day," such as the tale that the Atlanta Braves were being sold to Denver. Nobody laughed.

Atlanta Army Corps of Engineers public information officer Gene Brown said severely, "We have absolutely no plans to draw down or drain Lake Lanier. We got calls about it, and the Corps' lake office was flooded with calls." He said the calls came at the rate of about one a minute.

One caller was Mrs. Eileen White, who heads the Save the Lake Association, Inc., and is president of Lake Lanier Property Owners.

"I was told the rumor was false," she said. "But for a couple of days the phone went crazy . . . People called about property sales. You would be surprised how gullible people are."

Sutton agreed about the gullibility of listeners: "Lots of times what happens is that listeners hear only what they want to hear," he said. "People get upset. They call me and say, 'Hey, is that true?' And I always tell them no. Basically, it's done to test people's listening ability."

Nobody in Atlanta thanked him for the lesson.

Fictional Fashion Model Defends Her Reputation

What cub reporter scrabbling around the church news and police blotter circuit doesn't yearn to be a foreign correspondent?

A young society columnist for the *Amarillo Globe News* in Texas, whose beat was covering teas and lunches, decided to liven up the long list of a function's attendees. The reporter, Betty Ligon, typed in a fictional name: Mrs. Harrison Benudi.

The name went unnoticed when the paper came out. Growing bolder and more bored, Ligon began dropping the name into other lists until the day came when the formerly sleepy-eyed society mavens woke up. Who is Mrs. Harrison Benudi? they asked Ligon.

"Mrs. Harrison Benudi is a former New York fashion model, married to a Major Harrison Benudi stationed at the Amarillo military base," she wrote. And high society women thereafter began claiming they had invited her to lunch.

The publisher of the newspaper got wind of Ligon's little caper, and it amused him. He wrote a column for the paper, and one day he used it to announce that he had investigated Mrs. Benudi and learned that she was not a model and alleged she was a whore.

Society readers were of course surprised, but not as surprised as the publisher, who in short order received an outraged letter from a Major Benudi protesting the slander against his wife. Furious, the publisher ordered Ligon to move the Benudis out of town in her next column, and she did.

Ligon said she later discovered the letter from the "Major" had been written by a colleague, who was mad at the publisher for passing him up for a promotion.

No disciplinary action followed Ligon's hoax. She went on to become a free-lance entertainment columnist in El Paso. In commenting on her Amarillo gambol with her publisher, she said gleefully, "We got very power drunk."

Mencken Is Dead; Bathtub Will Live Forever

During World War I, the great American journalist, critic, and controversial figure, Henry Louis Mencken, who was known in different circles as "the Sage of Baltimore," "a dyed-in-the-world moron," and "the private secretary of God Almighty," grew greatly bored. In his newspaper stories, essays, and lectures he had championed Kaiser Wilhelm of Germany, using barbs tipped in acid to sting those in the United States who wanted to wage war against his beloved Germany.

Mencken's work did not sit well with the nation's editors after the U.S. declared war, and a lid was clamped on his journalistic efforts. Musing sullenly in his Baltimore home, he came up with a great story idea: the history of the bathtub. But where could he research such an arcane subject? Failing to find any information, he made some up, and sent the result to the *New York Evening Mail*, which published it.

The article, "A Neglected Anniversary," advised readers that December 10 of that year marked the seventy-fifth anniversary of the introduction of the bathtub to America. It was first seen in Cincinnati in 1832, he wrote, where one Adam Thompson, who had seen one in London, constructed his own—a splendid mahogany contraption lined with lead to prevent rot.

But a tempest of outrage greeted the innovation, Mencken wrote. Doctors called the bathtub dangerous to health; three cities charged extra for water used in the devices; Boston banned them, except under stringent medical supervision; and Philadelphia almost passed a law forbidding its use in the winter months. Then President Millard Fillmore bravely ordered one for the White House in 1851, Mencken continued, and the tub was "in."

Strewn throughout the piece were a hundred invented details, including names, dates, and publications. Newspaper editors, then magazine editors, and then editors of academic quarterlies rejoiced to see the Sage back in action. Before long the article's whimsical "facts" were preserved in many a staid volume as "history."

When Millard Fillmore's putative first found its way into standard reference books, alarms went off in Mencken's head. In 1926, he washed his hands of the story, admitting in print that it was a hoax (the master of the English language called it coyly "a burlesque") to entertain the masses.

One of the papers that carried his retraction was the venerable *Boston Herald*. Just three weeks later the same paper carried a reprint of the original bathtub story, as uncontested "real" news.

Over the years "facts" from the original article have regularly resurfaced. President Harry Truman used to allude to Fillmore and the first tub in the White House while showing visitors the lay of the Presidential abode, thirty-five years after the piece first appeared and twenty-six years after Mencken published a second retraction.

And these so-called facts still are around. Newspaper reporter Tom DiBacco wrote, on January 7, 1992, in a feature article in the *Washington Times*, that President Millard Fillmore brought the "first galvanized bathtub" into the White House.

No sweat, Tom. Just say, "Move over guys. Make room for me in the bathtub."

Duke's Bogus Baron

What does a guy do if he's just a nobody from El Paso, Texas, but he'd rather be a Baron de Rothschild? For starters, he enrolls at Duke University. Baron Maurice Jeffrey Locke de Rothschild found a happy home there.

He joined an exclusive fraternity, raised money for cancer victims, and even managed the school swim team, though he failed to manage his grades with the same finesse. After two years he flunked out of the University's continuing education program, then disappeared in a gathering swarm of rumors. The vanished Rothschild scion turned out to come, not from France, nor even from California—he said he couldn't speak French because his branch of the family was the California Rothschilds. But it turned out this Rothschild only came from West Texas, where he was more commonly known as Mauro Cortez, Jr.

How did he get away with it? "He fit in well here," the editor of the university newspaper explained. "This is the type of school where prestige is very important and social standing means a lot." But where did he get hold of that social standing, and how did he pay for it? Apparently, Rothschilds at Duke University needn't beetle their well-bred brow about any of that vulgar *argent* business.

Reflecting afterwards, the president of the *faux* Rothschild's fraternity observed, "It was questionable whether he could speak French or not. It was questionable about his car," a Honda. But the Baron's frat brothers came to believe his explanations that, either he didn't wish to draw undue attention to himself, or, if that didn't satisfy them, his regular carriage was in the shop—yes, for two years.

But surely a Baron needs pocket money, for the requisite *noblesse oblige*, and the odd *beau geste*? It turns out that money really isn't a Baron's problem. While managing the swim team, Baron Rothschild-Cortez hosted a grand reunion at the local Hilton hotel, and suggested in an airy way that his family would help sign off the details. It's unclear whether Cortez or his family ever put down a penny toward expenses, but somehow the bill was paid without an awkward word uttered.

However, it turns out that the phony-noble life isn't all crib-bage and cummerbunds. Cortez was indicted for embezzle-ment several months after he disappeared, having treated himself to the money he had been raising for cancer victims. These untoward trifles haven't diminished Cortez in the eyes of many Duke students, who think their school takes rank a bit too seriously. "He's almost the good guy," one student said. "People were sorry he got caught."

True Scoop on Royal Poop

Charles and Di—who don't have, or need, last names—had been rumored to be getting divorced. They've been getting di-vorced for years, and they never did, so who cares? And now it is confirmed, the royal couple is splitsville?

The royal tradition, of course, causes part of the problem. Traditional solutions to a bad marriage at Buckingham Palace—in which the good king abdicates his throne, or be-heads his queen, or settles his score with a war against her dad—these solutions are out of step with modern times. The times have changed so much that not even the Buckingham Palace Press Office knows how to handle contemporary royal news, especially the news of interest to what was traditionally called "the gutter press." Though the royal family expects deference from its subjects—who are not, after all, called "citizens"—their subjects increasingly consider the royal fami-ly just a hereditary line of show-biz swells. As Ross Benson, one of Britain's few respectable gossip columnists, observes, "There is a school of journalism in this country which has come round to the view that the royal family are fictional characters, and it doesn't matter what is said about them."

It used to matter. Reports of Edward VI's liaison with Wal-lace Simpson were cut out of foreign news magazines before they hit British streets in the 1930s. Such discretion—or, if you prefer, such censorship—is unthinkable today. All that's left is a dignified royal stonewall that disdains comment upon each and every breath or howl of scandal. The utter absence of confirmed facts, however, has resulted in a delirium of royal fictions. As the *New York Times Magazine* reported, without facts it takes craft to make a royal story—and especially a royal headline. At an Austrian fashion show the Princess of Wales asks what it's like to be a model; hearing "like" and "model," the royal rat-pack files to London that Di always wanted to be a model. At the Cannes Film Festival, a reporter asks the palace press secretary if Elizabeth Taylor is coming to dinner with Charles and Diana. Told no, he runs for the phones. "Superstar Elizabeth Taylor," he says, with all the teeth and lips the English use on foreign phones, "sensationally snubbed the Princess of Wales last night . . . . Buckingham Palace fights back, through a dignified veneer of lawsuits. The royal family won a $164,000 settlement against the *Sun* for publishing stolen photographs, and almost routinely files breach-of-confidence suits against tattling footmen. They demand contributions to charities and public apologies from misinforming media, when clear cases can be made against them.

But cases are often purposefully unclear. The recent Prime Minister, Margaret Thatcher, had governed Britain with huge, unprecedented micro-managed news and advertising campaigns that necessitated unofficial information conduits to the public, even as public disgust at journalists' invasions of privacy made libel actions ever more lucrative, and their underlying case law more confused. The whole truth seems to be that Charles and Di have had a dreadful marriage.

Pulitzer Prize-Winning Newspaper Turns Out to Be Fiction

The *Washington Post* article told readers what they already knew about drug addicts in the slums of the nation's capital, but with rare journalistic brio. "Jimmy's World" chronicled the life of an eight-year-old heroin addict with "needle marks freckling the baby-smooth skin of his thin brown arms," a boy who was addicted by his ex-prostitute mother's boyfriend, whose only ambition in life was to grow up to be a good dope dealer. With arresting eyewitness detail, the Pulitzer Prize-winning article told how the mother's boyfriend, "Ron," "grabs Jimmy's left arm just above the elbow, his massive hand tightly encircling the child's small limb . . . . The needle slides into the boy's soft skin like a straw pushed into the center of freshly baked cake. Liquid ebbs out of the syringe, replaced by bright red blood. The blood is then reinjected into the child." As he shot up the child, "Ron" said, "Pretty soon, you got to learn how to do this for yourself."

In response to public outcry, Washington police launched a citywide search for these arresting characters. But police thought the story was fishy, and said so—among other quibbles, they couldn't believe a junkie would give away drugs for three years for nothing. After a three-week investigation, the police department concluded that "the child, as described, did not exist." The *Post* defended its reporter, twenty-six-year-old Janet Cooke, and fought off subpoenas for sources and information on First Amendment grounds. Police doubts were ignored; the story circulated widely in the six months before it won Janet Cooke and the *Washington Post* the Pulitzer Prize for journalism.

Due to the publicity, Janet Cooke's fiction-writing abilities clearly shined. Vassar College let the *Post* know that, far from graduating *magna cum laude* as her published resumé claimed, Cooke had dropped out after a year. The University of Toledo pointed out that Cooke had received a B.A. from them, not an M.A.

Confronted with this news by her editors, Cooke at first stood by her story, which the *Post* hadn't verified by usual procedures because Cooke said she'd promised anonymity to her sources, and had received death threats from associated drug dealers. But when her city editor demanded that Cooke take him to the house where she said she interviewed the boy, Cooke broke down, confessed, and resigned. The Pulitzer Prize that ruined her career was passed on to a *Village Voice* writer who, ironically, had originally been chosen by the Prize jury. That choice had been overruled in Cooke's favor by the national Pulitzer board.

The next day the *Post* apologized in an editorial, and Mayor Marion Barry reminded reporters that "I was very firm in my conviction that Miss Cooke's article was part myth, part truth." Not long after, a writing instructor at San Diego State University abruptly changed a student's grade from B to F, for a short story the student submitted about a nine-year-old Chicago drug addict. The story was titled "Anthony's World." The instructor had thought it read more like a newspaper story than a piece of fiction, which was the only reason he hadn't given it an A.

After discovering the student's inspiration, the instructor told reporters, "What got me was, I gave the guy a B and he came up after class and argued that he deserved a better grade. He said he needed the grade to get into law school." Well, maybe he doesn't — until he wins a Pulitzer Prize.

Skaggs Scams Media to Make Social Comment

Joe Bones was a man with a product. He appeared on "Good Morning America" in 1986 along with six "fat commandos" and a former client, and explained to host David Hartman that he had a company called The Fat Squad, which could help anyone who had tried and failed to stay on a diet. For $300 dollars a day, Bones said, he would provide a twenty-four-hour rotation of "fat commandos" trained to prevent dieters from eating, period. They would keep watch outside the bedroom, stake out the refrigerator. While Joe Bones described his final solution to problem diets, the "Good Morning America" cameras panned over his six commandos, looking driven, glowering in front of an on-stage refrigerator.

This may sound slightly absurd to you, but David Hartman didn't seem to take it that way. The next day, the *New York Post* reported that "Good Morning America" had been hoaxed, by a forty-one-year-old artist and sculptor who dabbles in manipulating the media to make what he calls "social and political commentary."

His real name is Joey Skaggs. He explains, "If I wanted to do a book on all the scams and fraudulent people involved in dieting, it might take me a year or two to get an agent and publisher and then write the book. Instead, I use the vulnerable, gullible media to make my comments." And he gloats, "The kicker is that I'd already been on "Good Morning America" about a year earlier as Joey Skaggs, inventor of the fish tank condominium—aquariums complete with fully furnished living rooms, bathrooms, and kitchens. I called them condominiums for upwardly mobile guppies."

For years, Skaggs has been creating his mass-media art pieces: "The celebrity sperm bank, which I perpetrated in the mid-seventies, was a way of demonstrating how technology surpasses or at least challenges prevailing morality. We have test-tube babies and talk of cloning. So I used the availability of the media and created Guiseppi Scaggoli's celebrity sperm bank. We set an 'auction' of rock star sperm. I got calls from around the country from women who were willing to bid on Bob Dylan's sperm and Mick Jagger's and Paul McCartney's."

In 1981 he got into health care, with a parody of Franz Kafka's *Metamorphosis*. "I called for a press conference to announce I had developed a super strain of cockroach. I said I had been feeding toxins to the cockroaches, and when they developed immunities to the toxins, I said I extracted their hormones and developed a compound, which I made into a vitamin pill. My vitamins, I said, cured arthritis, acne, anemia, and menstrual cramps and made one invulnerable to nuclear radiation. I went from the press conference to a news show, where I wore a Panama suit, Panama hat, mirrored sunglasses, and a giant cockroach on my T-shirt that said 'Metamorphosis.'"

Though nobody got the joke, Skaggs got lots of ink. He turned himself in to the *Wall Street Journal* a few months later. No harm done — so long as he keeps it simple, and keeps up his media mailing list, Joey Skaggs has what the media wants.

Please Don't Keep Those Cards and Letters Coming

In 1989 an English boy was diagnosed as having a brain tumor and given little chance of survival. An American billionaire, John Kluge, arranged for him to be brought to the U.S. to have brain surgery performed in Charlottesburg, Virginia, and he invited the boy's family to join him for moral support.

Along the way Craig Shergold, twelve, let it be known that he wanted more than anything to get into the *Guinness Book of World Records* for receiving the most get-well cards of anybody in the world. And how many would that be? Craig didn't know, but it had to be a lot.

The operation succeeded. Craig made a brilliant recovery with an excellent prognosis predicting a long life. Then he went home to a future of hell.

The cards rolled in. The deluge grew and swelled. The house filled up with cards. So did the garage. A cry went out from Craig's mother to stop the flood.

The Children's Wish Foundation in Atlanta, which had spread the word in the first place, heard the call. A rumor, that Craig wanted to collect business cards, was emphatically denied by foundation president, Arthur Stein. "Craig never made such a request," he said.

By the time volunteers had counted thirty-three million cards in 1992, including cards from Ronald Reagan, President Bush, Margaret Thatcher in England, and Mikhail Gorbachev, Ann Landers was called in. She begged her readers not to heed new rumors or chain letters suggesting that Craig wanted cards.

For heaven's sake, she said, Craig recovered more than a year ago. "So, dear readers," she wrote, "please, please, if you receive any of these pesky things in the mail [pleas to send cards to Craig] . . . tear them up into little pieces and feed them to the fish."

Craig got his wish. He is listed in the *Guinness Book of World Records* as having received the most get-well cards of anybody in the world.

Murder Hoax Costs DJs Twelve Grand

On June 13, 1990, KROQ disc jockeys Kevin Ryder and Gene (Bean) Baxter received a phone call from a listener who appeared to be very upset. At first, the caller had a hard time talking. Words seemed to back up inside him and then pour forth like the spray from a stopped-up hose. He began to discuss his relationship with his girlfriend. Something terrible had happened. As he rambled on, his narrative became clearer and simpler. He spoke of an uncontrollable rage which had engulfed him. He told Kevin and Bean he had beaten his girlfriend to death.

The caller's confession was taken seriously by the Los Angeles police, KROQ's management, and Infinity Broadcasting, the radio conglomerate that owns KROQ. After all, Los Angeles is a huge city. Someone out there could definitely have beaten his girlfriend to death and then decided to confess on a live radio talk show hosted by a pair of comic DJs.

Unfortunately for Kevin and Bean, their hoax ended up costing them a pretty penny. Following disclosure of the fraud on April 11, 1991, the Los Angeles Police Department presented KROQ with a bill for $12,170, representing the 149 hours that a homicide detective had spent attempting to solve the murder case. KROQ in turn gave the bill to Kevin and Bean, who were made to pay the money out of their own pockets after returning from a six-day unpaid suspension. The DJs also agreed to perform 149 hours of community service.

"The fact that they're paying this out of their pockets is reflective of the fact that they are the culpable people," Infinity Broadcasting attorney Steven A. Lerman told the *Los Angeles Times*. "It was a lack of responsibility on the part of the disc jockeys and they've acknowledged that in their on-the-air apologies . . . They are taking on this community service thing at the company's suggestion, but they're happy to do it."

Lerman's statement seemed a bit sanctimonious. According to the *Los Angeles Times*, the corporation soon hired Doug Roberts, the Mesa, Arizona radio personality who played the murderer in Kevin and Bean's little skit. Roberts was hired four months after Kevin and Bean confessed their hoax, which prompted some tittering about KROQ management's possible role in all this.

Nevertheless, Lerman forcefully asserted there was no relationship between Roberts' participation in the hoax and his hiring at KROQ. "There was absolutely no nexus between his hiring and this incident," he told the *Los Angeles Times*. "The management had absolutely no inkling that he had anything to do with the hoax. Kevin and Bean did recommend him for the job. They had worked together [in Arizona]. Roberts had wanted for a long time to work for KROQ . . . he went through the normal review and hiring procedure."

Eskimos and Their 200 Words for Snow

You've heard it at cocktail parties, in lectures, and at plays. You've seen it repeated as an aside in editorials, articles, and books. It's a factoid in everyone's possession: The Eskimos — being specialists in the subject — have fifty, a hundred, or even two hundred words for snow.

Anthropologist Laura Martin of Cleveland State University first debunked the myth about the plethora of Eskimo words for snow in 1982. Unfortunately, like a lot of debunked rumors, word about the Eskimos' penchant for naming different classes of snow is still traveling.

The Eskimo snow myth got its start in 1911, with Franz Boas' *Handbook of North American Indians*. In making a point about Eskimo language, Boas wrote that just as English uses words with distinct etymological roots for different forms of water (such as liquid, lake, river, etc.), Eskimo language used distinct roots for *aput* " snow on the ground," *gana* "falling snow," *piqsirpoq* "drifting snow," and *qimuqsuq* "snow drift."

Boas' fairly academic comments were picked up in 1940 by Benjamin Lee Whorf, an amateur linguist who had made important contributions to the study of Mayan languages. Writing in the Massachusetts Institute of Technology's promotional magazine (he was an alumnus), Whorf expanded and changed the context of Boas' comments, explaining that it was the Eskimos' familiarity with snow which led to their variety of words for it in its many guises.

Whorf contended that, "To an Eskimo, this all-inclusive word [snow] would be almost unthinkable; he would say that falling snow, slushy snow, and so on, are sensuously and operationally different, different things to contend with; he uses different words for them and for other kinds of snow."

Of course, Whorf didn't mention in his article that English too has a variety of words for snow, including snow itself, sleet, slush, and blizzard.

From Whorf, the discussion of Eskimo words for snow went into a number of popular books on language, including Roger Brown's 1958 volume, *Words and Things*. From there it passed to non-scientific writers who were likely to repeat what they had read in secondary sources.

As the "facts" about the Eskimo words for snow passed further and further from scientific sources, the number of these words grew. In his 1978 play, *Fifth of July*, Lanford Wilson claimed the Eskimos had fifty words for snow. A *New York Times* editorial said there were one hundred, and a Cleveland TV weather forecast claimed there were two hundred.

Despite Martin's 1982 lecture and 1985 paper on the subject, and in spite of linguist Geoffrey Pullum's 1991 book *The Great Eskimo Vocabulary Hoax and Other Irreverent Essays on the Study of Language*, which pillories repeaters of the Eskimo factoid in its very title, the repeaters live on. We will probably never know how many words the Eskimos actually have for snow, for the same reason we can't accurately count our own words. Just consider, what *is* sleet anyway, and just when is it metamorphosed—linguistically or meteorologically—into slush? Are blizzards fundamentally snowy or windy? Is black ice snow? Besides, when the stuff's in our shoes and we use the words most distinctly, it isn't even snow anymore.

Omni Falls for New Scientist Hoax

Here's a marvel of science still uninvestigated: Just why are the media so endlessly gullible? In September of 1984, the popular science magazine *Omni* ran a story about an "amazing tomato-wheat-cow," a plant-animal hybrid that was described eighteen months earlier in the April Fool's issue of England's *New Scientist* magazine.

New Scientist had provided many clues that this plant—a hamburger-maker's dream—was a joke. *Omni* missed them all, reporting enthusiastically about the new advance, "With all the characteristics of a giant stalk of wheat, the skin can be tanned and used as leather, and several udder blossoms provide the grower with a steady supply of tomato juice."

To give *Omni* some credit (though not much), the *New Scientist* article was skillfully constructed and fooled two or three other news organs. It began, like all good hoaxes, with something believable: "Scientists have become so familiar with the fine structure of living cells that their manipulation and culture now appear commonplace. Intact chromosomes can be lifted out of cells for genetic studies; plant protoplasts . . . can be persuaded to grow into whole plants and much has been learned of plant metabolism by grafting experiments — for example, the grafting of tomato tops to potato tubers demonstrates the energy storing capacity of tubers."

Nothing earth-shattering so far, but here the editors of *Omni* should have began thinking of lunch, or at least a quick trip to Mickey D's. "Now Barry MacDonald and William Wimpey of the Department of Biology at the University of Hamburg have taken the research to its logical conclusion . . . creating the first hybrid from a plant and animal cell." To create the hybrid, Drs. "MacDonald" and "Wimpey" (Wimpey's is the biggest hamburger chain in England) used "heat-shock" and placed their materials in a "liquid culture medium containing glucose, monosodium glutamate, a mixture of vitamins, sodium chloride, and extracts of Raphanus brassica" — in other words, mustard.

Toward the end of the article, *New Scientist* really gives the trick away: "Using these techniques MacDonald and Wimpey have fused cells of Lycopersicon esculentum [tomato] with cells of Bostaurus [horse]. The resulting hybrid grows like its tomato parent but develops a tough, leathery skin. Field trials have shown that the mature 'plant' has an otherwise normal foliage, although its flowers are pollinated only by horseflies. After fertilization . . . the flowers develop extraordinary

113

clumps of discus-shaped bodies—microscopic examination shows that these bodies are a true hybrid of animal protein sandwiched between a thin envelope of tomato fruit. Attempts are now being made . . . to cross these hybrids with wheat cells, hopefully to produce a wheat-tomato-cow super-hybrid.

According to *Science Digest*, *Omni*'s fact checking was limited to leaving a message for Wimpey and MacDonald at the University of Hamburg . . . they were probably out to lunch.

California Spooks Sinclair Supporters with Phony Newsreels

California has been called "America in italics," the quintessential rumpled bed of the American dream. According to this view, California is the dream of all America, which explains its cultural authority over the rest of us. It is a place where fantasy drives reality. Obviously, California is the political hoaxter and con man's Promised Land.

Libraries are filled with tales of California political skullduggery. Here we focus on a historical high-point, which incidentally created, almost in its wake, an abiding American myth and archetype undoubted to this day. But our story begins with another California archetype, that of the famous author turned celebrity socialist, Upton Sinclair.

Sinclair was a longtime political dissenter and author of *The Jungle*, a celebrated exposé of Chicago's meat packing industry at the turn of the century. He parlayed his fame into a serious run for governor of California in 1934. His party went down in smoke amid a statewide propaganda barrage that included phony newsreels and manufactured news.

Movie mogul Irving Thalberg orchestrated many of the attacks. He saw Sinclair, perhaps correctly, as a dangerous Red who wanted to rob the rich to support the poor. He believed a Governor Sinclair would be bad for Hollywood, bad for himself, and probably bad for business in the nation. To prevent Sinclair's election, Thalberg used his resources to create anti-Sinclair newsreels, such as his "California Election Report" which featured interviews with hobos in a railyard, in which one dusty bum after another explains that he rode the rails to the Golden State just as soon as he heard the new governor-to-be was handing out free lunches. It was pure Hollywood, of course; the newsreel was one of many that ran in California theaters before the election, which Sinclair lost by a landslide.

These newsreels were early precursors of today's negative campaigning. Like the infamous Willie Horton ad of the 1988 Bush campaign, the "California Election Report" played on fears of the majority against a disadvantaged class. In the Horton case, the disadvantaged class was African-Americans. In the case of the newsreels, the disadvantaged class was the poor. Another similarly exploited group was the migrant Okies of song and story. These unfortunates were criminalized before they hit the state line by uncannily similar newsreels and political bamboozlers.

Sinclair probably would have gone down without Thalberg's efforts. Still, it's fun to note that on the day Thalberg's movie crew went out to a railroad yard, they couldn't find a single hobo. So the crew went back to MGM Studios and shot the sequence on a sound stage, with extras playing the parts of the California-dreaming hobos.

Actors Hoax Gabfests

Are the bizarre people who show up on television's daytime talkfests all real? The hosts and producers of these shows claim so. But they are not always easily authenticated. At least two people who have questionable credentials have appeared on three of TV's biggest gab sessions.

According to reports in the media between 1986 and 1988, Tani Freiwald and Wes Bailey posed as a sexual surrogate and her client on the talk shows of Sally Jessy Raphael, Geraldo Rivera, and Oprah Winfrey. Freiwald appeared on a talk show in 1986 when her employer, sex therapist Dr. Dean Dauw, refered her to the Oprah show for a program entitled "Women Who Hate Sex." Dauw, whose books include *Stranger In Your Bed* and *Sex Therapy Innovations*, often provided guests for talk shows on sexual aberrations. In this case, however, real guests were not forthcoming, so Freiwald, Dauw's office manager, claims he asked her to do a little acting. Dauw denies this.

However it began, Freiwald in turn asked Wes Bailey, a friend from an Omaha children's theater, to accompany her. The Oprah appearance went so well they began appearing on other shows. On Geraldo, Freiwald as "Rebecca" explained how she brought the virgin "George" (played by Bailey) to manhood at age thirty-five. In April of 1988, "Rebecca" appeared on Sally Jessy as a sexual surrogate to men over fifty. A month later she returned with Bailey who now presented himself as a young married man who'd become impotent, and whose wife, played by yet another actress, knew of and approved of "Rebecca's" "therapy."

Jim Flanery of the *Omaha World-Herald* unmasked the hoaxers in the summer of 1988. Predictably, no one in the talk show community was amused. The Winfrey show issued a statement that said in part: "We take every precaution to ensure a person's credibility. We trusted the referral of Chicago psychologist Dr. Dean Dauw." Sally Jessy Raphael said to Freiwald, "Tani, you have made me and, much more important, the audience, a laughingstock."

Raphael, who was at once indignant and aware that such controversy makes for good conversation, had the two back on her show. When asked why they did what they did, Bailey said he'd pulled off the frauds as an adventure, which he likened to white-water rafting. Freiwald said she couldn't pass up the challenge "to perform and be someone I wasn't, and do it convincingly — not just on the stage but as I came through the door, as I was picked up in the limo at the airport."

Raphael did not accept the explanations: "We help people. Of all the things to attack please attack the game show or soap opera. We have to feel our form of broadcasting is better than some of the pap — not that we're not pap. . . . Maybe we're pap with redeeming public values."

Kidney Heist in Central Park

Central Park can be a dangerous place to wander around. People are often hit by crime within its confines, and the stories can be horrendous: rapes, beatings, muggings, organ thefts. Organ thefts?

One story recounts how a group of friends enjoyed a night out in a Manhattan bar. They were having a wonderful time when one of the men managed to meet and become acquainted with a woman who was also visiting the establishment. After hours passed and night was turning into early morning, the group of friends decided to call it quits. The man who had made the female acquaintance decided that he wanted to stay and pursue it longer. He bid farewell to his friends, and they left the bar. But the story, of course, doesn't end there. The man who had stayed behind called one of the group a few days later, sounding sickly and desperate. He told his friend that he felt horrible and needed help right away. When his friend came to retrieve the sick man they went straight to the hospital. After examining the Casanova, the doctor announced his findings. He had found a long line of sutures on the man's back, and discovered that the man's kidney had been stolen.

This is the tale that has been heard many times over. The origin of the story can't be pinned down, as the victim of the heist is never found. Rather the story is told with extreme seriousness by someone who heard it from a "reliable" source. This source generally follows the pattern of the storyteller's daughter's boyfriend's gerbil's best friend's owner, or something along those lines.

A more definite source has been rumored to exist. A 1991 episode of a television show had a plot line in which a man got mugged in Central Park, woke up and discovered that someone had cut him open, made off with one of his kidneys and sewed him up. Sound familiar? Scriptwriters of this episode were said to be inspired by a colleague who suggested the story. The colleague said his idea had come from a newspaper story. Where is this newspaper story of a real, live kidney heist? The scriptwriter amended his story of the helpful colleague's newspaper clipping with the reflection, "I never found anyone who had actually seen it [the newspaper clipping]."

But, you say, it *could* be true. So many things happen these days. Besides, aren't organs very rare and in high demand? All that is true, which is probably why the rumor has caught on and continues to spread. The story most likely stemmed from an earlier version in which organs were stolen from people in the Third World. The rising disparity between rich and poor in America, as well as the inadequacy of the health care system for the poor, probably spurred the American Central Park revisions.

When the story comes to you, feel free to dispute it. Jan Brunvand, a specialist in urban myth, deems this story impossible because of the impracticality of storing and transporting human organs. "It's not like you can take them out, carry them around in a cooler and sell them on the streets of New York City."

Spaceman Makes Monkey of Press

In the summer of 1953, three locals who were roaming a southern rural highway in their pickup truck were halted by the presence of a foreign object smack in their path of travel. The humans involved in the story described the object as a flying saucer, an unidentified flying object. They were certain of this conclusion because the creatures next to the saucer were two small red men who returned to the craft upon seeing the three men. The craft then ascended into the sky with a display of flashing lights.

This startling event could easily be written off as a common occurrence on rural southern highways, except for the final twist of the story. The men began to drive away, but their truck struck one creature who was stranded by the sudden departure of its craft. Thus, the three men had in their possession physical evidence of their close encounter.

This exotic tale was told by the three to the local newspaper editor, who was convinced by their presentation of the physical evidence. And the story became front-page news, under the headline, "Hairless Critter Killed, Two Escape." With this headline, the men were propelled to fame. Newspapers in larger, non-rural, and non-southern cities also ran the shocking story of the locals' encounter. Interest in the story spread beyond the press, into military and scientific arenas.

The physical evidence was turned over to these high-level professionals. They performed batteries of tests and examinations. Then this batch of scientists reached a conclusion about the identity of the "alien creature." It was a rhesus monkey that had been shaved and deprived of its tail.

The three men had a bet with the local butcher and two local barbers involving their ability to get their names on the front page of the town paper. The amount of the wager? Fifty dollars. Their gain was the UFO-ologist's loss.

Radio Hoaxes Are Part of the Business

April Fool's Day has become an acknowledged, as well as an almost accepted, time for radio stations to pawn off hoaxes on the public, often while pulling promotional stunts. Many listeners look forward to learning just how they will be duped each year. On-air hoaxes can run the gamut from the purely entertaining to stories with potential to do damage.

Hoaxes in 1991 ranged from a mild WCXR-FM Washington broadcast that key players for the Redskins had been traded, to the mildly annoying WKLH-FM Milwaukee announcement that back taxes could be paid without penalties, to the downright irresponsible report by KSHE-FM St. Louis that parts of the United States were undergoing nuclear attack.

While the Federal Communication Commission (FCC) over the last few years has lightened its guidelines concerning on-air stunts, in an effort to change its image from one that was "heavy handed and censorious in telling broadcasters what they can and cannot do," according to Chuck Kelly, chief of the FCC Mass Media Bureau and Enforcement Division. He still requires that broadcasters "show good judgment and do not cross into areas that approach the severity of a *War of the Worlds* situation." Of KSHE-FM's reporting a nonexistent nuclear attack, Kelly says the FCC "still has rules that prohibit news slanting, distortion or falsification."

Naturally, KSHE-FM's program director/operations manager Rick Balis was less than pleased with the FCC's close examination following disc jockey John Ulet's announcement of a nuclear attack over the air. He said it was "most unenjoyable" and that "John made a major mistake, a major miscalculation, a major misjudgment in no uncertain terms." He added, speaking of how contrite the DJ felt, that "we suspended him without pay for a week, but any suspension without pay would have been dwarfed by what the man went through. Just because he made a bad mistake doesn't mean he should join the ranks of the unemployed."

Kelly said that he and the commission are concerned with those broadcasters who "seriously miscalculate what the community finds acceptable, and for the most part, we aren't concerned with April-fool type humor." Stations that show "over a continuing and long period of time a total disinclination to come straight with its audience" continue to be targets of FCC investigation, Kelly said. In short, the hoaxes the FCC is concerned with are those like the one that cost an Arizona station its license for claiming that one of its DJs had been kidnapped. It perpetuated the hoax even after police and other officials became involved in the manhunt.

While "various tort laws and other courses of action exist for those people who feel they, in some way, might be hurt by a program or a promotion," according to Barry Umansky, deputy general counsel at the National Association of Broadcasters in Washington, he says it's rare that a station puts itself in a position where it could be considered liable by the FCC.

A simple hoax, it seems, though not always appreciated by the public, has come to be accepted and, to a certain degree, expected by the FCC.

This Call's on Burt

When you get the urge to reach out and touch someone, wouldn't you like to have Burt Reynolds or some other rich celebrity foot the bill? That's exactly what thousands of long-distance callers have been trying to do, on and off, for years now.

In a rumor that has persisted since 1981, the one-time sex idol is purported to have stated on the "Tonight Show" that he had recently won a court settlement for a million dollars — against whom, the rumor varies, from the *National Enquirer* for libel, to the phone company itself for some unspecified transgression. Reynolds supposedly invited viewers to share his bounty by charging all their long-distance telephone calls to his number over a given amount of time.

Various fourteen-digit numbers, purported to be Reynold's phone credit card number, found their way into public circulation. Reynolds himself denied the story, the usual debunking newspaper articles came out, and AT&T made it clear that someone would pay for the calls, and it wouldn't be Burt Reynolds. Nevertheless, throughout the 1980s the rumor cropped up — often in letters to the editors of newspapers detailing how a "friend of a friend" had heard about the Burt bonanza. Variations attributed the telecommunicative generosity to Johnny Carson himself, as well as to Paul Newman, Robert Redford, and Sammy Davis, Jr.

Such seemingly harmless rumors shed light on a more frightening aspect of the budding "information age" — credit-card fraud and its ramifications. Sure, credit cards, telephone charge cards, and the like are easy to use — but they're also easy to abuse. A stolen credit card number opens up a whole world to the new breed of high-tech criminal, and creates a massive headache for the innocent plastic-money devotee. Few doubt that the economy of the next century will rely even more on electronic transactions, and no doubt such tales will continue. Now, if only we could get our hands on Burt's filofax...

Unreal Beach Bum Makes World His Oyster

In the summer of 1974, a weekly paper in the small Delaware beach town of Rehoboth reported the discovery of gigantic pearl-laden oysters in the surf off Rehoboth Beach. According to the paper, a local townsman, Sam "Hobo" Jones, a retired sheet-metal worker, and his wife, Ethel, waded into the water and filled two bushel baskets full of huge oysters, which, when split open, spewed out what seemed to be pearls of extremely high quality.

The Joneses, unsure of the value of their find, brought several of the oysters to the Rehoboth police department. The Rehoboth police chief, the paper reported, then contacted the Delaware Department of Interior, which in turn called upon the Smithsonian Institute in Washington, DC, and their resident Japanese pearl expert, Dr. Laernu Retsyo. Upon examining the oyster specimens, the doctor recognized them as the species "*Meleagrina gargantua*, which produced the largest, hardest, most brilliant pearls in the world." Each of the two to four super-pearls the oysters contained were reported to be worth between $500 and $1,000.

As the story of the giant oysters spread, crowds of East Coasters, trying desperately to keep up with the Joneses, flocked to Rehoboth in hopes of cashing in on the monster mollusks. But they scanned the surf in vain. No oysters were to be found. Had the Joneses scooped them all up? In fact, there were no oysters. The entire tale was a hoax, perpetrated by the fertile imagination of a newspaper editor attempting to bolster the beach town's flagging tourist season.

Close readers of the original story might have been tipped off by the unlikely name of the protagonist, "Hobo" Jones (whose nickname makes up part of "Rehoboth"). But even more telling is the name of the supposed Smithsonian pearl expert, "Laernu Retsyo", which, spelled backwards, is . . .

THE MILITARY MIGHT

All the MIAs Are Missing!

Missing in Action is one of the cruelest designations for parents whose child was lost in Vietnam. A mother can grieve for, and make peace with the memory of, a boy whose body was laid to rest in a pine box, but how can she give up hope on a son who might still be alive somewhere? Memories fade, but the picture of a boy languishing in a tropical prison when he ought to be growing into adulthood must be a heartbreak year after year.

The parents of a young man listed as missing in action are condemned to a life of waiting. That is why it is particularly disturbing to see their lives disrupted by a hoax.

In March of 1992, the family of Army Captain Donald G. Carr received a grainy photograph of a middle-aged man who bore a striking resemblance to their son, who was a pilot shot down over Laos in 1971. The man in the photograph looked so much like Carr that his relatives, like those of many of the 2,273 U.S. servicemen listed as missing in action, dared to believe that their loved one was still alive in Southeast Asia.

But like all such photographs that have been subject to thorough investigation, it turned out that the man in the photograph was not an MIA. In this instance the subject was a German national named Gunther Dittrich. Dittrich's identity, first reported by ABC News, was confirmed by Defense Department investigators who interviewed him in a German prison, where he was serving time for illegally exporting exotic Asian birds.

The phony photograph was sent to the Carr family by retired Air Force pilot Jack Bailey. Bailey claims he received the photo from an unidentified hoaxer and did not knowingly mislead the Carr family. Nevertheless, the Justice Department began an investigation of Operation Rescue, which Bailey formed to search for MIAs and which has raised over $3 million. The Department of Justice wants to know whether Operation Rescue is responsible for other fake MIA documents and photos.

The U.S. Senate has investigated Bailey's activities, as part of its inquiry into America's seemingly unending MIA heartbreak. With the full cooperation of the Viet Namese government, which desperately seeks to have rescinded the American trade embargo imposed during the Vietnam War, Senate investigators have not found a single piece of substantiated evidence that even one MIA survived the Vietnam War. But according to investigators, there is an overwhelming motive for manufacturing evidence to the contrary—money. Vietnam is desperately poor, squeezed between the Scylla of our trade embargo and the Charybdis of Communist economics. The only hard-currency commodities that routinely evade the U.S. embargo are the totems of undying hope and heartbreak that outlast every war.

Constellation Con

A giant wave of controversy washed over Baltimore's famed Inner Harbor and swept all the way to England in September 1991 when a naval historian said the city's prized tourist attraction, the United States Frigate *Constellation*—called the oldest navy ship still afloat—was a fake.

Respected naval historian Dana Wegner dropped the bombshell when he produced evidence supporting arguments voiced over the years that the 1797 frigate was actually scrapped in 1853, and its name given to a corvette under construction at the same time.

*Constellation*ites rallied quickly for a battle. Lovers of the USF *Constitution*, berthed in Boston Harbor, applauded. Built a month after the 1797 *Constellation*, the story, if true, would make "Old Ironsides" top gun in the navy. The navy wisely ducked the cannon shots by refusing to comment.

Constellation enthusiast Bill Cothron, of Bradenton, Florida, said "History, schmistory. It still looks like a pirate ship. So it wasn't the original one. So what? How many things in life are really original anyway?" Britishers complained that the HMS *Victory* (1765), on the decks of which Admiral Horatio Nelson died, is the oldest warship still in commission. To which Navy Lieutenant Len LaPorta replies, "Hey, it's not in the water. We don't count it."

Herbert Witz, president of the USF *Constellation* Foundation, was less cavalier in arguing against Wegner's findings. "The United States Navy has steadfastly maintained this is the one and only *Constellation*," he said. "Our position is simply what the navy says it is. And there are people of great repute who have always maintained this. We lay people, who are only volunteers, who are we to disagree with the experts in the navy?" Witz continued.

Wegner was drawn into the old argument after learning that the U.S. Naval Academy museum had a hull model of the ship in storage. Using computer analysis he concluded that the model did not match any of the 1797 drawings of the ship. Further research uncovered "seeming obvious forgeries" in twenty-one documents used to authenticate the 1797 theory, two of them phony letters written by Franklin Delano Roosevelt, a naval history buff and Assistant Secretary of the Navy in 1913, who went on to become commander in chief.

One of his supposed letters was written on a typewriter that didn't exist when Roosevelt was alive, the FBI found.

The ship also had nails fraudulently stamped 1797, "probably made with a device you could buy at any hardware store," Wegner said.

Why all the forgery hoopla? Wegner theorizes a *Constellation* curator probably was behind them, acting to save the ship after it was towed to Baltimore harbor years ago. The navy had plans to demolish the *Constellation*, "and the people of Baltimore had to act fast."

Rumors Fly in Noriega's Panama

Spring of 1989 was a season of discontent in Panama. The United States was ever more bluntly threatening the small Central American country, which bases its economy on the U.S.-controlled Panama Canal, and which owes its existence and independent history to the U.S. military. Panamanians were starved for news in those increasingly tense times, culminating in the most recent United States invasion of Panama. That action unseated the president of Panama, the drug-running ex-CIA-informer, General Manuel Noriega.

In Panama, as everywhere, discontent bred rumors. But the Panamanian rumor mill was unique, fed by word-of-mouth and telephone trees which were authoritative in the absence of a free press. President Noriega had suppressed the press at a time when late-breaking news could have been of life-and-death importance — it's unknown to this day how many hundreds, or perhaps thousands, of Panamanians died in the course of the 1989 U.S. invasion.

While President Reagan turned up the economic heat to force Noriega's ouster, rumors that the embattled ruler had fled the country flew from one end of the isthmus to the other. One rumor had him seeking asylum in Israel. In fact, Noriega hung tough in Panama.

Another *bola* (the Panamanians call their rumors "balls") said Noriega "had enough dirt" on Vice President George Bush to knock him out of the 1988 race for president, but that Noriega was waiting until after the Republican convention that summer to tell what he knew. Summer came and went with no new dirt on Bush.

For weeks Panamanians had heard of an international brigade of 1,200 soldiers — mostly Cubans and Nicaraguans — training secretly in the nation's jungles to fight for Noriega if the U.S. invaded the country.

"When I first heard that one," said an American born in Panama, "it was twelve hundred men. When I heard it a couple of hours later, it was twelve thousand I heard it from three different people that night, and [the brigade] kept getting bigger." Maybe it is still in the jungles. The soldiers never appeared in public.

The rumor, however, sparked rumors of shootings two nights in a row by U.S. marines guarding a petroleum tank storage facility near Panama City. Except for one marine killed in the crossfire of other marines, the U.S. said there were no casualties. Rumors persisted for days that four Cubans were killed in the incident and were taken out of the country secretly on a Cuban vessel traveling through the canal.

A marine at the scene later said the Americans did not chase the intruders into the jungle because one marine was already dead, and also he had heard a rumor that two air force guards were attacked in recent weeks at an oil-tank farm where fuel is stored. One was "hacked to death" with a machete and the other was "cut up pretty badly," he said. Surprised U.S. public affairs officers said "Bosh," and claimed that nothing like that happened.

Terrence Kneebone, public affairs officer at the U.S. Embassy in Panama, said, "There are no reliable sources of information in Panama, no reliable public media."

So, without a free press, rumors alone are left to carry the news, and so persuasive are some of them that even the international press corps is not immune to believing them.

One night during the season of discontent, reporters rushed outdoors around midnight to check out a rumor that there were tanks in the streets. They found no tanks. The Panama Defense Forces do not have any tanks.

Mussolini Says Hitler's Nuts?

One day in 1957 a mother and daughter walked into the offices of the Italian newspaper *Corriere Della Sera* and offered to sell thirty volumes of diaries they claimed were written by Benito Mussolini—draft dodger, vegetarian, and dictator of Italy for twenty-one years.

The daughter, Amalia Panvini, forty-three, said that one of the dictator's ministers had handed her father a package soon after the Italian underground captured and shot Mussolini and his girlfriend in 1945 near Lake Como, and hung them by the heels in Milan. The woman said the man told her father, "For the love of God, Panvini, hide them in a safe place." Her mother would vouch for her, the woman implied. The mother, Rosa, seventy-five, nodded.

Amalia said that despite the admonition given her father by the minister, she had now decided to sell the diaries because her family needed money. The old lady nodded again, this time emphatically.

"Ummm, good reading," the paper's editors decided after a hard look. The diaries contained passages characterizing Hitler as a madman. A call went out for the experts.

Vittorio Mussolini examined the handwriting in the letters and said it was his father's. An expert from Switzerland's University of Lausanne made chemical tests, compared the diaries with Mussolini's known handwriting, and pronounced them authentic.

"Thirty volumes of manuscript cannot be the work of a forger, but of a genius," he said. "You can falsify a few lines or even pages, but not a series of diaries."

Before anybody could buy the diaries, however, small details gave away the fraud, and police raided the Panvini home and charged the two women with forgery and fraud. The elder Panvini shouldered the blame. She said she had spent years perfecting her imitation of the dictator's handwriting and when the volumes were finished, enlisted her daughter's aid in selling the forged diaries. Both women got suspended sentences.

Unaware of this denouement in Italy, the *Sunday Times* of London bought a chunk of the volumes from the Panvinis eleven years later. After paying $71,400 for them, the editors learned of the hoax and stopped publication.

Amalia's mother died that year. Amalia waited until 1983 to say any more. No, they had not forged the diaries, she asserted. She had only confessed because of the prosecution's offer not to send her to jail if she did. Perhaps she yet hopes there's another scandal-mad nation out there—even further from Italy than England—that will properly appreciate her family's unique heirlooms.

Neo-Nazis Say Anne Frank is a Fraud

"Daddy began to talk of us going into hiding. I asked him why on earth he was beginning to talk like that."

So wrote Anne Frank almost fifty years ago in the family refuge, a small space above her father's shop on Prinsengracht in Amsterdam.

To her horror she was to learn why her father talked like that. In 1944 she and her family were seized by four Nazi policemen and sent to the Bergen-Belsen concentration camp, where Anne died of typhus three months before World War II ended. Her sister, Margot, was killed there, and her mother died of exhaustion. Otto Frank, her father, survived to spend the rest of his thirty-five remaining years editing and publishing his daughter's diary, which the Nazis had tossed aside when they routed the family.

In 1987, following publication of the most complete version of this acclaimed account of the most inhuman period in history, a rumor started in Vienna that the Dutch government had proof of the diary's falsity. Neo-Nazis in Germany picked up the rumor and spread it in their publications and by word-of-mouth, and soon those who wished to believe believed.

Actually, according to Vera Ebels, director of documentation at the Anne Frank Foundation, the Dutch government had, in fact, examined the diary and authenticated it by chemical, handwriting, and historical tests.

In fact, the Anne Frank Foundation is considering filing suit against the Nazi doubters, in the wake of a remarkable American court victory. In 1985, an associate of Holocaust historian, Elie Weisel, was awarded $90,000 in damages from the Institute for Historical Review in California, which had claimed to prove that the Holocaust was a hoax. Obviously, the life of Anne Frank is another document refuting such assertions.

Many who have read her diary require no documentation. Anne, remembered by her classmates as a humorous, likable girl who loved ping-pong, nice clothes, make-believe, and who collected pictures of movie stars, wrote of a deepening faith in life and in people as her outside world shrank and her inner world grew. The more hatred she saw, the greater became her courage and compassion. Only one who has lived through horror could have written as she did:

> In spite of everything I still believe that people are really good at heart ... I see the world gradually being turned into a wilderness, I hear the ever-approaching thunder, which will destroy us, too. I can feel the sufferings of millions, and yet, if I look up into the heavens, I think that it will all come right, that this cruelty too will end, and that peace and tranquillity will return again ...

Could anyone but a fifteen-year-old girl have written such a brave and simple paean to life?

Iraq Wins Again!

Jordanians had their choice of news sources throughout the 1991 Persian Gulf War. But in the cacophony of contradictory assertions, it was Radio Baghdad they believed. So they didn't know much about Scud missile attacks, for example, or of the one-sided barrage that ended the conflict. But they did hear many other war and news reports, with a perspective all their own.

One day they heard that Iran's president, Hashemi Rafsanjani, in blasting Iranian radicals, said it would be "suicide" for Iran to help Iraq keep Kuwait. But the same day, another report said Rafsanjani "made his position clear on Palestine — to destroy Israel. He said Iran wants Palestine in all the territory that is Israel, not just in parts." No mention was made in this report of "suicide."

The first report was made by Reuters, the BBC, and most Western news agencies. The second was made by Baghdad Radio. Which did the people of Amman believe? Man in the street Tureef Halaseb said just Baghdad Radio: "Iraq has made a point of telling the truth. They are dealing with the Arab masses, and the masses will not take it lightly if they are misled."

And the stories about Saddam Hussein having an atomic bomb, a cruise missile, and as many look-alikes as Elvis Presley, so the United States will never know if it gets him? All these rumors and reports were shot down time and again by the Western press and by American General Norman Schwarzkopf. "I pay no attention to Schwarzkopf," said another Ammanite, Khalid Abu Nuwar.

Jordanians also were told by Radio Baghdad, and believed, that Israel had itself set off explosives in Tel Aviv, and claimed they were Iraqi Scuds so that Israel would get emergency shipments of Patriot anti-missile missiles from the U.S. It must be said that, in fact, Israel did receive emergency airlifts of Patriot missiles immediately after the Scud attacks began.

Another Radio Baghdad report claimed that Colonel Muammar Qaddafi, a rival pan-Arab leader, was said to be hosting Syrian president Hafez Assad (Saddam Hussein's sworn enemy), and President Hosni Mubarak of Egypt (who dispatched Muslim troops against Saddam) at a mini-Yalta convened with the purpose of carving up the Arab world.

And what was Radio Baghdad's explanation for the Americans coming into the Gulf? They want to control King Fahd of Saudi Arabia, who is custodian of the Arab world's two holiest places, and therefore control the minds of 800 million Muslims. The infidels ordered Iraq to invade Kuwait so they could intervene, and the Kuwaitis, who aren't the country's legitimate rulers anyway, knuckled under.

No, the story doesn't make much sense, but it seemed to many Western listeners that what Radio Baghdad broadcast best was static.

MIA "Evidence" for Sale

There have been many cruel hoaxes concerning sightings of Americans still listed as missing in action almost two decades after the conflict in Vietnam ended.

Along Dong Khoi Street on any afternoon in Ho Chi Minh City, formerly Saigon, one can find a bazaar abounding with American artifacts from the war, all for sale: dog tags, letters home and letters meant to have gone home, books with nameplates, Zippo lighters with favorite nicknames engraved on them.

The question arises: If you were a local looking for some easy money, why not gather some of these objects and use them for raw material to fabricate sightings of MIAs, the facts of which you will send by parcel post?

Such hoaxes have become a cottage industry in Vietnam. In 1990, the U.S. State Department forwarded to Vietnamese authorities a handwritten letter from a U.S. serviceman saying he was alive in Vietnam. With the letter was a blurred photo showing the American writing at a table.

The letter said, "If you want to see me you have to send money," recalled Dang Nghiem Bai, an official at the Vietnamese Foreign Ministry in Hanoi. An investigation disclosed that the black man shown at the table was the offspring of a liaison between a black American soldier and a Vietnamese woman during the war.

Bai said that up to $1 million has been offered over time as a reward for information on POWs and MIAs. Given the poverty of the nation as a whole, he said, "It is unlikely that no one would come forward if such evidence exists."

An American official familiar with the catalog of hoaxes on MIAs said, "While live sightings reach us with amazing regularity . . . not one report has ever panned out to the satisfaction of authorities who are hoping against hope that it is true."

An American diplomat added, "No one has ever offered a rational explanation for why the Vietnamese would continue to keep prisoners of war when they stand to lose nothing from it and in fact stand to lose substantially if it ever were proven."

As the MIA marketplace is investigated more deeply, it becomes more and more clear that some Americans, no less than Vietnamese, have profited from this desperate commerce in false hope.

Great War Photos Shot Down

The Great War—which got its name changed after the second, even greater one—ended with the 1918 Armistice. But in popular memory and media it lived on, especially in the glamorous images of wartime heroes that were endlessly recycled through the troubled peace that followed. The most glamorous heroes were the World War I flying aces who so daringly lifted individual combat from the old fields of honor, into the sky. Small wonder that the first Academy Award was won in 1928 by a piece of Hollywood shop work called *Wings*.

Three years later, the popular imagery of aerial dogfights got much better. A collection of fifty-seven spectacular air-combat photos received rave reviews in New York. Documenting with unprecedented clarity and drama skies thick with planes and flames, the photos were all the more piquant for being taken by an actual downed, dead hero, whose identity was not revealed because he had violated strict Royal Air Force rules against fiddling with cameras while defending British soil.

Surely a forgivable peccadillo: The House of Commons clamored that posthumous honors be rendered the heroic photographer, and the British Air Ministry assured all and sundry that he would not be disciplined if his identity were revealed. But the flying photographer's widow, a mysterious Mrs. Richard W. Cockburn-Lange who shunned the public eye and communicated only through her literary agent and travel agency, ignored the clamor with ladylike decorum.

Some flyers and experts were in fact skeptical of the photos and the attendant hullabaloo. All the planes dated from the last year of the war, and it seemed unbelievable that one man could have seen, let alone shot, so much action in so brief a time. But the critics were silenced in 1933, when the diary of the anonymous hero was published, along with his famous pictures, in the acclaimed bestseller *Death in the Air*.

The diary described the familiar comradery and gore of war, and also explained how the photos came to be taken. It even detailed a long, clever struggle to design a shutter that would trip automatically when the airplane's guns were fired. No more controversy: The Cockburn-Lange photographs became archetypal Great War images, and disappeared from common view only when they were outmoded by World War II.

So matters stood until 1984, when a few suitcases filled with flying memorabilia were donated to the Smithsonian Institution. They caught the eye of Peter Grosz, who was until then researching reconnaissance aircraft of the late Austro-Hungarian Empire. Grosz had grown up in the thrall of the Cockburn-Lange photos, and suddenly his research interests shifted. Through archival sleuthing, Grosz followed a paper trail that ultimately led to Wesley Archer, a restless American who had served in the RAF and, while knocking around after the war, served a stint as a pioneer Hollywood special-effects man. His specialties were set design and model-making.

Photo researchers say he had an impressive flair for superimposing multiple negatives (one of his photos contains fourteen variously arresting airplanes), and he had a pretty good hand at retouching wires barely detectable in negatives. Wesley Archer and his wife Betty—a.k.a. Gladys Maud Cockburn-

Lange — made $20,000 in 1930s dollars from their fraud, and persisted in their rather knockabout ways until their deaths in the 1950s, still undetected. The researcher who helped Grosz unmask them says, "the Archers were really good people in their way, and their hoax was a genial one. You have to admire them both."

Hitler's Diaries, Doubtful

It was a world-wide publishing sensation when the brash West German photo weekly *Stern* announced in 1983 that it had uncovered sixty-two volumes of Adolf Hitler's diaries chronicling the Fuhrer's years from 1932 to 1945.

They were found, the weekly said, by farmers after a plane carrying Hitler's personal effects crashed near Dresden at the close of World War II. The plane was one of ten carrying his staff and priority cargo from the bunker in Berlin where he killed himself nine days later ("Must close now. Borman wants all my documents sent away," the last entry reads).

Newspapers and magazines in England, France, and the U.S. offered millions for the privilege of reprinting the diaries. *Stern* saluted them and reached out for the money.

But first, the customary documentation. Cambridge historian and Nazi scholar Hugh Trevor-Roper, also a director of one of the news organizations bidding for the reprint rights, examined some of the books of the diary and wrote, "When I turned the pages of those volumes, my doubts gradually dissolved. I am now satisfied they are authentic." At that point he should have put the cover back on his typewriter. But like so many writers who have already made their point, he went on to say that he would stake his reputation on his conclusion.

Newsweek consultant Gerhard Weinberg also looked at the books, since the magazine considered spending big bucks to reprint. Weinberg liked what he saw but had reservations. *Newsweek* pulled out of the negotiations.

British historian David Irving switched from skeptic to true believer. He'd earlier interrupted a *Stern* press conference by leaping up and shouting, "Ink, ink, ink." But he calmed down after further study of the diaries and pronounced them genuine.

Stern's presses started to roll.

Researchers continued to nag *Stern*. How come such unlikely comments in the diaries as "Must get tickets to Olympic games for Eva Braun," and the complaint "On my feet all day long"? And how about the diaries saying Hitler (forty-eight years old at the time) received congratulations on his fiftieth birthday from a general who was celebrating his own fiftieth birthday?

Other nuisances were pointed out: Hitler had always dictated his thoughts and messages; moreover, he had suffered progressive palsy which made his writing hand greatly shake. None of the diaries showed this wavering.

With negative evidence mounting, the issue was decided by a devastating analysis report that polyester and other post-war fibers were in the books. Trevor-Roper, seeing his until-then august reputation at stake, reported his second thoughts: "I must have misunderstood," he wrote. ". . . I am now convinced that some documents in that collection were forgeries."

Stern had been duped, and cried "hoax" and "forgery." It stopped the presses, returned the money collected from the bidders, and four editors and three executives from *Stern*'s parent company, Gruner & Jahr, were fired.

The Armistice that Wasn't Quite Yet

In the fall of 1918, the German army, in full retreat along the Western front and with their homeland in upheaval, began sending out feelers to the Allies about an armistice to bring an end to World War I, the most devastating conflict the world had yet seen. Finally, on the morning of November 7, an official German delegation passed through the French lines to negotiate a general cease-fire.

Shortly thereafter, the French Intelligence Bureau received an erroneous report that the armistice had been signed at 11 a.m. and that all fighting would cease at 2 p.m. that afternoon. This news was passed on to Captain Stanton of the American Liaison Service, who, before confirming the report, sent it on to his chief in Paris, Captain H.J. Whitehouse. Whitehouse, in turn, relayed the information to American Army Intelligence in Paris, which expressed extreme doubt that the armistice could have been signed so quickly, despite Whitehouse's assertion that the story was "absolutely reliable and authentic." Unswayed, Army Intelligence passed the rumor on to General Pershing's headquarters with a great deal of reserve, where it should, in fact, have died.

Meanwhile, though, Stanton was relaying the story to French and American officials. A telegraph message with the bogus tale reached the office of American Admiral Henry Wilson in Brest just as the head of United Press, Roy Howard, was paying the admiral a courtesy call. Howard, recognizing the story of a lifetime, asked permission to use it, which Wilson hesitantly granted. The U.P. chief hastily prepared a cable to be sent to his New York office, but since only his head European reporter, William Philip Simms, was authorized to send a collect cable through the Brest office, Howard added Simms' name to the bottom. The cable operator, assuming the dispatch had been censored and therefore approved in Paris, added a Paris dateline to the cable. At 11:56 a.m. Eastern Standard Time, the Western Union cable office in New York received the report. Three minutes later, the New York censor approved the dispatch for release — it must be authentic, he presumed, since it carried the name of the president of U.P. and its chief European correspondent; the Paris dateline further assured its censorship by the French. The news was promptly relayed to the U.P. office. Thus through a most byzantine chain of unconfirmed reports and faulty presumptions was the false news of the war's end relayed to America.

New York exploded with celebration. Offices, stores, and factories emptied as people spilled onto the streets, joyously embracing and marching arm-in-arm with complete strangers in impromptu parades. Confetti and ticker tape rained down on happy mobs of revelers as they sang patriotic tunes and toasted the Allies and their leaders. The Stock Exchange shut down a half-hour early; the telephone company carried more calls between one and three than in any two hours in its prior history.

Meanwhile, U.P. headquarters began to become skeptical. No other press service had the story. The hapless Howard, learning that the report was "unconfirmed," urgently cabled New York to that effect at about 2 p.m., which should have been early enough for the afternoon papers to dampen the effect of the story. The censor in New York, however, first channeled the cable to Washington, allowing the tale further time to travel across the country.

Not until the next day did the truth bring the nation back to reality. In an editorial entitled, "The Thief of Joy," the *New York Tribune* mused, "When the news of peace arrives, shall we have another celebration as good and joyous as those first hours? Hardly, we think. The edge has been taken off."

Navy Intelligence Officer Uses Disinformation to Protect SMU Football

University presidents and trustees often talk about wresting control from over-eager boosters and integrating football into academic life. But the fact is that in many cases the tail is still wagging the dog.

Take, for example, Southern Methodist University. Anxious to cash in on ticket demand, SMU moved home games from its thirty-thousand-seat Ownby stadium on campus to Texas Stadium, which holds sixty-five thousand and is home to the Dallas Cowboys. In the mid-1980s, SMU got into trouble for recruitment violations. Some said players had been paid. Others said special do-nothing classes had been created to help football players keep their grades up. In the wake of these violations, the National Collegiate Athletic Association (NCAA) put SMU on probation.

The boosters and SMU officials—hardly fazed by the probation—soldiered on, setting up a slush fund which they used to pay players. But when the NCAA got wind of the new slush fund, their game plans went situation-red.

According to the *Chicago Tribune*, school officials contacted Kevin Lerner, who claimed to be a navy intelligence agent assigned to spy on foreign students at SMU. Lerner soon began to cloud the issue of SMU's behavior by spreading rumors about the school.

He began by making anonymous phone calls to the press. He told reporters that the scandal went beyond a slush fund. He alleged that other students were organized by boosters to take tests for athletes and that boosters paid women students to have sex with athletes.

Lerner's ruse provoked some stories in the *Dallas Times-Herald* but did not in any significant way derail the NCAA investigation, which eventually resulted in a two-year suspension of the SMU football program.

Meanwhile, an SMU committee recommended a way to reestablish the academic integrity of the football program and the school. The committee advocated that athletes have at least thirteen secondary-school credits, rank in the top half of their high school class, and have a comprehensive score of at least 800 on their SATs. The minimum NCAA standards are a 700 on the SAT and a 2.0 grade-point average.

"What we're talking about is strong internal control," SMU interim president William Stallcup told the *Chicago Tribune*. "We want the dog to start wagging the tail."

The Iraqi Baby Killers

It's said the first casualty in war is truth. The truth of the maxim was clear to see in the United States' biggest foray into armed international-dispute resolution, the liberation of the occupied Middle Eastern state of Kuwait. Saddam Hussein's invasion of his peaceful Persian Gulf neighbor had rightfully shocked the world. As stories of the Iraqis' brutal occupation of the tiny oil-rich kingdom began to leak out from occupied Kuwait — most vivid was the tale of Iraqi soldiers tearing Kuwaiti newborns from their incubators and leaving them to die — the community of nations coalesced in indignation and outrage. "This will not stand," President Bush intoned, drawing a line in the sand and daring Saddam to cross it.

In the months that followed, the world debated what course of action to take in response to the Iraqis' aggression. Immediately after the invasion of Kuwait, president Bush sent a large contingent of American troops to Saudi Arabia to dissuade Saddam from any temptation to keep his troops moving into what would have been a much bigger prize. That, it seemed, was where the proverbial line in the sand had been drawn. In October, as reports of atrocities in Kuwait continued, the U.S. Congress was treated to an emotional spectacle as a teenage Kuwaiti girl calling herself only "Nayirah" (she didn't reveal her full name, presumably to protect her family still in Kuwait) tearfully recounted the incubator story, telling Congress she personally saw fifteen Kuwaiti babies dumped to their deaths. She recounted other tales of horror also widely broadcast.

The congressmen were moved to tears. Bush was moved to double the American troop presence in the Gulf. Clearly, instead of a defense of Saudi Arabia, the Americans were now preparing for an invasion of Kuwait to evict the Iraqis. Amnesty International picked up the story in its eighty-eight-page report on human rights abuses in Kuwait, and the president cited the report repeatedly as rhetoric heated up and his deadlines came due.

But was the incubator story, the tale that gripped the U.S. most strongly and solidified the president's basis for action, true? Who was this Nayirah?

Though truth suffers in war, it often makes a quick recovery once the boys—and now girls—come home. In the May 1991 edition of the *Progressive* magazine, shortly after the fighting ended, Arthur E. Rowse uncovered the real story behind the purported baby butchery. The weepy Nayirah, it turns out, was the daughter of the Kuwaiti ambassador to the United States. She hadn't been in Kuwait during the occupation, much less witnessed the Iraqis pulling incubator plugs. And doctors at the main Kuwait City hospital disavowed any knowledge of such atrocities; the few newborns who perished in the first days of the invasion, it seems, suffered chiefly because 90 percent of Kuwait City's doctors fled the country before or shortly after the invasion.

Man's Inhumanity to Man, Good for Rumor

Post-war Berlin was ravaged by many plagues—hunger, homelessness, poverty, political turmoil. And, in the minds of most Berliners, something of a much more barbaric nature.

This story was prevalent throughout the summer of 1946, when many Berliners were on the verge of starvation: A young woman bumped into a gaunt old man feeling his way down the sidewalk of a Berlin street with a cane — a blind man. The plump girl, feeling sympathy for the poor, sightless soul, offered her assistance. He gave her an envelope, asking her to deliver the letter inside it to the address on the envelope. The girl, noticing the address was quite a distance away and that she was passing that way, said she would be glad to take the letter with her.

As she walked off, she happened to glance back to check on the man's progress; what she saw was the presumed invalid making off rapidly in the other direction, cane tucked under his arm. Fearing a ruse, she delivered the letter not to the address on the envelope but to the police, who went to the apartment indicated. There they found two men and a woman with a virtual butcher's shop of fresh meat. A doctor inspecting the meat and declared it . . . human flesh! The envelope, when opened, consisted of a single sentence scrawled on a sheet of paper: "This is the last one I am sending you today."

The credulity of the Berlin public, 95 percent of whom are said to have believed the tale, may be traced to the tale of the Ogre of Hanover, a *real* cannibal. He was executed in 1925 for murdering several dozen young Hanover men and selling choice cuts of their bodies to the public. The entire town of Hanover became strict vegetarians for several years afterward.

Serbs and Croatians Both Claim Same Massacre

In time of war, it's difficult or impossible to find out what's really going on. Troops move through neighboring towns, bombed houses set blocks on fire, electricity fails, food becomes short. Is the enemy close at hand or far away? Is your side winning or are you about to lose, or die? People living in a war zone are more vulnerable to rumors than anyone. Rumor-peddlers, both official and amateur, find a ready audience in a war zone—an audience desperate for information and more than willing to be whipped into an emotional frenzy against the enemy.

During the war between Croatia and Serbia, rumors of atrocities circulated wildly. Some were true, but many were either total fabrications or half-truths staged and twisted by the two governments. First we'll look at Croatian rumors, which were loudly disseminated by a nascent national government eager to win the sympathy of the West in its bid for independence.

Some of the rumors were meant to portray the opposition as inhuman brutes bent on destroying and humiliating Croatia and her forces. One story told of Serb militants who cracked open the skull of a Croatian guardsman they had taken prisoner. After the soldier died, the Serbs purportedly scooped his brains out of his skull with a bayonet and forced another captured guardsman to eat them. When he choked, the rumor said, the Serbs shot him in the head.

Another type of rumor involved the way officials portrayed events that actually happened. Croatian TV viewers were shown graphic scenes of what an announcer described as a massacre of Croatian villagers by Serb guardsmen. Later that same night, the same footage was shown on Serb television— but the Belgrade broadcaster claimed that it was a Croatian massacre of Serbs. The truth isn't known.

Throughout the conflict, the Croatian government attempted to portray itself in a sympathetic light. It characterized Serb forces as "terrorists." Their activities were "war crimes." Croatians injured or killed in the conflict were not casualties but "victims."

In war, rumors come with the territory and they work against as well as for governments. The common impulse is to believe that everyone is lying, and to try to guess what the truth really is. In the former Yugoslavia, this impulse was made worse by the conflicting reports of the two governments. In the town of Split, a Croatian woman was worried by news reports that warned residents to expect attacks from Serb militants who would kill even women and children. Rather than consider that the reports might be exaggerated, the woman contended the government was not telling "even one sixth of the truth."

On the Serbian side, a rumor spread widely that the Croats were buying their weapons by selling the organs of Serb soldiers to the Germans. Most outside observers saw Serbia, by far the strongest nation within the former Yugoslavia and the dominant power in the Yugoslav army, as the aggressor in the conflict raging across its borders. But many Serbians see themselves differently, and rumors have helped them to do so. The rumors have ranged from the atrocity stories common in every war to specific disinformation campaigns fostered by the Serbian government to put itself in a good light.

One common rumor held that Croatian soldiers were shown on television playing football with the skulls of Serbian babies. We know that Serbian TV viewers saw graphic scenes of what an announcer described as a massacre of Serbian villagers by Croatian guardsmen—the same scenes that, earlier that same night, were shown on Croatian television as a Serbian massacre of Croats. Serbian president Slobodan Milosevic, who had used fiery nationalist rhetoric to consolidate his power while the other nations of Yugoslavia looked on nervously, used the electronic media to spread one-sided information, prop up Serb moral, and demoralize the enemy. As Serbian forces moved into Croatian territory, Milosevic used bombastic satellite television broadcasts to paint Serbian nationalists and the federal army as victims of brutal Croatian aggression.

Likewise, the Serbian press worked to sanitize their country's activities by the use of such phrases as "defending our hearth," "liberation," and "volunteer units."

All these rumors functioned to alienate Serbs from their Croatian neighbors. Before the war, Serbs and Croats had commonly lived in the same towns and on the same streets. Intermarriage was common and many of the younger generation thought of themselves as Yugoslavs rather than Serbs or Croats. The rumors helped to change all that, and make neighbors enemies.

More recently, a far more dreadful disinformation campaign has undergirded the terrible fighting and "ethnic cleansing" perpetrated by Serbian forces in Bosnia, the mixed-ethnic nation nestled between Serbia and Croatia. Bosnian Serbs widely believe that their Muslim neighbors are in cahoots with Arab terrorists and Islam fundamentalists to turn the tide of Western civilization. They believe, on the basis of such rumors, that the Serbs of Bosnia stand on the embattled ramparts of all Christendom, and that Western ingratitude is not their just due.

Bosnian Muslims, it must be noted emphatically, consider these convictions to be nonsense. No evidence has been presented to support any of them. For the Serbian irregulars attacking their former friends and neighbors, none is needed.

On a related front, United Nations observers have concluded, after researching widespread rumors of massive, systematic rapes of Muslim women and children by Serbian forces in Bosnia, that the stories have a horrifying basis in truth. Serbia stands accused of using civilian terror, with terrifying rumor-mongering in its wake, as deliberate weapons of war.

Chiang Kai-Shek Needs a New Watch?

A story sprang up during the visit of Madame Chiang Kai-Shek to the United States in 1943. It seemed her secretary entered a jewelry store in Baltimore and asked for a $500 watch. The dealer recoiled; he didn't have such an expensive watch, but he assured her he did have some good ones. He showed several to the secretary. In all, the secretary selected $7,000 in watches and jewelry and told the proprietor to wrap them up. "And how," the jeweler asked, will you pay for this?"

"Just charge them to Lend-Lease," the secretary replied.

In World War II America, the story hit a nerve. Some citizens were already suspicious of Lend-Lease, a U.S. aid program that offered food, munitions, and other goods to nations fighting the Axis powers. And rumors were already were flying that Chiang had ripped off millions in money and materiel the U.S. had sent him to prop up his shaky regime.

Rumor scholars Gordon W. Allport and Leo Postman analyzed this historic rumor in some depth, in a lengthy 1949 *Public Opinion* article. They made several discrete points worth separating:

First, Allport and Postman called this a characteristic World War II "wedge-driving" rumor, which tended to divide the U.S. from its allies. Such stories circulated only among a "limited rumor-public," such as people who hated China or President Roosevelt, especially those who resented the "free-lunch" that they considered Lend-Lease to be offering mooching foreigners.

They theorized the rumor was "a product of frustration from shortages and high taxes, and its result was displacement of that frustration on Washington." It represented "a subtle fusion of antipathies and frustrations, and explains and justifies our political animosities," the authors said.

Moreover, it helped people on the home front to deal with their "guilt evasion." Many people stateside made a lot of money and spent it on themselves during the war, stashing away bags of rationed sugar and gas coupons while men were dying on the battlefields, on the sea and in the air. But this was easily forgiven "in the face of the blatant self-indulgence of one of the most prominent wartime personages, wantonly wasting our national funds in the purchase of fabulous luxuries."

The rumor also featured more common tall-tale characteristics, such as its "pseudo-authority of detail." Those precise amounts, $500 and $7,000, gave the story more plausibility. Also, specifying a well-known figure personalizes the rumor itself, and assimilates it "to common and conventional subject matter, of current interest."

And, of course, whether friend or foe, it makes Chiang Kaishek a more interesting villain.

OUT OF THIS WORLD

———————

Authentic Space Junk Inspires Kansas Boosters

On April 8, 1992, Kansas highway worker Charles Hodges noticed something near the side of the road. He walked over for a look and found a piece of twisted and burned metal, embedded in a field outside a state maintenance building. There was a backwards "R" inscribed on the metal and the grass around it was burnt and charred.

Not knowing what to make of his discovery, Hodges notified the Kansas State Police, who in turn handed the matter over to the Kansas Cosmosphere and Space Center (KCSC) in Hutchison. The KCSC, which local officials started in 1976 in hopes of creating a tourist attraction, already had a large collection of outer-space memorabilia. Museum experts, an astronomer, and an aeronautical engineer deemed the metal "consistent" with rocket fragments fallen from space. Moreover, a call to the air force revealed that a Soviet rocket booster had re-entered the atmosphere that morning. By evening, local television stations announced that a piece of Soviet space junk had dropped in the middle of Kansas and that Cosmosphere officials had it.

The story was not totally unbelievable, but in this case it was totally untrue. Shocked by how far his prank had gone, an unnamed highway worker informed his superiors at the Kansas Turnpike Authority that he had planted the piece of metal as a joke on Hodges. The supposed Soviet booster fragment had come from a diesel tank and not from outer space.

At the Cosmosphere and Space Center, embarrassed officials tried to back away from what was reported to be their original position. Max Ary, the Center's executive director, told the *Wall Street Journal*, "The most we ever said was that it could be a piece of space junk — the media overstated our position, but sure, we're embarrassed."

Besides blaming the media for misreporting what he said, Ary claimed that it was the Kansas Highway Patrol that led him astray. "Usually," he explained, "we devote 50 percent of an investigation to the circumstances of discovery. But when something is brought to you by the Kansas Highway Patrol, and when they assure you it's a legitimate story, you tend to believe them."

Landscape Painters Hoax Countryside

For several years in the late 1980s, crop circles were taken seriously as evidence of either extraterrestrial landing or some difficult-to-explain meteorological activity.

The crop circles were first noticed in 1981 when observers reported them to the press, which promptly served them up as evidence of extraterrestrial visitors. Each year, several more crop circles appeared in the English countryside and soon crop circles were appearing in isolated places on the continent of Europe.

Extraterrestrials were the most common explanation, but believers in the paranormal claimed the circles radiated mysterious energy forces. Others associated with the privately funded Circles Effect Research Unit (CERU) argued that a still unverified weather phenomenon was often responsible for the weird damage. Physicist Terence Meaden, who heads

CERU, claimed that when whirling columns of air pick up electrically charged matter, they flatten crops and produce the bright lights some observers saw above the circles.

A Japanese team led by physicist Yoshi-Hiko Ohtsuki visited the sight and theorized that a form of ball lighting generated by microwaves in the atmosphere flattened the crop. Ohtsuki's work was picked up by the British journal *Nature* and repeated in the national newsweekly, the *Economist*.

It was only after the circle enthusiasts – or "cereologists," as experts in the field style themselves – began seeking government funding that the hoax's perpetrators, landscape painters David Chorley and Douglas Bower, admitted that they had created the circles.

Chorley and Bower hatched the hoax in 1978. They were having a couple of beers in a pub named the Cheesefoot Head and wondering what they could do "for a bit of a laugh," when they recalled the circles Australian farmers had created a few years previously. It occurred to them they could have a little fun at the expense of UFO enthusiasts if they created a few of those circles in England.

They made a scale drawing of the pattern they wanted and devised a scheme for execution which involved a four-foot-long board and some wire attached to a visor, which they dragged in circles over pastures and fields. Oddly, though they created twenty or thirty of these circles a year, the first one wasn't discovered for three years. When one was finally found, the reaction to it was worth all their work. "We laughed so much that time," Chorley told *Time*, "we had to stop the car because Doug was in stitches so much he couldn't drive."

Cereologists for their part have reacted with some skepticism to Chorley and Bower's revelations. Pat Delgado, co-author of *Circular Evidence*, a bestselling book on the subject, told *Time*, "These two gents may have hoaxed some of the circles, but the phenomenon is still there, and we will carry on research."

Giant Octopus or Big Squid?

Almost a century ago on a Florida beach a man named Doc Webb found "a giant octopus" two hundred feet wide and weighing five tons. Comparable to a twenty-foot-tall person, it was the largest such creature ever seen by man.

Webb, a respected St. Augustine physician and founder of the local scientific society, announced his discovery, and the furor over what the creature really was and what to do with five tons of octopus began.

Webb himself assembled four horses, six volunteers, and much necessary rigging; he moved the creature forty feet over to some railroad ties, to save it from the tides. Talk began of turning it into a tourist attraction, but the hulk stank. The Florida sun only made the stink worse and also made the creature begin to shrink (possibly from dehydration).

Naming his proud find Octopus Giganteus, Webb sent a sample of it to A.E. Verrill, a Yale University scientist, who concluded that it indeed was an octopus, and immediately sat down to write about it (publish or perish even back then?). His article landed in the respected *American Journal of Science* and critics began lashing out at Verrill. The find, they said almost unanimously, was a whale or squid, which are known to grow much larger than octopuses.

After examining the creature F.A. Lucas, a curator at the Smithsonian Institution, said, "The substance looks like blubber and it is blubber, nothing more or less." Verrill then changed his mind. In another article in *Science* the headline ran, "The Supposed Great Octopus of Florida: Certainly Not A Cephalopod," (cephalopod being the octopus genus).

End of monster myth. Or was it?

In 1957, Dr. Joseph Gennaro, an anatomy professor at the University of Florida, heard about the monster from a researcher and decided to look into it. He obtained a small slice of the specimen which had wound up at the Smithsonian, stored in a three-foot-tall can, later lost by the institution. Gennaro's tests concluded that the sample was part of an octopus.

In the mid-1970s Kenneth Gruber, a student of Gennaro's at Harvard University, conducted some amino acid tests on the sample, and also concluded that it came from an octopus.

Neither Gennaro nor Gruber received any support from the scientific community for their findings, and the Giganteus sank into obscurity. Gennaro gave the sample, all that remains of the creature, to the St. Augustine Historical Society, whose director, Page Edwards, still calls it a squid.

Edwards said he had heard about the monster for years, calling it "one of the myths that has been around."

The Great UFO Conspiracy

William L. Moore, a UFO researcher, in May 1987 made public documents showing that President Harry Truman created a special unit called Majestic 12 to study the crash of a UFO in which four alien passengers were killed.

Moore said his research team had found a key White House paper in the National Archives dated July 14, 1954, which mentioned in passing a change in plans for a Majestic 12 briefing for President Eisenhower. The report appeared to have been prepared for the air force by Robert Culter, a White House aide.

In another document, President Truman ordered Secretary of Defense James Forrestal to create Majestic 12. A third document, which Moore said was obtained from an anonymous source, was a purported briefing paper for President-elect Dwight Eisenhower describing the 1947 crash, as if the then-Army Chief of Staff had never heard of it.

All this was heady stuff, and immediately the dogs were set loose.

Phillip J. Klass, the Washington editor of *Aviation Week & Space Technology* magazine and a leading debunker of UFOs, led the withering fire aimed at the documents. He prepared a report released by the Committee for the Scientific Investigation of Claims of the Paranormal which called the documents "clumsy counterfeits."

The chairman of Klass's committee, Paul Kurtz, a University of Buffalo philosophy professor, saw them more heinously. He said the documents represented "one of the most deliberate acts of deception ever perpetrated against the news media and the public."

First of all, the committee's report said, the man who prepared the report to the air force, Culter, was not in Washington when the report supposedly was written, but had left for Europe eleven days earlier.

As for the National Archives being the source for one of the documents, Klass said, it does not bear a top secret number and is marked "Top Secret Restricted Information," a designation not used until the Nixon Administration.

Furthermore, the document Truman supposedly wrote to Forrestal did not follow the format the president used to address his cabinet members in writing, and was created by superimposing the message on a photograph of an authentic Truman letter, Klass said.

It is worth noting that since the committee's report was published, several new books on the alleged UFO crash and cover-up have been published. Presentations on the subject are perennial favorites at UFO-phile conventions.

Nostradamus Is Always Right — Vaguely

The sixteenth-century seer whose deliberately murky four-line poems in his book *Centuries* — written at night after sitting for hours gazing into a brass bowl of water mounted on a tripod — are said to have predicted such things as the Great Fire of London in 1666, the rise of Hitler and his break with Italy, the sinking of the Luisitania, the Chicago Cubs' National League division championship in 1984, and the defeat of President Bush in 1992, among other events.

Like so many obscure riddles in the Bible, *Centuries*, the collected quatrains of Nostradamus, is a book of prophecies so wisely ambiguous that Nostradamus scholars can apply them to almost anything.

Nostradamus's influence remains so pervasive, especially to those who have heard his reputation but never read *Centuries*, that people get edgy from time to time when somebody unveils a new reading of prophecies that can be turned toward current events.

So it happened in Los Angeles in 1988, when Nostradamus was said to have predicted that the city would be hit by an earthquake caused by "planetary realignment." Los Angeles' Griffith Observatory and Cal Tech's seismology office were immediately inundated by callers asking if it were true.

Two events influenced the virulence of the rumor: One, an earthquake had struck the city the previous October; and two, a 1981 movie about the French stargazer called *The Man Who Saw Tomorrow* had recently been reviewed on a syndicated TV-movie review show. It had become a hot number at the city's video shops.

At Griffith Observatory, program supervisor John E. Mosley explained, sorry, there was no planetary lineup that spring. Sorry, planetary lineups do not cause quakes. And sorry, Nostradamus hadn't predicted an earthquake, he'd predicted a hailstorm with hail "larger than an egg," (this was his own reading of the seer's message). Cal Tech spokespeople debunked the possibility of the quake as well.

A Mountain of Lies

The Himalayan Mountains are the highest in the world. They've inspired many an adventurer, visionary, and blowhard to seek challenge, Shangri-la, and truth among their abiding mysteries. Science journals are now unveiling an alleged fraud of Himalayan proportions which may force geologists to rethink and rewrite the geologic history of "the roof of the world."

The individual amid the controversy is Viswa Jit Gupta of Panjab University who has published literally hundreds of articles on Himalayan geology over more than twenty-five years. They have been seminal in scholarly reconstructions of how the Indian subcontinent has slammed into the flank of Asia, raising mountains as it continues to move north on its tectonic plate.

But John A. Talent, of Macquarie University in Australia, has despairingly concluded that the fossil worm jaws which Gupta claimed to have found in the high Himalayas actually came from Amsdell Creek, New York, and have nothing to do with mountain-making. What's more, he believes Gupta's "Himalayan" fossil mollusk shells must actually have come from Morocco. As a result, says the Australian paleontologist, Himalayan geology "from one end to the other has been mucked up."

Dr. Gupta replies that the charges are "far from the truth," and stem from "malicious bias and professional jealousy." In the meantime, Gupta's many scientific collaborators are scrambling for more secure, if less Himalayan, high ground. Some have pointed out that, while Gupta's collaborators identified the fossils that Gupta presented them, Gupta himself retained sole responsibility for where they came from, and for theorizing how they got there. Therefore his collaborators stand by their identifications, while admitting that they may not have been sufficiently skeptical of the fossil's similarities to other, known specimens.

It was the specificity of some fossil types that pointed to Gupta's alleged fraud. The most suspicious fossils were conodonts — that's the common name for pinhead-sized, conical, toothlike shapes found in limestone. These conodonts are thought to be the remains of jaws once attached to segmented worms that lived in the Devonian Age, about 360 million years ago. Amsdell Creek, New York, contains a well known type of conodont, thought unique to the area. Moreover, Amsdell Creek limestone formations contain conodonts from four distinct periods within the Devonian Age, which is highly unusual. The Amsdell Creek conodonts are so well "fingerprinted" with distinct time periods that, according to Talent, "it is statistically beyond the bounds of possibility" that such strata could be found elsewhere — except in geology labs the world over, where they are commonly used for teaching and research.

In the case of the old Moroccan mollusks, called ammonoids, Talent says that these fossils too were distinctively fingerprinted, by desert weathering which could not have occurred in the high Himalayas. Gupta claimed he found the ammonoids proximate with the conodonts in the Himalayan mountains, though mineral analysis indicates that the two fossil types are fifteen million years different in age. Excising any erroneous information from the scientific record would take years, and might well leave behind an abiding strata of geologic error. Himalayan theory has returned to earth.

The Piltdown Man Returns to Dust

It's the most famous and consequential scientific fraud of the twentieth century. Because of it, for fifty years ancient human fossils found in Africa were virtually ignored by science—they contradicted theories built from the bones of the famous Piltdown Man. But in 1953, fifty-one years after the Piltdown Man was discovered, his head proved to be nothing more than an old human cranium—perhaps three centuries old—that was plopped atop the jawbone of an orangutan. The fraud exposed, science was freed to discover man's African genesis among much older bones in eastern Africa. Over the last forty years the Piltdown Man's remaining vestiges have been swept from the halls of science.

But still they're fascinating: Who pulled off this fabulously successful hoax? Why, and how? Eminent Oxford scholars have been implicated in theories of careerism and revenge; Sir Arthur Conan Doyle has not been above elementary suspicion; even the Jesuit mystic Pierre Tielhard de Chardin has been accused of knowing more than he told. A new book by anthropology professor Frank Spencer, *Piltdown: A Scientific Forgery*, runs through the alibis of the usual suspects, and delves as deep as we're likely to go to the bottom of the Piltdown mystery.

Spencer's suspicions center on one of the lesser suspects, Sir Arthur Keith, an ambitious, socially prominent Young Turk in turn-of-the-century science. From his position as anatomist and conservator at the Hunterian Museum of the Royal College of Surgeons, Keith was an early advocate of the theory that the human brain is the nexus of human evolution. He argued that humans had existed much earlier than was supposed, and that what first distinguished humans from other primates must have been an enlarged brain.

So Keith dismissed Neanderthal Man and Java Man, the small-minded protohominids then known to science. Sir Arthur was after proof positive for his theories, and he concocted nothing less than the Holy Grail sought by paleontologists and deep Darwinians alike: the "missing link" that clearly connected, with intermediating features, man and ape.

Seen in this light, his Piltdown Man could be compared to the mythical Northwest Passage around North America, which was often illustrated, though it didn't exist, on early explorers' maps: Piltdown Man was created because he *must* exist. His modern, English, brain cavity, paired with an obviously more primitive ape jaw, triumphantly confirmed Darwin's—and Keith's—theories, and bolstered as well darker Social-Darwinian persuasions concerning the burdened white man's evolutionary superiority over the peoples he was everywhere colonizing. The missing link provided by Piltdown Man ennobled an entire ascendant race, and brilliantly fulfilled a few individual careers along the way. The rise and fall of the Piltdown Man says volumes about the objectivity of Western science, and Western scientists, for good and ill.

Popular Science in the Age of Exploration

In the late summer of 1835, readers of the New York *Sun* were thrilled to learn that there actually are men on the moon. The men were revealed to be batlike, winged and furry, on average about four feet tall, yet, reassuringly, "their attitude in walking was both erect and dignified." What's more, lunar cranes and pelicans were also seen through the largest telescope on earth, and goats and buffalo. The day of the most amazing revelations, the *Sun* sold almost twenty thousand copies, achieving the highest newspaper circulation in the world.

How were these astounding assertions proven? Well, they weren't, exactly, for perfectly plausible reasons that involved the greatest astronomical dynasty of England. Founding father Sir William Herschel discovered Uranus in 1781, and his sister Caroline described three nebulas and eight comets; after receiving the king's patronage the two stargazers constructed an unprecedented, forty-foot-long telescope through which they promptly discovered Saturn.

Sir William's son, Sir John Herschel, out of filial devotion persevered in the family vocation after his father's death. In 1833 he and his family set sail for the Cape of Good Hope, where for the next four years he mapped the largely unknown southern skies, cataloging 68,948 stars.

Sir John was so far from Fleet Street that he labored in considerable obscurity during these years. This provided the main chance for Richard Adams Locke, an enterprising journalist for the New York *Sun*, who began his hoax with three articles, said to have been culled from respectable Edinburgh journals, on Sir John's lunar observations. His fourth article began to describe life on the moon, and his fifth caused a public sensation.

As viewed through Sir John's super-duper telescope, Locke revealed that moon men "were covered except on the face with short and glossy copper-colored hair, and had wings composed of a thin membrane without hair, lying snugly upon their backs from the top of the shoulders to the calves of the legs. The face, which was a yellowish flesh color was a slight improvement upon that of the large orangutan. . ." Their wings "possessed great expansion and were similar in structure to those of the bat, being a semitransparent membrane expanded in curvilinear divisions by means of straight radii, united at the back by the dorsal integuments." They shook these wings to dry after bathing like ducks.

Sadly, Locke reported two weeks later that Sir John's African laboratory burnt down, ending his work—though a group of Baptist ministers had already made inquiries to the reporter about possible means of propelling the Gospel to the moon. In another two weeks, the *Sun* gleefully admitted that its story was pure moonshine, and a good laugh was had by all—almost. A struggling hack writer named Edgar Allen Poe complained—quite unfairly—that the story was stolen out of his *oeuvres*.

Nine years later, the *Sun* made good to Poe: Its next hugely successful hoax, concerning adventurers who crossed the Atlantic to South Carolina by balloon, was penned by none other than the mollified Mr. Poe. Poe's hoax was richy praised by yet another starving writer, named Fyodor Dostoyevski.

Rain Forest Watergate Unfolds

Jaded anthropologists and *National Geographic* readers in 1971 were thrilled to encounter in a cover story a hitherto unknown tribe: the timid, Stone-Age Tasaday of the southernmost Philippines. Eating grubs, wearing orchid leaves, and as ignorant of agriculture and art as of weaponry, they were celebrated as "the most primitive people on Earth."

Their reputation foundered in 1986. Several journalists from Switzerland and Germany who trekked through the rain forest found wooden beads, metal knives, and colored T-shirts among the Tasaday they interviewed; they reported that the entire tribe was a hoax, perpetrated by the discredited Marcos regime in order to pillage nearby mahogany stands while seeming to befriend Philippine tribesmen. The hoax was arranged, according to the journalists, by Manuel Elizaide, Jr., the head of a government agency in charge of defending minority rights. His agency had rigid controls over access to the Tasaday homelands, and helicoptered scholars on-site for only a few hours at a time.

A scholarly spitting contest has ensued, with no clear victor. The original, allegedly duped anthropologists concede that the Tasaday aren't Stone-Age relics after all, but insist that the tribe is indeed distinct from its neighbors. Linguistic anthropologists disagree on whether the Tasaday speak a distinct language or a regional dialect. Neighboring dialects use words of Sanskrit, Chinese, Spanish, and English origin, while the Tasaday don't; this suggests to some that the small tribe may have broken contact with its neighbors two centuries ago, for reasons still entirely obscure. Equally obscure is whether a tribe of hunter-gatherers could live without agriculture in the Philippine rain forest.

A panel of the American Anthropological Association will review the controversy, but can't be expected to clear it up. The forests of southern Mindanao are thick with fugitive soldiers of the Marcos regime, Communist guerrillas, and understandably armed tribal groups. Any and all of them might be suspicious of errant anthropologists. Meanwhile, the existing fifty-thousand-acre Tasaday forest preserve would be eliminated if its home tribe is determined not to exist, so lobbying pressures that further politicize the Tasaday's existence are building force, while the population of southern Mindanao expands, and the international mahogany market scavenges the world for remaining old-growth trees.

What all this boils down to, according to Berkeley anthropologist Gerald Berreman, is "a rain-forest Watergate." Fellow anthropologist William Longacre of the University of Arizona in Tucson says, "It would take a competent archeologist a matter of hours to examine the Tasaday caves and determine whether they had been inhabited for days or for generations." So it's easy, right? "I wouldn't touch that study with a ten-foot pole," he concludes. The facts are the least of the controversy.

California Isn't Going Anywhere Very Quickly

People who have lived through earthquakes describe the experience in vivid terms. They tell of the shaking and shuddering of the usually immobile earth. The ground swells, surges, and breaks, causing structures to lose their foundation. California has the unfortunate distinction of being a frequent site for these disturbances.

Rumors are plentiful regarding California's likely situation after "The Big One," because of its oceanside location. Many people believe, or suspect, that California will break off the rest of the United States and sink into the Pacific Ocean. Can it be that Beverly Hills, Hollywood, and all of Lotusland are going to dramatically plunge underwater and disappear forever?

Experts say no. The San Andreas fault is to blame for most of the earthquakes that plague California. The fault runs through parts of the western section of the state from the Gulf of California in Mexico to a small coastal town called Manchester in the north. But the fault is a small part of an entire fault zone between two much larger pieces of the earth's crust—the Pacific Plate and the North American Plate. The movement of these two plates relative to each other is what causes earthquakes. The plates are not moving up and down, but rather they are sliding against each other. During a large quake, the parts of the state on the western side of the San Andreas Fault move northwest of those on the eastern side.

What this means is that if California is separated from the rest of the country, it will not sink. The part west of the fault will simply veer off and become an island or peninsula, comparable to Mexico's Baja California. But the process should take tens of millions of years, and, when it gets there, there will be even more beaches for everyone.

Another Earthquake Shake-up

In the fall of 1990 a New Mexico scientist predicted that the New Madrid Fault might break into the news again. New Madrid, a tiny hamlet in the Missouri territory, was flattened in 1815 by a huge earthquake that was felt as far away as the East Coast. Since then, only Midwestern geologists had thought about the obscure seismic fault running through the town and up the northern Mississippi valley—it has been quiet, and theoretically quite mysterious, until Dr. Iben Browning made his prediction. He calculated a 50 percent probability of a strong earthquake along one of four faults, including New Madrid, within forty-eight hours of December 3, 1990.

Admittedly, that sounds vague, but the scientific study and prediction of earthquakes is, to say the least, a shaky business. Browning's claim to have predicted the 1989 Loma Prieta quake made a lot of Midwesterners think twice about how solid the ground was under their feet, and in Southeastern Missouri, recently-developed emergency preparedness plans were publicized and practiced as a result of his announcement. Employees received a Federal Emergency Management Agency safety checklist and enacted evacuation drills. The town of New Madrid undertook its own emergency planning—which had been discouraged until then, in the belief that it was better not to advertise the town's possible earth-shaking predilections.

Though the date passed with no tremors, all in all the scare had beneficial effects. Disaster response plans, not limited to earthquakes, were coordinated and organized for any and all future needs. As it turned out, no one—not even Dr. Browning—knows when they will come in handy.

Radium Therapy: the High-Tone Miracle Cure

Eben MacBurney Byers, the well-known socialite steel mogul, was returning from the 1927 Harvard-Yale football game when he fell out of bed in his Pullman compartment, apparently while engaged in intimate revelry with a female foot-

ball fan. Byers was forty-seven, rich, and into every enthusiasm and excess that the Roaring '20s roared to satisfy.
He felt run-down after his accident, and was advised to take
Radithor, an over-the-counter health nostrum that was
making a name among the smart set. Though the tonic was
quite expensive — a dollar a bottle — Byers drank two or three
bottles a day.

Radithor was marketed as a general pick-me-up and, more
discreetly, as an all-purpose aphrodisiac. One serving contained a half-ounce of distilled water, tinctured with two
microcuries of radium. Byers swore by the stuff for two years,
recommending it to friends and lovers, until he complained to
his doctor that he'd lost "that toned-up feeling," and went off
the treatment. He died of massive radium poisoning a year
and a half later.

By then Radithor was off the shelves, and its promoter was
out of business. Regulatory agencies hadn't been remiss all
this time: The Federal Trade Commission had established
that Radithor indeed contained radium, and so satisfied
federal truth-in-advertising statutes. But Radithor eventually
fell afoul of the law by continuing to advertise itself as harmless, while more and more people seemed to die of it. This
could constitute untruthful advertising; the Federal Trade
Commission swung into action.

The FTC invited Eben MacBurney Byers to testify. Told that
the socialite was too sick to travel, an FTC lawyer went up to
Byers' Long Island estate to take his statement. The lawyer
said Byers' "whole upper jaw, excepting two front teeth, and
most of his lower jaw had been removed. All the remaining
bone tissue of his body was disintegrating, and holes were actually forming in his skull." Even after Radithor sales were
banned, some people — including New York City mayor
James J. Walker — continued to swear by it. So it was front-
page news when Byers died, and the official cause of death in
his autopsy report was radium poisoning.

Fallout from the Radithor controversy killed off the radioactive patent medicine business. But the marketing genius who pitched Radithor—at a 400 percent markup—protested his innocence to the end, noting that he'd probably drunk more of the stuff than anyone, and he felt great. He died of bladder cancer in 1949. Almost twenty years later his bones were exhumed by medical researchers. If good for nothing else, his Radithor still toned up a Geiger counter.

THE PROS AND THE CONS

Herrlinger Targets Dayton Hudson for Hoax

In the go-go eighties, the takeover was the big thing. Lots of money changed hands as rumors of mega-deals swirled through financial markets.

It's easy to understand the psychology of the hours or days preceding a takeover. If, for example, the stock of company A is trading at $28 a share, say Company B estimates the true value of Company A as $50 a share. In the interest of making a profit, B offers to buy all the outstanding shares of A for $40 a share. Reuters or Dow Jones gets wind of the offer and puts it on their wires. Investors large and small see they can make a quick bundle if they can grab stock in company A for, say, $35 a share. So the price of shares in Company A suddenly shoots sky-high.

The risk for investors is that the takeover might not come off and they'll be stuck with shares they bought at $35, while the stock's price falls back to $28 or even lower as dismayed speculators unload. In purchases of thousands, tens of thousands, or hundreds of thousands of shares of stock, a $5 per share loss can be quite expensive.

At 9:49 a.m. on June 23, 1987, Dow Jones tickers tapped out just such a takeover offer: A Cincinnati "private investment company" called Stone Inc. was offering $70 a share in cash for Dayton Hudson Corporation, a Minneapolis-based retailer whose holdings included Target department stores. The $6.8 billion dollar offer was unusual in coming from a company no one had ever heard of. Perhaps some investors who read the report reasoned that Stone Inc. must in some way be related to Cincinnati's wealthy Stone family.

The price of Dayton Hudson promptly shot up ten points, with one "lucky" investor grabbing 131,500 shares at $63 each. Unfortunately for that investor, the takeover offer was a hoax concocted by Paul David Herrlinger, a wealthy Cincinnati portfolio manager related by marriage to the Stone family.

Herrlinger first gave the news to the Pittsburgh bureau of the *Wall Street Journal* which, after checking with Herrlinger's boss at Capital Management Corp. and confirming that, according to *Journal* news services vice-president William R. Clabby, "[Herrlinger] was a man of substance" passed it on to the *Journal*'s corporate parent, the Dow Jones wire service.

Initially, Dayton Hudson refused to comment on the "offer." Buy orders flooded the market and at 11:35 when a 655,000-share block changed hands, the price had reached $59 a share. The price softened to $55 after 12:40, when Dow Jones reported that "circumstances surrounding the offer remain cloudy." Finally, at 3:30, Herrlinger's lawyer announced "David is not feeling right. He is a man who made a mistake," the price sank to $53⅛, down ⅞.

Why did Herrlinger do what he did? The hoax may have been simple mischief—or an attempt to manipulate the market, something the Securities & Exchange Commission inconclusively looked into. In any case, the Herrlinger hoax was part of a general speculation in Dayton Hudson stock, which at the time was often cited as a likely target of takeover attempts.

Agency Feels Sheepish About Sheila

The scent induces a mood; the wearer feels attractive; her admirer is intoxicated by her fragrance. It is "Sheila," a perfume, a pure luxury. And . . . it kills flies!

Sheila will make you feel good about yourself, attract that man you've been longing for and, get this, kill any flies that happen to be hanging around your person. Sound attractive? It did to hundreds of Londoners who besieged that city's department stores and finer boutiques with questions about the mysterious perfume that was suddenly being advertised on thousands of bus shelters around the city.

Those eager shoppers might have saved themselves the trouble: The ads were a hoax, albeit an innocently intentioned one. There was no Sheila. The posters were being used to test public reaction to advertising under certain conditions of lighting and location.

The creation of English ad agency More O'Ferrell, the Sheila posters, like most perfume ads, created a seductive aura of sex and mystery. But unlike other posters in the perfume genre, the agency had printed "ALSO KILLS FLIES" across the bottom of each poster.

More O'Ferrell marketing director Francis Goodwin explained to the *London Daily Telegraph* that the line about the flies was meant as a tip-off to the public. Unfortunately, Goodwin admitted to the *Telegraph*, the public did not notice that the ads were offered tongue-in-cheek. For days on end, they harried larger department stores and luxury shops seeking the new perfume that also kills flies. Who could have known there was such a market for a fly-killing perfume?

The ads proved that you never know what will succeed. When they appeared and were met with such a positive reaction in the spring of 1989, More O'Ferrell executives faced an odd problem — they had created brand awareness and demand but they had no product. According to the *Telegraph*, an Australian company had tried to market a scent named Sheila in Britain several years previously but it had "faded like a vanishing perfume."

An Old-Fashioned Rumor Still Makes a Bank Run

Rumors have the power not only to sway men but also to fell businesses. Some rumors are based on gossip and overheard conversations and predict business stories before they occur. Others, however, are not grounded in fact, but are still able to cause panic and chaos. "The bank is closing" is among these types of rumor.

Long lines, panicked bank customers withdrawing the contents of their accounts, fears of bank closings—all sound reminiscent of the 1930s during America's Great Depression. But wait, this happened in 1992 in Kansas City, Missouri. A rumor began to circulate around town that a local bank, Metro North State Bank, was to be closed by regulators, and that federal bank insurance would not be valid. There was a massive run on the bank, customers overflowed the lobbies and mobbed the drive-up windows, all demanding their money. The bank was forced to stay open two hours after its usual closing time in order to accommodate all the panicked depositors.

The bank tried to dissuade customers from withdrawing their funds by distributing a memo from the chairman of the bank to all depositors, which explicitly stated that the rumor was false and the bank was secure. This had only a minor influence on the panic. The Missouri Commissioner of Finance publicly announced that the state had no intentions of closing the bank. Officials from the Missouri state regulators as well as the Federal Deposit Insurance Corporation visited the bank to set customers' minds at ease about their bank. But the customers kept pouring in to take out their money before they lost it forever.

The exact source of the damaging rumor was not uncovered, but recent events made the bank fertile for speculation. The individual who controlled Metro North had recently turned over control of another bank he controlled, Home Federal. The Resolution Trust Company closed Home Federal and took several days to return funds to its customers. This sparked fear among bank customers. Another incident on the day of panic further spurred the rumors. A branch of the rumored bank had been robbed and was subject to a brief closing as a result. Customers visiting the bank under the fear of the rumor could have been further panicked by finding their branch closed.

This bank managed to avoid financial devastation and accommodate all customer requests. The rumor, however, did cause damage to the bank and its credibility. It is quite a task to rebuild customer confidence in a bank that was rumored to be on the verge of closing down for good.

Coke: The Real What?

Does the drink that brings the world together in perfect harmony also get it high? Is there more to the energy boost of a glass of Coca-Cola than just caffeine? Is Coca-Cola really made with cocaine? Rumors have circulated about the ingredients of the beverage for many years now, and have never fully faded. The Coca-Cola company has always protected the secret formula of its popular product. Only a chosen few know the details of the modern-day ambrosia. Coke's production line is set up in different stations so that even those who produce the magical formula only know some of its ingredients. This level of secrecy leaves the company wide open to speculation, and what often grows from such speculation is juicy rumors.

Stories abound of the capabilities of Coke. The drink was nicknamed "dope" in the South of the 1890s because of its rumored narcotic content. In the 1960s, popular belief held that the mixture of aspirin and Coke would make the consumer high. College students believed that if the drink were mixed with ammonia it would provide an energy boost of the kind they needed to pull all-nighters.

Coca-Cola was first manufactured in the late 1800s and sold at soda fountains. It became part of the fountain tradition. The beverage included extracts from kola nuts – the source of its caffeine – and from coca leaves – the natural source of cocaine. Coca-Cola was not, however, unusual in its use of the coca leaf. Many beverages used it as an ingredient. So this early version of Coca-Cola may have contained a trace of cocaine. The Coca-Cola company puts the emphasis on "may have" in their official response to the cocaine rumors. In any case, medicines of the time also regularly contained traces of various now-illicit drugs.

Society turned against the use of these drugs in the early twentieth century, and Coca-Cola revised its recipe. It began to use de-cocainized coca leaves in its formula to appease the rising disapproval of cocaine. The drink remained as popular and as well-loved as ever.

The stories of the mystical capabilities of Coca-Cola are utterly false. The active ingredients in the beverage are actually quite predictable – carbonated water, sugar, caffeine, caramel, and phosphoric acid. Whatever the extra ingredients are that make Coca-Cola such a popular beverage, they definitely are not cocaine or any other addictive drug. The mystery of what *really* makes the world sing in perfect harmony, alas, remains.

Cookie Was Steep Even for Neiman-Marcus

Think of the many times you have gone to the mechanic and received an extraordinary bill for what you thought was quite ordinary work. Or the movie theater where you can buy a ten-ounce soda for the unreasonable price of two dollars. Or the prime example of all, the retail store where you can find a $10 can opener. These days gripes about business and prices are quite regular, but one story takes these themes to the limit.

It goes like this: A man, Ron DeRocher, and his daughter were lunching at a Neiman-Marcus store in Dallas. They were happy with their meal and decided to top it with dessert. The waitress brought out Neiman-Marcus chocolate chip cookies which Ron and his daughter thought were excellent. He was so struck by their taste that he asked the waitress for the recipe. He was rather rudely refused, so he offered to buy the recipe. The waitress greeted this suggestion much more warmly (the miracle of the dollar!) and named the price at "two-fifty." The man accepted and asked the waitress to add the recipe onto his meal bill. Ron and his daughter finished up their luncheon, collected the new treasure, went home, and thought little of the episode until about a month later.

The shock arrived with his Neiman-Marcus monthly statement. Instead of the two dollars and fifty cents which he expected to be charged for the recipe, he was billed a whopping $250. The disgruntled cookie connoisseur called Neiman-Marcus to rectify the situation, believing that $250 was a ridiculous figure for cookies, even Neiman-Marcus cookies. The world of big business as played by Neiman-Marcus refused the man's request and claimed that it was a done deal.

Ron was not, however, a passive man. Rather than accept being a small fish in the ocean of big business and big money, he decided to fight back. He used an item as characteristic of modern life as overpricing — modern technology. He logged on to a computer bulletin board, which is a hi-tech method of sharing information and insights. Ron shared his valuable Neiman-Marcus chocolate chip cookie recipe with all of the bulletin board's users, for free.

This tale is not only believable, but also laudable. Ron manages to get revenge on the corporation that tries to rip him off. The problem is the tale isn't true. Neiman-Marcus can't understand its association with the story, since it's willing to share any of its recipes with customers at no charge. This story is traveling the country, and the name of the corporation changes with the territory. Several department stores as well as Mrs. Field's cookie company have been struck by the stinging story. The story will most likely continue to travel through the rumor mills as long as consumers are being overcharged.

Dead Cat Legends Have More Than Nine Lives

The death of a pet is a traumatic experience for a family, especially if the pet is well loved. The problem of disposing of the pet's corpse is also substantial — at least according to a popular story of a dead cat. The cat can't be flushed down the toilet, or tossed in the garbage. The solution may be to wrap up the once-loved pet, and arrange for its burial elsewhere. This solution can prove extremely difficult, if one is to believe tales.

An article appeared in the Bloomington, Indiana, *Daily Herald-Telephone*, on May 28, 1959, telling of a pet-disposal ordeal. The city of Bloomington had an ordinance against burying the bodies of pets within its confines, so a family that lost its pet decided to bury it out in the country. The woman of the house called a country friend and asked for her help. Her friend obliged, and they arranged to meet in a downtown department store.

On the day of the meeting, the catless woman decided to combine her trip with a little shopping. She packaged the dead cat in a brown paper bag, and went to a store. While doing her errands, she happened to lay the parcel on a counter. When she returned the bag was missing! The saleswoman told her that shoplifting had become a problem at the store, and there was not much to do. Confused, but relieved, the woman left the store. After all, her problem was solved. Outside the store, a large crowd had gathered. The woman made her way through it and saw a large woman unconscious on the ground. On top of her lay the carefully wrapped brown paper bag, with the head of the cat sticking out! The story was reported as true on the front page of the paper, but it is most likely just an urban legend. It bears many similarities to other stories and versions.

Another version was also published in a newspaper, the *San Francisco Chronicle*, in 1963. This one, however, was told as a legend and not a true story. This story also took place at a department store, where a store detective found the shoplifter in the bathroom. She has once again passed out, with the package on her lap. Stories featuring the cat problem also include versions in which the package is not stolen, but replaced with a different bag. Various stories have it become a ham, or a leg of mutton. Other stories appeared later. They tell of a woman who spots a cat who had been run over. She picks up the cat out of pity, and plans to bury it, but leaves it in her car while finishing shopping. She then sees a thief steal the package from the car, run away, and then open it and faint. This tale generally finishes with an ambulance that comes to rescue the fainted thief, and a kindly citizen who places the package in the ambulance with her. The thief just can't get rid of her loot.

The story has had a long life, also. Versions have been around since the early 1950s, and have been found in many cities, including London. Apparently the problem of dead pet disposal plagues the Western world. The woman shoplifter is a constant, as is her fainting. And what's the moral? Crime just doesn't pay, and dead cats don't go away.

Death Car Story Never Dies

Good deals, bargains, free stuff, getting something for nothing — these are all things we hope for. After all, if we don't have to work for it, why should we? A perfect example of this sentiment is the story of "the death car." A man in Los Angeles found an incredible sports car for a bargain price. The car was a Porsche Targa, and the going price was a paltry $500. He bought the car. But, of course, there is no such thing as a free lunch. The price turned out to be so drastically reduced because the car had been stranded in the Mojave Desert for a week, with a dead man rotting in it. The stench of decaying flesh could not be removed from the car, the story concludes.

Or . . . there's the story of the car dealer who specialized in repossessed cars. He had found a red Corvette with an interesting story. The past owner of the car had been murdered and hidden in the sports car's trunk. Then the car was given up for repossession. The dealer completely refurnished the car — new paint, new carpet in the trunk, the whole works. He sold the car easily, since it was still, after all, a red Corvette, but the buyer returned it in a week, saying there was a smell he just couldn't get rid off. The dealer sold the car to another buyer, and the same thing happened. In fact, the same thing kept happening. The dealer still has the car and the price is only $100, but he just can't get rid of it.

This story has been popular since the 1940s, in various versions. The car may be a Ford Thunderbird, an MG, or a 'Vette, but its price is always dirt cheap. The price has kept up with the times, though. That part of the story has varied with inflation. The car had sold for about $50 in the 1940s, up to about $500 in the 1960s and 1970s. Prices really aren't what they used to be — even in rumors. The story has not been steadily popular, but rather has had ups and downs. It gains popularity again when some young kid gets wind of the dirt cheap sports car.

The story has been traced back to the small black community of Mecosta, Michigan, in 1938. Here the story was a firsthand account of an event. A group of individuals known in the community had been involved in a suicide. The suicide was hidden for three months, and a unique 1929 Ford automobile was involved. This story may well have been the source of all the modern versions, yet although the story has true origins, most if not all of the versions are baseless rumors.

Still, the story tells well. After all, cars are among our most coveted possessions, and red sports cars are even higher on the list. To be able to get one for such a paltry sum would be great, maybe even worth the stench. Something for nothing — can't beat that! But alas, it is not true, and there is no such thing as a free lunch, nor a $500 Porsche Targa.

The Story's Tripe, but Sales Plummet

On January 2, 1987, two brothers and their wives sat down to a shared dinner in their home in Southern California. The fare was nothing elaborate, just a canned Mexican stew called menudo. The item, manufactured by Juanita's Foods, is ordinarily comprised of beef tripe in a hominy base. But the couples found an added ingredient in their can of menudo — a human finger with an attached fingernail. The dining companions did the reasonable thing: They threw away the rest of the stew. And they saved the finger to take to nearby Glendora Community Hospital for analysis. At the hospital, they say the pathologist identified the object as a finger. The family then went to report their finding to the police.

Then the shock waves and rumors were set in motion. The police did their duty — they took the item and delivered it to federal food inspectors for identification and investigation. The supermarket where the family purchased their dinner took all cans of menudo off their shelves. And the media got involved. A radio station announced that the menudo was being removed from grocery stores in the area because a human finger had been discovered in one can. A local paper wrote an article based on the police report saying that a finger had been found in menudo. The United Press International picked up the story and spread it all over the world. The story was sent to cities around the United States and in South America. And a local television station ran the story on its news complete with an interview with the family, and an assertion that the object was a human finger. All this had been accomplished before the three-day federal investigation was complete.

Then the results were released—investigators concluded that the "human finger" was actually a type of connective tissue found in tripe, the cow stomach that is menudo's main ingredient. The hospital that the family claimed positively identified the object as a finger denied ever making such a claim. Juanita's Foods held a press conference to announce that previous reports were wrong. The radio personality who had mentioned the incident told his listeners the results of the investigation. The television station that had run the story aired a correction in which the federal findings were reported, although this story ran during the late newscast.

This all may have been too little, too late: Juanita's Foods suffered great damage and losses from the rumor. Within a month of the rumor and its debunking, the company lost 50 to 80 percent of its menudo business in Southern California. Menudo was 80 percent of Juanita's Foods sales. As a result, the company expected to lose between $1 million and $3 million in sales for the year.

The company hired a "crisis consultation" firm to help manage the negative rumors. They also planned to spend a large portion of their advertising budget to counteract the story. Juanita's no doubt wishes that the family hadn't "lifted a finger" to help!

Rumors of a Claiborne Cult

In the field of fashion, word-of-mouth is considered the best kind of advertising among designers and manufacturers. But back in late 1990, officials at fashion plate Liz Claiborne's company were trying to stamp out whispers that the outfit was in cahoots with the devil: It was supposedly shelling out some of those natty profits to a satanic cult.

"Have you heard the rumor?" the *Chicago Tribune* quoted a major retailer complaining of the spate of consumers who had returned Claiborne clothes. "They say they heard Liz Claiborne was on the "Oprah Winfrey Show" and she said some of the company profits go to a satanic cult," explained the retailer, who asked not to be identified.

The rumor had begun popping up in different parts of the country though the publicly-held company was quick to deny the rumor, and to assure its shareholders and customers that Claiborne's sales of more than $1 billion a year had not been affected. Nevertheless, the rumor hung over the company's image. It became especially worrisome to retailers who were beginning to feel the pangs of a nervous economy.

Ironically, Liz Claiborne, already retired from the company she founded, had never even appeared on the Oprah show. How about the "Phil Donahue Show"? Yes, but that was in the early 1980s when she commentated a fashion show. The program had never been rebroadcast.

The company decided to combat the rumor mill with a one-on-one strategy rather than a corporate announcement. Claiborne's public relations manager had personally answered questions from the press and consumers. Sometimes there were five queries in a day; other times, none. What set the rumor off? Corporate officials had refused to speculate, noting only that Claiborne has a large and visible company.

"This is a very unfortunate situation," opined a publicist for the syndicated "Oprah Winfrey Show." "People call and literally say 'I saw her [Claiborne] on your show yesterday,' but it's just not possible. It just goes to show how damaging a rumor can be and how quickly it spreads."

Devilish Man in the Moon Haunts P&G

During the 1980s Procter & Gamble — maker of Ivory soap, Folger's coffee, and Crest toothpaste — the nation's biggest advertiser of consumer packaged goods, was besieged by rumors that its familiar moon-and-stars logo was a satanic symbol.

Procter & Gamble's trademark began around 1851, a time when most products didn't carry a visible brand name. A wharf hand had painted a crude cross hand on a box of P&G's Star brand candles. The symbol was more than mere decoration. It helped customers who couldn't read identify the company's brand on shipping crates. In time, the cross evolved into an encircled star, reflecting part of the rivermen's shipping sign language. Then that star multiplied into thirteen stars — representing the thirteen American colonies — enclosed in a crescent. Next came the Man in the Moon, a popular decorative fancy of the 1800s.

During the 1860s, in fact, P&G tried to eliminate the symbol from its trademark, but it was too late. Its customers apparently were already moonstruck. A down-river merchant rejected a shipment of Star Candles, chiding P&G in a letter for sending imitations. The moon was promptly back on products, and in 1882 a refined model of the "Moon and Stars" was registered in the U.S. Patent Office. By 1902 the trademark displayed some of the gingerbread frills typical of the turn of the century. Twenty years later the logo was streamlined with little fundamental change from the original design. Finally, in 1930, a sculptor was commissioned by P&G to design the authorized version of the moon and stars.

After years of deflecting the satanic rumors, the Cincinnati-based consumer giant made yet another logo change in 1991. The new design straightened out the curlicues in the man in the moon's beard. The change eliminated hairs that could be taken to resemble the number six. The sixes had fueled rumors that P&G supported Satan, because the number 666 is linked with the devil in the Book of Revelation in the Bible.

But it wasn't the beard that made boycotters in the South spread those Satanic rumors. It was the stars. If the logo's thirteen stars were connected, according to religious groups circulating boycott fliers, you would see 666. P&G insists it didn't cave in to the rumor. After all, the logo still displays the thirteen stars. And though the company's business cards and stationery continue to use the corporate symbol as a trademark, the company will use "Procter & Gamble" or "P&G" in a new script.

Five-Wheeled Car Eliminates
Bone-Shattering Vibrations

When Audi of America marketing director Tony Kirton began receiving information about a new five-wheeled car that was making a splash in Argentina and was getting ready to take the big plunge into the American market, he took the news of a new competitor quite seriously. After all, if Yugoslavia could crack the American nut with what many considered to be the sub-par Yugo, why couldn't Argentina become a player with a revolutionary five-wheel drive?

Kirton was far from alone in worrying about the effects of this new player in the import market. "We literally thought, 'not another [competitor] coming in,'" George Garbutt, vice president and general manager of Maserati Automobiles Inc., told the *Wall Street Journal.* Infiniti, the luxury car division of Japanese automobile giant Nissan, was likewise ready to protect its flank from any upstart South American competitor.

And why shouldn't these upscale car makers have been nervous? Industrialized South American nations such as Argentina already have car industries — though most plants are controlled by world manufacturers like Ford. It really wouldn't have been a huge step for an Argentine capitalist to create a car from existing components, add an extra wheel, and put the whole thing under a sleek new body.

For three consecutive days in late March of 1990, car company executives received Federal Express packages containing copies of ads for the Caballo XL. The text described how the Caballo XL, the "world's first and only five-wheel drive" car, "integrated the steering wheel to the seat," thus eliminating "all of the bone-shattering vibrations" that can rob drivers of control. The ads also included nature scenes, rather like Nissan Motor Company's Infiniti ads, and an illustration of an attractive red coupe.

Audi's Kirton told the *Journal*, "I looked at it and wondered if this [technology] really works." To find out, he sent copies of the ads to Audi's product planners for examination. Had he waited a couple of days, he might have saved himself the trouble.

Around April 1, letters from Hoffman York & Compton, a small Milwaukee advertising firm, began appearing on the desks of the fifty-six automobile executives who had received the Caballo promotional materials. These letters revealed that there was no Caballo XL and that the ads had been a promotional gimmick for Hoffman York & Compton, which had had difficulty in obtaining automobile accounts.

"Everybody is interested in what a competitor is doing," Tom Jordan, Hoffman York's creative director, told the *Journal*. "We figured that if we could convince real auto makers about the existence of a car they'd never heard of before, we might win some business."

Hoffman York & Compton was certainly successful in convincing people the Caballo XL existed. It remains to be seen if their hoax will win them some real automobile accounts.

Serial Killer Epidemic: Cured!

In this day of tabloid journalism and "reality" television, nothing makes better copy than a good string of unsolved murders, especially those perpetrated by an unknown assailant with a catchy nickname such as Son of Sam or the Zodiac Killer. Beginning in the early 1980s and for several years running, the airwaves and print media flooded the American public with shocking reports of an "epidemic" of serial killing in the United States.

With our broad, open spaces in which to lose oneself, with our easy access to guns and drugs, and with our lax social mores that promoted uninhibited sexuality, the U.S. seemed to have become the perfect spawning ground for nameless, faceless, murderers without a soul who drift from town to town, preying on society's outcasts and innocents.

The serial killer story began to take shape in the late '70s, with the mightily publicized Son of Sam and Atlanta child murders. These cases planted the idea of a serial killer epidemic. The true panic that ensued can be blamed on convicted murderer and arsonist Henry Lee Lucas, who in the fall of 1983 began confessing to law enforcement officials a larger and larger number of murders, eventually more than three hundred.

The cases subsequently evaporated, and only ten murders, then three, could be pinned on Lucas—who had enjoyed all the attention—but it was too late. The media avalanche had begun. The *New York Times* ran a front-page story in January 1984 officially proclaiming the epidemic. Serial killers, the *Times* article stated, may account for as many as 20 percent of all homicides in the United States—some four thousand a year.

The story went on to paint the now-familiar picture of the serial killer as aimless, psychotic drifter created by exposure to violent or sexually explicit material. Knowing a good story when they see one, the editors of magazines such as *Life* and *Newsweek* and the producers of network news magazines like "60 Minutes" all followed up with their own stories of the murder rampage sweeping the nation. Americans were finding serial killers under every bed. As final evidence of a true societal trend, the inevitable TV movies followed.

The truth is, no such epidemic existed. The most telling and widely repeated figure in the media coverage of the supposed epidemic was the figure of "as many as four thousand" serial murders a year in the United States. Where did that figure come from?

Although the number of murders in the U.S. has indeed escalated alarmingly, it's not to be blamed on an army of Ted Bundys and John Wayne Gacys. As Philip Jenkins of Penn State University pointed out in the *Criminal Justice Research Bulletin*, in 1982, the year before the "epidemic" began, there were twenty-three thousand murders in the United States, of which the Justice Department classified 4,118 as "motiveless" or "unsolved." By the mid-1980s when the spate of articles and television segments began to appear, that figure was estimated to have increased to five thousand. Experts would comment that "as many as two-thirds" of those unsolved cases may have been serial in nature. Others would simply state the four thousand or five thousand figure, leaving the reader or viewer to infer that *all* of those cases were serial murders.

In fact, a closer analysis, such as the one performed by Jenkins, reveals that the increase in "unsolved" murders that the Justice Department has reported is a product primarily of the reporting system itself. After a murder, the police are required to file a report to the Justice Department, which keeps data on crime in the U.S., within the first five days after the crime has become known. The report asks the police to identify the offender and the motive. At such an early stage, the police often know neither. Once a case is resolved, though — weeks or months later — it is up to the police department in question to file an updated report with the Justice Department. Some do; but given the amount of paperwork already burdening most big-city police departments, many follow-up reports are never filed. Thus many solved cases will remain "unsolved" in Justice Department data. Unless the perpetrator is discovered and identified immediately, the report of a murder's solution may well fall into bureaucratic limbo. In fact, the surprising thing as that so many cases *are* reported solved.

Cases where the suspect is immediately identified are preponderantly those in which the victim knew his or her assailant — a family member, friend, or lover. The percentage of such murders in this country has declined — from about 60 percent in 1976 to only 10 percent in 1986, but don't blame the serial killer. The evidence is overwhelming that the increase in murder by strangers is largely a product of the growing violence of the drug trade.

A 1983 Justice Department study identified thirty serial killers who had murdered at least six people from 1973 to 1983. As Jenkins reports, even if that number were larger, it is extremely rare, and in fact quite difficult, for a serial killer to commit more than six homicides in any particular year. That puts the number of Americans murdered by serial killers at between two hundred and three hundred per year at the most — shocking, but not an epidemic. Jenkins himself found only seventy-one cases between 1971 and 1987 in which a killer claimed six or more victims in separate episodes, accounting for between 950 and one thousand victims in all — or about fifty a year. Even if some cases have escaped attention, serial murderers account for at most two to three percent of the murders in the country, and more likely far fewer.

We've seen the ease with which rumors can take hold and spread throughout a community with little or no factual evidence to support them. Once a gruesome story strikes a receptive audience, it gets passed along—and often embellished—unquestioningly. Such is the case, on a much grander scale, with the purported serial killer epidemic of the mid-'80s. The story shows all the signs of a classic "panic" rumor, except in this instance the vehicle for the rumor was not the people of a small community passing along stories by word of mouth, but the vast network of communications that is the news media.

"Astronaut" Cons Yuppie Honey

Ann Sweeney was twenty-three. She graduated from the University of Rochester with an optical engineering degree and got a good job with Polaroid. All that was missing from her life was love, and that changed in a hurry.

In May of 1989, a retired Marine Corps colonel she knew introduced her to his son, a dashing ex-marine who had become a police detective in Cambridge, Massachusetts. The young man was so kind and considerate that Ann was swept off her feet. Within a few weeks, she felt she'd known him a lifetime. By August, they were married.

After a beautiful honeymoon they settled into a comfortable Medford, Massachusetts condominium. There Ann learned that her dream man was even more extraordinary than she had thought. He regaled her with stories of air combat above Libya. He took her to Annapolis, where he told her he had graduated first in his class. He took out his full-dress uniform—sword and all—and brought Ann to a Washington,

D.C. Marine Corps ball. One day he dug up an authentic space helmet with his name on it, and told her about the missions he had flown for NASA.

No expense was too great for him to please her. He flew her to Montreal in a private jet. They visited the Bahamas and Florida, and during a trip to Ireland, Dublin mayor Benjamin Briscoe awarded her wonderful husband honorary citizenship. All the while he told her how good it felt to love one person and how tired he was of the groupies who had followed him around when he was a pilot.

Then, less than six months after their marriage, a Massachusetts state trooper and a Medford police officer knocked on their door, and arrested Ann and her dream husband on charges of larceny and fraud.

Ann Sweeney would soon find out more about Robert Hunt. Among the allegations made against him were: He had never been a marine or attended Annapolis, he had no pilot's license, he wasn't a member of the Cambridge Police Department. Nor, it turned out, had Hunt paid for any of the couple's many trips. The tab for these lavish excursions had allegedly gone on Ann Sweeney's corporate credit card, or onto the credit cards of Hunt's previous wives.

"Twenty minutes after we got to the police station, the police explained everything they had found," Sweeney told *People*. "I was really in a state of shock. It was almost like watching somebody die. Here was this person I thought I knew, and bit by bit, in the course of an hour, he just dissolved, just disappeared. I loved the person I thought he was but that person never really existed."

The charges against Sweeney were dropped when police were convinced she had not been part of the alleged scam. But she lost her job all the same, and was allegedly saddled with $24,000 in American Express charges. Hunt for his part faced charges that could result in up to twenty years in prison.

SEX, LIES, AND . . .

Playboy Hoisted on Its Own Petard

Playboy magazine, from its off-the-cuff beginnings in the basement of an old building on the Near North Side of Chicago to its corporate offices in a Michigan Avenue skyscraper, has been the target of thousands of rumors. Most of them, of course, have been aimed at its founder, Hugh Hefner.

The longest-lived subject of rumor in *Playboy*'s history concerned the question, "What issue would the magazine confront reality and show *it* (female genitalia)? "Every month for years, eager readers would open the magazine to the centerfold, driven by a new rumor that this was the month. Then readers would race to the newsstands again the next month, spurred on by a fresh batch of rumors. When the magazine finally took what was a natural step forward to meet their readers' growing lust for knowledge, the more sophisticated among them gave the fold a glance and turned the page.

One spate of rumors, however, had nothing to do with the editors or the content of the magazine. It rose from a device planted in the 1960s on the cover of every issue by the marketing department — a series of little stars next to the "P" in the magazine's title.

Word had it that the stars represented how many times Hefner had bedded the Playmate of the Month. Hefner's daughter, Christie Hefner, now the chairman of Playboy Enterprises, figured in rumors, too — the stars were said to represent parental blessings upon predictable milestones in her life. Other rumors identified the stars as some sort of area code, or as the number of printings a given issue had gone through. In February 1972, the magazine finally put the speculation to rest in answer to a reader's query as follows:

> To paraphrase William Shakespeare, the clues to Hefner's personal life, dear reader, are not in our stars. Hence, these are not galactic goodies signifying some kind of droit du seigneur regarding the Playmate; they're identifications of our regional editions. All editions are, of course, identical in editorial matter, but each is distributed only in a specific area as a convenience to advertisers who wish to reach that area.

It then went on at length to list the twelve areas in the U.S. the magazine targets for its advertisers, but that has nothing to do with rumors or lies.

Royal Tattler Gets Tales Told

No move the Princess makes fails to attract the attention of the British scandal sheets. And early in 1992 the limelight migrated from the yellow sheets into books when a scandalous biography of Princess Diana appeared in the stalls and quickly crossed the Atlantic to the U.S..

Entitled *Diana in Private*, it purports to explore her sex life. She and Prince Charles were lovers before they were married, the book alleges. Further, it says that she became pregnant with her first child so she could get out of her royal duties, that she had sexual fun with a royal bodyguard who subsequently died in a traffic accident, and that she has had other private "confidantes," as has her husband.

But the British press takes its scandal and spicy scuttlebutt wherever it can get it, and in short order, newsmen were nearly as intrigued with the source of the new rumors as with the juicy allegations themselves. What was the background of "Lady Colin Campbell?" the royal poopsters wondered, and soon marveled at what they heard. Married briefly to Lord Colin Campbell, hence her title, Georgia Campbell, forty-two years old, boasted that she had moved in royal circles since she was twenty-two.

While Buckingham Palace dismissed *Diana In Private* as "a spurious mixture of rumors and unsubstantiated innuendo," the press got busy giving Campbell a dash of her own medicine. "And when exactly did you become a girl?" one journalist snipped at her during a press conference at London's Ritz Hotel.

"My dear," Campbell replied. "I absolutely never discuss it . . . I would end up stripping myself of all my dignity. Everyone knows I had a very odd upbringing." Parenthetically, Georgia's previous book was *How To Be A Modern Lady*.

Indeed she may have had an odd upbringing. Widely published reports have said that the Jamaican-born Campbell underwent a sex change operation as a young person, that she was christened George at birth, and spent the first eighteen years of her life as a boy. The dark-haired, exotic-looking woman subsequently denied the allegations and sued the publications that printed the bizarre story.

When questioned about her sources for *Diana in Private* and whether she knew the difference between gossip and fact, she replied testily that her job was to be "a conduit for accurate information. I leave speculation to the gutter press."

With that, she closed her press conference.

Safe Phone Sex Still a Little Scary

In these days of AIDS and the search for safe sex, where does a man go for a one-night stand that won't jeopardize his family, his offspring, and possibly his life?

Well, there are the porno shops and triple-X videos . . . or one could dial any of hundreds of advertised phone numbers and actually talk through the sex act with a honey-voiced lady who will variously describe herself as a "long-haired blonde," "sex-hungry brunette with long, warm, legs," or "a redhead filled with enough desire to set you on fire."

Often the lady spoken to is actually sitting in a room containing a battery of phones with several other women doing the same thing. It's a living, they say.

This was true for "Raven," a woman with a gift for gab and a silken voice that easily stoked the fantasies conjured up in her caller's heads. She said she had to feed her family.

"Raven" carried on over a Nevada romance line so well that she was considered a hit in the office. One man called her twenty-six times in one day. Three sent her love letters. Somebody in West Virginia asked her to marry him. But finally, in January 1992 after eight months on the job, she called it quits, stepped out of the phone room, and revealed herself to be Darryl Malone, a 165-pound National Guardsman and the father of four children, who planned to sue Northwest Nevada Telco for sex discrimination.

Because he is a man, he claims, he had been passed over for raises and promotions.

"You must be wondering how an ex-marine could talk sex to men," he said after his disclosure. "I had to feed my family. There was a point when I thought Raven was going to take over my life. After I hung up the phone, I had to take a shower because I felt so dirty." When his wife first suggested the idea, he thought, "Who would be better for the job, since a man knows what a man wants?" His clients, who weren't contacted for their reactions when the story broke, may agree.

Grand Jury Investigated

It started innocently enough, as such things go. Another credit union collapsed.

In Omaha, Nebraska in 1988 the Franklin Community Credit Union, headed by free-spending party-giver Lawrence E. King, Jr., went belly-up, with $34 million missing from its till. King was charged with forty counts of misusing credit union funds, given a competency hearing, and found sane. He was tried, convicted, and sent to prison for fifteen years.

In the meantime, rumors of child sexual abuse began swirling around town involving a publisher, a newspaper columnist, a police official, a judge, and a millionaire. And then an investigator for the Franklin committee was killed in a still-unexplained plane crash in Illinois during the credit-union investigation.

Often entertained by King, who had been a rising star in the Nebraska Republican Party, the publisher, the columnist, the police official, and the others were accused in the rumors of sexually abusing young people from Boys' Town, an Omaha institution for troubled boys. They were said to have transported the boys out of state, doped them up, and forced them to perform in pornographic movies.

Those rumors were further fueled by a memo to a local reporter from a former state senator naming the five "powerful and rich public personalities" as "central figures" in the credit union case. The memo charged that the state was afraid to prosecute.

But the county wasn't. In 1990 a county grand jury looked at the evidence and called the accusations "a carefully crafted hoax"; it slapped the wrist of the ex-senator, deciding that his memo was written "for personal political gain and possible revenge for past actions alleged against him."

The grand jury further concluded that a state investigator looking for a link between the porn rumors and the credit union fiasco was duped by an executive who had been fired from Boys' Town. Details remained murky.

Was it all a hoax or not? Can grand juries be believed? Can the rich and powerful commit mayhem and buy their way out? You bet they can, according to call-in polls of Omahans taken after the verdict by a TV and a radio station. TV viewers scorned the grand jury's report by ten to one; "incredulous," said 72 percent of the radio listeners.

Unsolved Hoax Links Elizabeth Taylor with Young Actor Julian Lee Hobbs

Tabloids regularly link Liz—the most beautiful woman in biker leather in the world—to gentlemen and other men she hasn't necessarily even laid eyes on. From sumo wrestlers to rock stars, nothing is too bizarre. In fact, there was a time when no issue of the *Weekly World News* was complete without a picture of Liz and that little space alien from *Close Encounters of the Third Kind*.

In contrast, conventional newspapers and wire services have infrequently printed unconfirmed rumors about Taylor's love life. One lapse occurred in June of 1990, when both the Associated Press and United Press International fell victim to an elaborate hoax and sent stories to hundreds of local newspapers linking Liz to Julian Lee Hobbs, an actor who was then twenty-three.

At the time, Taylor was in a Santa Monica hospital. Rumors connecting hospitalization, a biopsy, and a new love interest began popping up overseas. Foreign newspapers and news organizations began calling wire services in Los Angeles for confirmation. The wire services in turn called St. John's Hospital and Health Center in Santa Monica, but since Taylor had left instructions for the hospital not to divulge information, reporters called her longtime publicist Chen Sam. But it was Sunday, and Sam's office was closed. The wire services left messages with her answering service.

By posing as "Lisa," one of Sam's employees, the hoaxers gained a list of names, numbers, and messages from her service. A person who said she was Sam returned United Press International's call, and someone who said she was "Lisa Flowers" from Sam's agency called the Associated Press. Having the rumors confirmed by Taylor's publicist was enough. Both services sent out stories to member papers.

By Sunday evening AP was becoming suspicious and sent a note, called a "withhold," to members. UPI sent no such note. "We had no reason to doubt it," UPI bureau manager Robert A. Martin told *Editor and Publisher* magazine. "We called Chen Sam, and we thought she called us back."

As the story made newspapers, first overseas and then domestically, editors and eventually wire service officials began receiving angry phone calls from the real Chen Sam, who denied any link between Taylor and Hobbs. By Monday morning both wire services were running stories about the hoax.

Hobbs, who is also known as Rory Emerald, denied any involvement with the hoax in an interview with "Entertainment Tonight."

How Great Was She? . . . The Catherine Scandals

The scandals surrounding royal families are numerous and well-publicized. Modern-day stories generally involve illicit affairs or ill-mannered behavior. One royal figure from the past has been hounded by rumors of a much greater shock level. Catherine the Great of Russia has long been rumored to have had strange sexual preferences and behavior. The story is that she met her maker when her servants were lowering a horse on top of her for a most unorthodox ride, and that the horse dropped too quickly. Although widespread, this story is not true. Catherine the Great actually died from an attack of apoplexy while sitting on her commode, from which she died two days later, at age sixty-seven.

The stories probably started because of Catherine's behavior. She became Empress of Russia in 1762 after ousting her husband Peter III. Her husband died in prison, which left the Empress free to act however she wished. She had many lovers while she was reigning over Russia, but animals were not among them.

Her active sex life left the door open for French historians, who were decidedly anti-Russian, to fabricate stories of promiscuity and bestiality. The story of her death was one of many false tales.

One story maintained that she had all lovers tested for venereal disease before allowing them in her bed. Another tells of two ladies of the court who were used as testers to ensure that Catherine's prospective lovers were up to speed in their sexual prowess. French historians have also created a story which tells of saved silver horseshoes in the shape of hearts which were worn by Catherine's favorite horse.

Despite the lasting impact of these stories, they are false. Catherine may have had her share of lovers, but they were human, and they did not lead to her demise.

Gossip Hook Is the Only Hook

Teenagers have the ability not only to tell stories, but to spread them across the country. One story has been labeled "The Hook." It's known by adults who were teenagers in the 1950s and 1960s, and each knows the story as it was adapted to their hometown. Most would insist that the tale did happen in their hometown, not elsewhere.

A young couple, the story goes, pulled up an old lane in a wooded area—the favorite make-out spot in town. The boy tuned the car radio to some romantic, mood-setting music, and the couple got comfortable. Just then, an announcer's voice came over the radio. He said an escaped convict was roaming the area. The prisoner had served time for rape and robbery, and had a hook in place of his right hand. The couple got frightened and sped away—just in case. When they arrived at the girl's home, the boy walked around to her door to open it, and found a hook on the door handle. The convict obviously had been about to open the car door when the boy sped off—the result was that the convict had lost his hook to the car.

Variations on the theme include detailed descriptions of the make-out site—usually depending on where the teller comes from. Other changes might be that the escaped man was from an insane asylum, not a prison, and that only the girl was scared, and she begged her partner to take her home. In this last revision, the boy gets angry and speeds off, tearing off the man's hook hand. Versions of this story have scared teenagers from Maryland, Wisconsin, Indiana, Illinois, Kansas, Texas, Arkansas, Oregon, and Canada. The first version mentioned here was in a letter written to Dear Abby, and published in that column on November 8, 1960. The point of the letter and story, written by a teenage girl, was to warn other teenagers not to park and make out. By that time, the story was well known by teenagers around the country.

The story, of course, is not true. It is much too similar to a horror movie to resemble reality. Also, the story relies on too-perfect timing. How is it that an escaped convict would appear just as the announcement of his existence aired on the radio? How is it that the boy drove off at the exact instant the hookman tried to open the door?

Why did the creepy tale catch on among teenagers? Because the story relates to teenagers and the things they do, namely making out in parked cars. The possibility of the hook story being true is interesting enough to teenagers to tell other teenagers — and so the cycle goes.

One interesting interpretation of the story gives it a Freudian twist. The hook is taken to be a phallic symbol that manages to make contact with the girl's door, but is torn off when she becomes afraid. In the context of the story itself — a car parked in the lonely dark for sexual reasons — it may be that the girl is afraid of an overly zealous date.

Whatever hidden meaning the story may have, some things remain clear. It is clear that teenagers continued to spread the story because it related to them and was interesting enough to scare them. It's also clear that if a parent had started this rumor, it was the best way to make sure their kids weren't doing anything they didn't want them to!

Another Royal Rumor

In the summer of 1990, perspicacious paparazzi caught British Princess Di planting a peck on the cheek of her hunky Italian chauffeur, who had been her "escort" on a Charlesless weekend romp through Venice. It was, for royal-watchers, perhaps the picture of the year, confirming as it did what many feel is Di's disloyalty, her penchant for Latin Lotharios at the expense of her husband and future king.

But the picture the camera-hounds haven't gotten yet, the one that would really set the tabloids screaming, is the one catching Charles' younger brother, Prince Edward, *in flagrante delicto* with *his* hunk.

If the notoriously nasty British tabloids are right, the only man Prince Charles should not fear his wife falling for is young Edward. "Royal observers say girlish Prince Edward is much closer to becoming a queen than future King of England," the *Sun* recently reported. Citing "insiders" — those steadfast sources that pump the rumor mill surrounding high-profile people — the papers reported that Edward's supposed link with a Brit bombshell, actress Ruthie Henshall, was a mere smoke screen to cover an affair with an actor friend who was appearing in a London stage hit for which Edward helped out behind the scenes.

"I'm not gay," the Prince responded bluntly, in a breech of royal etiquette that shocked his fellow first-estaters almost as much as Di's Venetian indiscretions.

TRUE BELIEVERS

——————————

Sales of Entenmann's Cakes Fall After Rumor Links Company with Unification Church

In 1981 a bewildered Entenmann's delivery man was assaulted by an angry Connecticut opponent of Reverend Sun Myung Moon's Unification Church. This was the culmination of mysterious rumors that the "Moonies" owned Entenmann's. The rumors began appearing in Nassau County, Long Island, in the late 1970s soon after the conglomerate Warner Lambert bought the old-line purveyor of baked goods, which itself had been in existence since before the turn of the century.

"Two years ago we heard a rumor that the Unification Church had bought the bakery and we all laughed," company chairman Robert Entenmann told the *Boston Globe* in November of 1981. The joke ceased to be funny, however, as sales dropped and opponents of the Unification Church began harassing truck drivers and sales representatives.

Spurred by a spoof on "Saturday Night Live," the rumor spread as far west as Chicago and reached its most virulent state in New England, where anxiety about the church's tactics reached its highest pitch.

Moon, a Korean minister with messianic tendencies, inspired a great deal of fear in the Northeast. He came to the United States in the early 1970s and made much of a meeting with President Nixon and a mass wedding he performed in New York's Madison Square Garden. As time passed however, he gained a reputation for converting mixed-up kids, getting them to sign away their possessions, and sending them out on the street to sell flowers. Critics claimed he used mind control techniques and that "deprogramming" methods were necessary to reclaim children from the Unification Church.

To combat the rumor, Entenmann's began printing the Warner Lambert logo on its boxes. It sent letters to fifteen hundred church groups in New England and held a news conference in Boston, where Robert Entenmann said, "Our reputation has spread by word of mouth, and now the rumor has spread the same way we advertise our cakes."

According to the *Globe*, Joy Irvine, director of public affairs for the Unification Church, denied any relationship between the Church and the bakery but said negative attitudes toward the church represented "the same kind of bigoted stereotypes that Catholics encountered when they came to Boston." Asked if the rumor had hurt the church she said, "No way. Their food's great."

As of the early 1990s, the Unification Church was still very much in existence, though Moon himself was sent to jail for tax evasion.

Rumor Claims Satanists Will Kill Prom Goers

Toward the end of May 1987, students at Panther Valley High School in Lansford, Pennsylvania, began hearing that a satanic cult was planning a violent disruption of their school's upcoming prom. According to the journal *Western Folklore*, one form of this story held that among the first six people to enter the prom, three would be murdered and three would commit suicide. Other forms of the story claimed the first four entrants would die or that the first five to leave would die. Some students heard that girls wearing pink would be killed or that satanists would open fire during the dance of the king and queen. Others rumors claimed that refreshments would be laced with drugs or that the prom would erupt in an orgy of stabbing and shooting.

Echoes of these stories spread to nearby McAdoo, Lansdale, Lehighton, and Jim Thorpe high schools, while on the day of Hazleton High School's prom, similar stories erupted there. Students even claimed they had heard stories of animal sacrifice in the Conyngham Valley, where Hafey High School's prom had been conducted.

Given the dire nature of these rumors and the many frantic phone calls they prompted from concerned parents, it is surprising that students attended the proms at all. The Panther Valley principal, Phillip Rader, defused the situation in cooperation with state officials, by holding conferences to assure press and public that fears were unfounded.

But Rader took no chances: He had metal detectors installed at the door of the banquet room where the prom was held, and undercover agents mingled with students, while state police cruised the roads outside. No incidents were recorded at Panther Valley or any of the other schools where the rumor had become a point of controversy.

According Bill Ellis, writing in *Western Folklore*, there is a growing network of police officials who specialize in detecting "satanic" involvement in rural communities and who, through newsletters and personal communications, encourage law enforcement agencies and other community officials to interpret innocent rumors and events in terms of dangerous cults.

FCC Petitioned in the Most Unholy Way

In 1975, the Federal Communications Commission (FCC) received a petition asking it to cease granting religious organizations new licenses for noncommercial television and radio stations. Since granting such a petition would infringe upon freedoms of religion and expression, FCC governors dismissed the petition on August 1, 1975.

The story of the petition was picked up and passed along by a network of ministers and church papers, which neglected to mention that the FCC had dismissed the petition. As the story traveled, it became more exaggerated and extreme. By autumn of 1975, church activists around the country were warning that a massive response was the only way to prevent the FCC from granting atheist Madalyn Murray O'Hair's petition to ban all religious broadcasting.

Ms. O'Hair had never had anything to do with the petition, but whoever attached her name to the story knew how to give a rumor instant credibility. O'Hair had often brought suit on issues of church and state separation, and was well-known in religious circles. She was widely believed to be capable of making such a petition, and many people feared she had the influence to make it stick. Some of the more extreme religious elements viewed her as the handmaiden of the devil and believed that her petition was one of the first steps in the final, apocalyptic struggle between good and evil.

Stories about the rumor's falsity appeared in *TV Guide* and in national newspapers, and in the national religious press as well. Nevertheless, ministers and church bulletins continued to repeat the rumor and to urge their congregations to write letters of protest to the FCC. Hundreds, then thousands, of letters began arriving at the FCC every day, coming from every American region and denomination. By the first half of 1979 concerned Christians were sending the commission more than fifteen thousand letters each day.

National leaders began to worry that the rumor could cripple the FCC's credibility. In mid-1979, President Carter signed into law a bill that gave the FCC a quarter of a million dollars to combat the rumor. The FCC sent thirty thousand explanatory letters to clergy, churches, and religious organizations. Remaining moneys paid for extra staff personnel to answer individual letters.

The tactic seemed to work, though not completely. Daily letters fell to 361 a day in September of 1979, rose to 534 in October, went down to 392 in November, and then rose to more than one thousand in December. In early 1980, the commission was still getting three to four hundred letters a day. Denominational and regular news services exaggerated when they reported that the tide of letters was reduced to a trickle. If the commission had been getting that many letters on any other subject, it would have been called a "major response." Pundits were quick to point out that rumors about the death of the rumor were greatly exaggerated.

Town Bids for Soul of Con Man and Loses

Difficult as it is to believe, residents of the town of Newick, England, of their own free will, gave a stranger $324,000 to fight his self-declared satanic impulses, unquestioningly supplied the man with money and resources (including a $55,000 Rolls-Royce Camargue) to penetrate and dismantle England's satanic underground, and continued to press packages of money into his hands, even as he laid out $4,500 for a champagne drinking cruise up the River Thames with one hundred associates.

In the countryside south of London, John Baker, vicar of the Church of St. Mary, threw his entire town's resources behind Derry Mainwaring Knight, an alleged con man and convicted felon who had concocted a story about satanic possession.

Though Baker believed Knight, Knight could not believe Baker. "Every time I told him about a debt, he got money," Knight told *People*. "We talked about witchcraft and satanism because he was interested in that sort of thing. It got out of hand. I tried to back out, but he just would not let me. He and his group had this fixation about destroying the devil's organization, and no matter what you said, they just did not listen. Every time I saw him, he kept giving me brown paper parcels of money," Knight said.

Knight first appeared in Newick in the mid-1980s, handing out Christian tracts. He began attending Baker's bible study class and soon confided in Baker that he was deeply in debt. An unhesitant Baker promised to help, and within twenty-four hours provided Knight with more than $5,000.

Sensing Baker's resources, Knight invented the story that bilked Baker and the town of $324,000. Knight told Baker that when he was eight his grandmother told him he was destined to lead a vast satanic movement. To help him communicate with the devil, he said, she had two platinum disks implanted in his head. According to Knight, he had struggled against satanic impulses all his life and now he needed money to fight satanic organizations in England.

Baker was again unhesitant. "I felt the Lord was asking me a question," he said later, "How much would it cost to redeem a man from the depths of hell?" Wealthy and powerful congregants were also ready to help. Susan Sainsbury, wife of supermarket magnate Tim Sainsbury, gave almost $120,000. Farmer Michael Warren contributed more than $83,000, and Lord Hampden, Anthony David Brand, bought a Rolls for Knight's personal use.

Where did the money go? Knight bought fancy cars and outfits to fit in with his "satanist friends." He bought satanist pendants, bracelets, and necklaces which he had local jewelers melt down for him. He even threw a golden scepter into the Thames.

The residents of Newick were more than willing to go on, but the Bishop of Chichester, Dr. Eric Kemp, got wind of Knight's activities and called the police. The police arrested Knight and a jury found him guilty of obtaining money by deception.

Though a judge eventually sentenced Knight to seven years in prison and a $75,000 fine in 1986, Baker still believes in what he and his congregants were doing. "If we had been allowed to succeed," he told *People*, "what we were doing would have dealt a body blow to satanism in this country."

Two-Toed Vampire Terrorizes City

When Teresita Beronqui showed off her foot, with its three missing toes, the people in a large barrio of Manila wondered whether she was the feared local vampire *manananggal* or its victim.

Many people in the Quezon City District believe in ghosts, faith healers, nymphs, and vampires. One of the vampires is the legendary long-tongued *manananggal*, a beast that can suck an unborn baby from a pregnant woman's womb. It can also cut its own body in two, with the top half flying off in search of babies. Legend says that the two parts of the body must be rejoined by daybreak.

"This is the first time in 50 years I heard that a *manananggal* lives in Manila," said Asuncion Albor. "They usually live in the provinces." Meaning, by provinces, any other of the seven hundred islands that make up the Philippines.

Among those who have seen the vampire is Quezon City resident Martina Santa Rosa, who said she had fought with it. "It was naked. It had long, scraggly hair, long arms, and sharp fangs," she said.

With that, up went the garlic on the walls of the houses and the painted crosses on the doors.

"If a woman is pregnant, it's best to put coal dust on her belly and to sleep with a bullet on a string around her neck or waist," Albor said.

Another resident, Elvira Militante, said, "My mother said she often saw my grandfather, Augusta, fly over the house as a *manananggal*. First he rubbed himself down with his magic oil. No woman goes out after dark in my village."

So, considering the temper of the area, it should come as no surprise that, after a number of local women suffered miscarriages, the woman with three toes missing became suspect. Alderman Alfonso Bernardo told the press, "We saw the *manananggal* fly from her house." The contention that it accually happened brought the Manila TV crews flying to the scene.

There the reporters found only Teresita Beronqui, pointing to her mangled foot and insisting that she was a victim of the vampire, and not the *manananggal* herself.

Manananggal experts among the villagers remained unconvinced. She obviously had changed back into human form in such a rush that she forgot her three toes, they said.

In Soweto, the Revolution Drifts, Morticians are Slaughtered

As in Salem, Massachusetts, in the late sixteenth century, so in Soweto, South Africa, in 1988. To those who believe that witches exist, and that it is their job to put an end to devil-driven shenanigans, the very word "witchcraft" drives some to commit mayhem.

In March of 1988, crowds of youths in Soweto burned hearses and killed five undertakers' employees after rumors surfaced that funeral homes were kidnapping children to use as witch-bait.

"All black undertakers are being attacked," said scared funeral director Daniel Kopane. Kopane lost a brother and a cousin when the rampaging youths burned one of his hearses and killed its three crew members in northern Soweto.

Another hearse belonging to a rival firm also was burned and its two occupants stabbed to death in the central area of the sprawling black township near Johannesburg, police reported.

Soweto residents who kept a distance from the disturbances told reporters that the youths used knives and stones to attack the hearses and the men inside. They burned the coffins in the hearses, the residents said, driven by rumors that undertakers were kidnapping Soweto children to use their bodies in witchcraft rituals.

Kopane saw a more sinister motive behind the rumors and the slayings. "It seems to me," he said, "that somebody is trying to destroy our black businesses. All black undertakers who are doing well are being attacked."

Groups of young leftist "comrades" were recruited to escort all his hearses, Kopane added. His firm was sympathetic to the leftist youth and their organization, the anti-apartheid United Democratic Front. In revolutionary times, when society's familiar structures are called into question, even seemingly outdated notions such as witchcraft can take root and flourish.

Has the Virgin Come to Quezon City?

Thousands of Filipinos swarmed around an urban house one day in February 1988 to watch the Virgin Mary, made patroness of the Philippines by the Spanish during their 350 years as colonial rulers, descend from heaven.

Just after 5 p.m. on February 2, some people in the frenzied crowd became transfixed, gaping at an olive tree in the front yard.

"The Virgin is here!" shouted a woman in the crowd, gazing skyward over the house, which sits between an Italian restaurant and a whorehouse in the Manila suburb of Quezon City. But most of the other worshipers agreed there was no virgin in the sky. Yet several thousand people did see quite a strange apparition — the afternoon sun danced and spun for several minutes.

Subsequently the city's daily newspapers filled with many more such sightings, and the city's entrepreneurs, ever on the lookout for more business, dreamed of Manila becoming another pilgrimage center such as Lourdes in France and Fatima in Portugal.

Cardinal Jaie Sin played down the sightings, and attributed the apparitions to hunger — 43 percent of the adult Filipino population is jobless. But the cardinal quietly ordered the Church's Permanent Committee on Extraordinary Visions and Phenomena to investigate.

The cardinal told reporters soon after the alleged miracle, "When you are hungry, you see visions. So my first advice is to eat. When you are not hungry anymore, you will not see visions." A church spokesman said about the investigation, "It will take a long time" to confirm or deny.

Amidst a gathering national hoopla, the church issued additional cautions in an official statement: "Irresponsible mongers of sensationalism are trying to focus public attention on fantasies that caricature the apocalypse with predictions of bloodshed, darkness, and other disasters. We warn the faithful against a thirst for an easy acceptance of visions and visionaries with a concomitant danger of paying a less-than-prudent credulity to strange pronouncements, threats, or promises. Ignore these rumors, and practice instead prayers and penance."

The statement concluded with thanks to the many scientists who had explained to reporters and the public at large that the "dancing sun" is a fairly common phenomenon, caused by cloud crystals interacting with air pollution.

But reporter Ike Gutierrez of the *Manila Bulletin* wrote in response to the cardinal's advice about eating, "When I craned my neck skyward I was neither hungry nor sick, and believe me, I did see the sun dance.

"I was not sure whether those with me had taken lunch or not. Most of them were ordinary people — government employees, taxi drivers, cigarette vendors — who do not eat lunch in a plush villa.

"When our stomachs are empty, not due to laziness but to the inequities and hypocrisies of our so-called Christian society, we lean on faith."

Over time, we tend to lean on evidence. A church spokesman, Father Socrates Villgas, acknowledged that "it will take a long time" to pass final judgment on the truth of the vision. He pointed out that "if it perseveres, it must really be from God." In this vein, he noted that four years passed after her apparition at Lourdes before the Blessed Virgin's appearance there became an official miracle. At Fatima, her appearances weren't accepted as genuine by the Vatican for twenty years. In the Philippines, many are watching and waiting.

"Medicine Woman" a Shaman or a Charlatan?

Lynn V. Andrews of Beverly Hills and New Mexico, author and horse breeder, has made a fortune relating her experiences in spiritual self-discovery through mystical aboriginal practices.

One of her five works, *Crystal Woman*, made the *New York Times* bestseller list. That volume and her other four, *Medicine Woman, Flight to the Seventh Moon, Jaguar Woman,* and *Star Women,* are frequently are stolen from library shelves and were "steady backlist sellers," according to a Canadian distributor — until 1988, when Andrews' books became engulfed in international controversy. Canadians and Australians charged that she wrote about customs and sexual ceremonies in their countries that simply do not happen.

In *Medicine Woman*, set in Canada's Manitoba province, she wrote of herself as "a bridge between the Indian world and the white world," and in one episode she claimed to have been told by Cree Indians to strip before a group of elders in a tepee. The practice is unheard of and offensive to Manitoba Indians.

Andrews also said in that book that she had been brought into a "Sisterhood of the Shields," a group representing "different indigenous cultures from around the world." She was brought into the sisterhood, she said, by two Manitoba Cree women named Agnes Whistling Elk and Ruby Plenty Chiefs. But according to Eva McKay, a Cree elder, "Plenty Chiefs is a name from Montana, and Whistling Elk is another American name."

Andrews turned her attention to Australian aborigines in her book *Crystal Woman: The Sisters of the Dreamtime*, and got into more trouble. Aborigines there joined Canadians in hectoring the author over such passages as this:

> Ginevee, Agnes, and I stood naked within a large circle of women. The women, girls, and children dipped their hands into a strong-smelling substance called bandicoot grease and quickly began to rub us all over with the stuff . . . they touched our breasts, our faces, our vaginas, our legs . . . In turn, we examined them with equal care . . . then we got up and touched our bellies, each in turn, to the bellies of every person in the village.

Andrews claimed the event happened, but she refused to say where except that it was in central Australia. She also would not divulge the names of her friends in the Sisterhood of the Shields.

Yami Lester, chairman of Australia's Pitjantjatjara Aborigine Council, said there is no record of Andrews' visit to his people's lands in central Australia and no one had any memory of her visit.

According to Australian immigration records, a Lynn Andrews entered the country on June 24, 1986, and left it on July 9 — a stay of only sixteen days.

The bandicoot? Lester said he had not seen one of the rat-like marsupials in thirty years. And Ginevee? He had never heard a name like that. All in all, he said he and other tribal elders found the whole book laughable. But the controversy hasn't stopped the prolific writer's production. Since then she's published *Windhorse Woman*, *The Women of Wyrrd*, and *Shakai*.

The Columbus Curse

The name Christopher Columbus is capable of generating quite a flap in the United States these days, but nothing to compare to the panic his name evokes in the Dominican Republic, on the island of Santo Domingo or Hispaniola. Dominicans agree — the name is a curse and to say it is to summon bad luck. They refer to Columbus when they must as the "Great Admiral."

Columbus spent much of his time in the New World on the island of Santo Domingo. During his stay, most native inhabitants were effectively enslaved, or killed. The islanders believe that the Columbus curse began during his lifetime, and persists on the island. Columbus's settlement known as La Navidad was ravaged and destroyed by Indians within a short time of its founding. Later, Columbus became involved in a dispute with Spanish colonists and was held captive in a dungeon called the Well of Sorrows, and returned to Spain in shame. He eventually died a penniless pauper in Spain.

The bad luck brought to the island by Columbus endured after his departure — Dominican and Haitian history is riddled with disaster. The Indian population of the island was wiped out in a generation by Spanish diseases and settlers. The capital of Santo Domingo had to be relocated after it was ravaged by ants. There have been centuries of civil wars, coups, foreign invasions, and tyrannical dictators.

Unfortunately, according to the islanders, the curse of Columbus did not end in history. Rather, it lives on in present Santo Domingo, ready to be summoned by any who speak the name of the Great Admiral. The people and scholars have observed the wrath of this curse. In 1937, a fund-raising project for a lighthouse named after Columbus included a fly-over of three planes named the Nina, the Pinta, and the Santa Maria. All three planes crashed and their pilots were killed. On August 4, 1946, Columbus's urn was opened at a ceremony celebrating the 450th anniversary of the city. At the same time an earthquake of record proportions struck the island, causing two towns to disappear into the sea. In a 1948 ceremony introducing the Columbus lighthouse, the official heading the project got his car crushed by a boulder. Yet more evidence of the curse involves an honor bestowed by the country, entitled the Order of Columbus. The medal itself pricked a 1940s recipient during his investiture ceremony, and resulted in his death from infection. Another of those honored was kidnapped and killed by leftist guerrillas after receiving the medal. An ambassador to the Dominican Republic has rejected the curse, but since he began writing a negative book about Columbus, he has suffered two accidents, many broken ribs, and a broken hip.

There are those who refuse to believe the legendary curse. The U.S. Ambassador spoke the dreaded name three times in a speech, causing many in his audience to protect themselves by knocking on wood. The most notable disbeliever is the president himself, Joaquin Balaguer, who has constructed a massive illuminated lighthouse and cross in honor of the Great Admiral.

Whether or not the story is true, many residents of the island would agree with German Ornes, a newspaper owner, who stated "I don't believe in the curse, but the best thing is not to defy it."

Philippine's Psychic Surgeons Above Board?

Hundreds, perhaps thousands, of Americans have gone to the Philippines to undergo psychic surgery. With the patient fully conscious, the practitioner opens and enters the patient's body using only his hands, and removes bloody tissue said to be causing the patient's problems. The skin is never cut and no scars are left, though the operation is usually a bloody business.

The comedian Andy Kaufman, who was diagnosed with terminal lung cancer in 1984, underwent this treatment, and was reported in the *National Enquirer* to have enthused upon his return, "The doctors don't know everything." On the other hand, he died a few weeks later.

According to another journal, the *Star*, Kaufman paid $25 for each operation, twice a day, at the hands of Ramon "Jun" Labo, one of about fifty such surgeons in the Philippine Islands. Kaufman's girlfriend, who was "not a foot away," made sure everything was above board. She went on, "We saw Jun cure a man with an eye problem. He actually removed the eye, and you could see the empty socket. And then he put the eye back in." Surgeons modestly riposte that this operation can be performed by anyone who can do card tricks.

These Philippine surgeons have received so much media play that, back in 1975, the Federal Trade Commission enjoined several California travel agencies from promoting Philippine tours for sick people. The FTC said "Because we are dealing here with desperate consumers with terminal illnesses who want to believe psychic surgery will cure them, no amount of disclosure will suffice to drive home to all the point that psychic surgery is nothing but a total hoax." As with the worthless wonder drug laetrile, which many terminal cancer patients went to Mexico to obtain in the 1970s, so with psychic surgery today: Expert discouragement doesn't discourage the desperate.

Russian Royal Family Is Gone but Not Forgotten

Ever since 1918 when the Bolsheviks executed Czar Nicholas II and his family, the mystery of Anastasia has lingered like a Siberian winter. Over the years, the daughter of Russia's last czar was said to have appeared in Berlin, America, and a half dozen other places, prompting one historian to characterize her as "Russia's equivalent of Elvis sightings." The "sightings" have included a play by Marcelle Maurette, the book *Anastasia: the Riddle of Anna Anderson* by Peter Kurth, the television mini-series *Anastasia: The Mystery of Anna*, adapted by James Goldman, and the motion picture *Anastasia*, written for the screen by playwright Arthur Laurents, based on Maurette's play. The movie won a best actress Oscar for Ingrid Bergman in the title role.

Still, no one knew for sure if there was a royal pretender still making her claims somewhere, or if the seventeen-year-old Anastasia had not miraculously escaped the fusillade of bullets that cut her family down late in the night, in the city of Yekaterinburg in the Ural Mountains, on July 17, 1918. In recent years a swarm of researchers, including historians, anthropologists, archaeologists, geneticists, and even dentists have swept over the tiny hamlet like a horde of Cossacks, looking for clues to bring back to life what happened on that fateful night.

According to historian Edvard Radzinsky, who spent twenty-five years researching *The Last Tsar*, the killers spent twenty minutes blasting away at the Romanovs. Strangely, the bullets seemed to ricochet off their bodies, so the victims were stabbed with bayonets to make sure the job was done. The Romanovs had died hard, the executioners discovered when removing the bodies, because the women had sewn diamonds, pearl necklaces, and gold coins into corsets and bras, creating a kind of bulletproof armor.

Were there any survivors? Could Anastasia have lived? Most investigators think it very unlikely—yet possible. In a grave unearthed in July 1991 in Yekaterinburg, archeologists found what they believed were the remains of Czar Nicholas II, his wife Alexandra, three of their four daughters, several servants, and the family doctor. Experts studied the bones with a computer to match skulls and teeth. The skeleton thought to be that of the czarina, Alexandra, was identified partly due to dental work— porcelain and platinum crowns—that wouldn't have been available to most Russians of the era. Their study identified the skeletons of the Czar Nicholas, his wife, their eldest children Olga, Maria and Tatyana, and their family doctor, Sergei Botkin.

But none of the skeletons was young enough to have been Anastasia, who was seventeen at the time of the assassination, nor of her brother Alexei, then thirteen. Did the brother and sister escape alive, as legend has it? The scientists speculate that their bodies were probably cremated. But a fire pit has yet to be found.

Some believe there is a suitcase somewhere packed with answers. This suitcase, said to have been smuggled to Europe by the White Army more than seventy years ago, is said to contain a trove of Romanov family data that includes x-rays, medical records, dental records, and other vital information.

Rumor has it that the suitcase is buried in a Russian emigre cemetery in Paris. Others stories put it in a church or museum in Brussels. The suitcase could even contain some remains of Alexei and Anastasia.

Meanwhile, using DNA sequencing to authenticate the remains found in Yekaterinburg, forensic experts were busy trying to identify the genetic pattern unique to members of a family—even for relatives of different generations. This is done by cross-checking samples of DNA from the old bones with the DNA of known descendants of the Romanov family who live in Great Britain and other countries. And so it goes for the graveyard sleuths who are trying to reconstruct a tale from the crypt that has haunted the world since the Russian monarchy was buried.

Puritan Vampires Discovered

Vampires in the twentieth century have been reduced to Halloween figures with black capes, bright red lips, and fanglike teeth. Some early Americans, however, counted them among their many difficulties—in addition to hostile natives, a harsh climate, rough new terrain . . . now vampires.

Vampire cults formed in several areas of New England, mainly in Connecticut and parts of Rhode Island. They were a reaction to the death and disease that plagued early settlers. People began to believe that the dead of the town became vampires who plagued the living and inflicted awful diseases upon them. Suspicion of vampire activity began in families that experienced the deaths of many of their young. The first dead relative, a defenseless scapegoat, would often be blamed for bringing the epidemic to its living family. Acting on this story, settlers would visit the cemetery, dig up the buried bodies, and mutilate them in order to rid the living of the curse of the dead. This practice was only recently unearthed.

In one instance, several members of the Ray family died in the six years between 1845 and 1851. In 1854, another member of the family fell ill. The family came to believe stories of their dead relatives becoming vicious vampires, and acted to protect their ailing kin. The family, its friends, and its neighbors unearthed the bodies of all dead relatives and burned them. The ill man was restored to health.

A public vampire exorcism was also employed in Manchester, Vermont, in 1793. A man there had had repeated bad luck with wives: Captain Isaac Burton married one woman in 1790, and she died of tuberculosis. He married another woman who also fell ill after the nuptial. Determined not to lose this wife too, the Captain planned to rid himself and his wife of their vampire relatives. A ceremony was held in which over one thousand people watched the body of the Captain's old wife dug up. Her organs were removed and burned. This didn't change the Captain's luck, however; his second wife also died.

In 1990, a graveyard was found in Connecticut where a gravel pit was being dug. Four boys found a family graveyard while playing in the site of the new pit. Archaeologists determined that the cemetery was that of the Walton family, who lived in the area until 1830. The Waltons arrived in the area in 1690 and farmed the land until moving on to more fertile ground. They then abandoned the cemetery. Archaeologists found twenty-nine bodies in the family lot, many of them children who had not survived the hardships of early America. The body of one male may have been the victim of the vampire scare. His body had been dug up ten years after his burial. His chest had been opened and his organs removed.

Scientists are now using modern-day DNA techniques to determine if the Walton male was the victim of a vampire scare.

Haunted House Drives Family Away

Tales of haunted houses are as old as houses and tale-tellers. Are these familiar stories of ghosts and poltergeists, creaks and bumps, and haunting homes only the fare of preteen slumber parties and Halloween? Do ghosts exist, and if so do they haunt the homes of humans? Most such tales are dismissed as the work of sensation-seeking spooks, but some people in Connecticut have been discussing the subject with utmost gravity. A family had a harrowing experience with their Connecticut house that can only be described as supernatural.

The Gerald Gooden family rented the newly renovated house in Bridgeport in 1986. The house was in good condition, spacious, and in an ideal location on Lindley Street. They realized just before moving in that the house had been a funeral home: It contained many remnants of the funeral days, such as crucifixes lying around a doorway, and a room full of leftover funeral paraphernalia. The parents got rid of the equipment before allowing their children to move in. This didn't stop their son from exclaiming that he wanted to leave the house because it was full of evil. Fear of the house spread to the other children in the family as well.

Then the family began to experience more than just negative feelings. The children claimed that three men appeared in their bedroom, and when the parents came to check they found physical evidence of visitors. What they were not able to discern, however, was the manner of entry to the house, as all entrances were locked. Mystery number one for rumor-lovers to ponder.

Then the odd experiences began. They heard strange noises. They experienced constant funeral music, a ringing phone, a door opening and closing. No explanation covered the extent of the occurrences. Mystery number two.

The experiences of a teenage niece convinced the couple definitively that something out of the ordinary was going on. The girl was found screaming in reaction to an invisible attack. The woman of the house suddenly saw a hazy figure — a disembodied hand — attacking the girl. Mystery number three.

The Goodens then took action against the forces of the house. They resorted to their religion for protection — first in reciting the rosary, then having Catholic masses held at the house. The couple also enlisted the aid of two professional supernatural investigators, Ed and Lorraine Warren who concluded that non-human forces were indeed plaguing the house. Finally, the couple held an exorcism of the house. The procedure was declared a success, but the family left the house within days.

They now live in another area and have no further problems with spirits. Subsequent tenants of the "haunted" house have had no problems. The former owners of the house deny that any mysterious events ever took place.

Fact or fiction? This can't be conclusively answered, but is it worth challenging the spirits on a guess? Isn't it worth whispering about, anyway?

KKK Kenya Mission a Hoax

The Ku Klux Klan, missionaries, and foreign governments — it sounds like the stuff of a spy thriller, but in 1987 a true saga featured them all, although this real-life drama had strongly fictional elements. The story is set in Kenya and involves American missionaries, especially one from Carrollton, Georgia.

In 1987, all three of Kenya's national newspapers ran the same front-page story, which sent the country into an uproar of fear and confusion. They alleged that missionaries from the

United States were there not to spread the word of God, but rather the word of destruction and racism. A letter was reproduced in the article that purported to be from the missionaries to the Ku Klux Klan. It requested $20 million dollars from the KKK to destroy the governments of Kenya, Tanzania, Zimbabwe, and Zambia. This would accord with the goals of the KKK, since these governments threatened white rule in South Africa.

The workers of the Lord were forthwith deported from Kenya due to their alleged collaboration with the KKK. Quite a legitimate reason, if the story were true. Did racists, bent on destroying the existing order of the country, really enter Kenya disguised as missionaries?

The United States government said no. The U.S. Embassy in Kenya said the letter was a forgery and claimed the whole setup was a malicious hoax. The FBI traced the letter back to David Kimweli of Carrollton, Georgia. The FBI asserted that Kimweli wrote the letter. There was a suspicion that he was angry at the missionairies for alleging that he defrauded them, which was his motive for writing the letter.

Kimweli had recruited some of the deported missionaries to Kenya, but when they arrived ready to serve, they were told by Kimweli that they did not have sponsor churches in the country. Some of these disgruntled missionaries went to the U.S. Embassy with their complaint. Soon it was discovered that back home Kimweli's had a prior history of inventing Kenyan churches: The Smoky Mountain Church of Sevierville, Tennessee, had taken action against Kimweli for raising money for non-existent churches.

Kimweli, not surprisingly, denied all allegations. First he claimed ignorance of the plight of the expelled missionaries. Then he claimed ignorance of the Ku Klux Klan. Finally, he told of his own good deeds. He said he had been raising money to help the people of Kenya and had already provided much clothing to the country; he maintained that he was not raising money to overthrow its leadership.

Raising money for missionary work abroad remains a popular gambit, unfortunately denigrating the difficult work of true missionaries and hurting the needy people who would benefit from charitable contributions.

Satanists in Media Soup, Stirred by Police

Sallie Breslin was walking her dog in a state park near her home in Allenstown, New Hampshire, when the dog ran off the trail. Sallie ran after him, but he soon returned with a treasure. It was a mutilated animal, a dead skinned beaver with its ribs sticking out. Unsure of what her dog had uncovered, Sally took it to the police.

Then an announcement went out — a satanic cult might be active at the Bear Brook State Park. Their activities might include sacrificing pets and wildlife. The police were flooded with responses to this announcement. It seemed everyone in town had witnessed some form of satanic cult activity, or could attribute their problems to it. There were many complaints of missing pets, and quite a few friends of teenagers called to report cult activity among teenagers.

Panic spread beyond Allenstown into the neighboring cities of Wolfeboro and Manchester. Police attributed a grave-robbing incident to cults in Wolfeboro. In Manchester, a panicked mayor tried to ban the rock group Metallica from performing because these type of groups "are into cults and satanic worship."

While the rumors and reports continued to spiral, the Allenstown police announced a new explanation for Sallie's dog's findings — trappers who are allowed to work in the park must have left behind the beaver. The police had explanations for the other incidents as well. And with that, the cult scare died down.

Tales of mutilated animals and devil worshipers have become common across the country. They are not just the fare of the paranoid: More and more police officers are trained to react to clues with the same first instinct — it must be satanists.

An example of this instinct happened in Scituate, Massachusetts. Police raided a World War II ammunition bunker in the woods of Wompatuck State Park on the suspicion that it was used by cultists. Inside they discovered an animal skull, daggers, candles, and a table. Nearby they found a group of teenagers wearing medieval garb. Had the police uncovered a dangerous satanic group and saved the community from its malevolent deeds? Actually, what the police interrupted was a group of diligent students. They had been working on an advertising layout for a class at Northeastern University.

It's unclear whether satanic cults are growing, or whether the public is just latching on to the idea of these cults. There have always been some satanists and some cult activity, but media reports and television talk shows have recently drawn attention to the idea.

Science Investigates the Shroud of Turin

Is it true or could it be a hoax? Did the Shroud of Turin in fact cover Christ? Were there practical hoaxers as long ago as the 1350s? Is it possible that in Turin, Italy, the French knight Geoffrey de Charny was running a religious scam of epic proportions?

When this medieval knight opened the doors of his newly built church in the Italian town of Turin, visitors were startled by the sight of a stained and seared sheet of linen. Even more shocking than the contrast of such a seemingly old cloth in such a new church, was the form, imprinted into the relic, of a bearded man wearing a cross of thorns, with puncture wounds in his wrists. The people believed this was the very shroud that for three days covered Christ after his crucifixion, and his visage had been scorched into the linen when he rose from the dead. While the Catholic church never definitively claimed the Shroud to have been the burial cloth of Christ, it became the best-known relic of Roman Catholicism.

In 1988, after decades of pressure on the Vatican from scientists who wished to run a carbon-14 analysis on the sacred linen and date it scientifically, the Vatican succumbed. Most of the Vatican's resistance stemmed from the fact that until 1986 it would have been impossible to calculate radioactive decay from anything smaller than a handkerchief-sized piece of the cloth, and to have validated the results, scientists needed at least three handkerchief-sized swatches of the Shroud of Turin.

But due to advances in technology, in 1986 it became possible to measure degrees of radioactive decay in swatches no larger than postage stamps, allowing the scientists to bring much more reasonable demands to the table when they began negotiations with the Vatican.

In April of 1988, the Vatican sent sets of identical samples to three different laboratories in Zurich, at Oxford, and at the University of Arizona. Once the studies were completed, before the results were even released, rumors began to buzz. In August of 1988, the *London Evening Standard* claimed that the tests showed the linen of the Shroud to have been woven around 1350. London's *Sunday Times* reported that "All three laboratories have independently placed the age of the linen in the same period of medieval history." The reports set the shroud's birth date more than a millennium too late to be Christ's burial cloth, and put an end to a belief six centuries old.

The Vatican still values the Shroud of Turin, if no longer as an archaeological relic, then as an artistic treasure, saying that the faithful will still venerate the cloth "just as they might a beautiful painting by Raphael."

Controversy Erupts Over Crying Icon

St. Irene Chrysovalantou Greek Orthodox Church in Astoria, Queens was swept by religious fervor when their missing icon was returned through the mail five days after it was stolen. The icon, a 6" x 8" painting on wood of St. Irene, the church's patron saint, was stolen at gunpoint—presumably for its gold-wrought and jeweled frame, which had been donated by parishioners and appraised at $800,000.

St. Irene is patroness of peace and the sick, but it seems she wasn't heisted for her healing powers; the painting itself was returned, the frame was not. Parishioners believe that in 1991 as the United States headed to war in the Persian Gulf, the image of St. Irene on the icon shed tears of grief, in addition to performing miracles of healing.

The return of the painting was met with thanksgiving. Parishioners offered jewelry, even their own wedding rings, to be used in replacing the missing frame. The church's leader, Bishop Vikentios of Avlon, promised special services to celebrate the icon's return every morning and every evening for forty days. Adding to the uproar inside the church, both New York City Mayor David Dinkins and the Speaker of the City Council, Peter Vallone, along with a hoard of reporters, attended the service.

Dinkins and Vallone were given reproductions of the icon. The icon was then carried by church officials outside and paraded through the rainy streets of Queens. While Mayor Dinkins' speech, in which he pledged the thieves would be brought to justice, was relatively short, not all of the on-lookers were pleased. As flashbulbs exploded and the hoopla rose to a crescendo, one woman snapped "This is a church!" The controversy did not end there.

The incident seems to have spawned an argument between the church and two Greek-language newspapers, *Proini* and the *National Herald*. Bishop Vikentios says the church will charge the papers with slander and defamation for articles that lead readers to believe the church was running a scam, and the theft was nothing more than a hoax. One of the articles published by the *National Herald* before the return of the icon said, according to a parish translator:

> The new episode of Chrysovalantou is being played successfully. Since the bells toll mournfully, the prayer services are followed by one after another. Candles are sold continuously. The atmosphere is electrified particularly now with the holiday season. The curiosity will be inflamed and the confusion will continue climbing its peak, until someone will 'dream' the discovery of the 'miraculous icon.'

The publisher of the *National Herald*, Antonio Diamataris, said: "We are expressing reservations. Did the icon cry? Frankly I have grave reservations. Was it stolen? Frankly I do not know. But I haven't accused anyone of any hoax."

What exactly the *National Herald* is accusing the church of seems to be lost in the translation.

TRICKS OF THE
POLITICAL TRADE

Trickster's Hoax Jams Dukakis' Line

Dirty tricks never die. They just get new phone numbers.

Governor Michael Dukakis rode the Massachusetts miracle to the top of the 1988 Democratic ticket where, as we all know, he was walloped by then Vice-President George Herbert Walker Bush. In late March of that year, when the outcome of the primary season was still in doubt, someone in the anti-Dukakis camp pulled a dirty trick that ground his campaign to a temporary stop and spread egg on the faces of the nation's top newspapers.

The hoax involved a simple help-wanted advertisement. The ad read: "Electricians and helpers. Commercial and residential wiring. Company benefits. For more information call (800) 872-6453." Unfortunately for Dukakis, the phone number listed was the toll-free number of his national campaign office in Boston, not the number of an electrical contractor.

The ad and several variants ran on March 30 in Honolulu, Los Angeles, San Francisco, Denver, Detroit, Houston, Chicago, Miami, and New York. In one instance an impostor placed an ad using the name of Dukakis' deceased father, Panos, for billing purposes.

Within hours of the ad's publication, phone calls inundated the Dukakis campaign's "1-800-USA-MIKE" line. Campaign staffers were stuck explaining to disappointed job seekers that no there were no wiring jobs available, that the whole thing was a cruel prank, and that they had reached the Dukakis presidential campaign, not an electrical contractor.

According to *Editor and Publisher* magazine, most of the newspapers killed the ads as soon as the hoax was discovered. *New York Times* spokesman Bill Adler told *E&P* that *Times* proofreaders "scan" classified ads for obvious irregularities but that "something very brief and innocuous like this is hard to spot." At the *San Francisco Examiner,* classified supervisor Tonia Bell traced the ad to a development company listed in Daly City, California. That company's phone number was found to be non-working.

As for the Dukakis campaign, it lost time and money to the prankster and his errant callers. Staffers had the number disconnected on April 8. Commenting on the incident, Dukakis spokesman Steven Akey was not amused. He told *E&P*, "It's really a lame joke at the expense of people who are out of work and looking at these ads."

As a dirty trick, the phony help wanted ads did not nearly reach the depths of cruelty or damage attained by Richard Nixon and his predecessors. Nevertheless, it was the kind of hoax that could temporarily demoralize and impart a sense of futility to a fledgling organization.

Photographer Gets Caught
Creating Crime Scene

It's true, no democratic society can long survive without a free press. But tricksters seem to have an equally sacred calling, regularly bursting the press's self-important bubbles.

Early in 1989, the Japanese tabloid *Asahi Shimbun* broke a story of corruption in then-Prime Minister Noburo Takeshita's inner circle. The story of the scandal was a coup that the newspaper rode to high circulation figures and milked for weeks. In May of 1989, the paper was hitting near-record circulation figures by making daily calls for Takeshita's resignation.

Takeshita was still in power when a nasty little scandal broke out on *Asahi Shimbun*'s own pages. Searching for a new crusade to keep its sales high, the paper printed a page-one article and photograph reporting that scuba divers had defaced an environmentally precious coral reef by carving the initials "KY" in the coral. The reef in question was at Iriomotejima Island, near Okinawa off the southern coast of Japan.

The reef story was designed to appeal to a cross section of environmentally aware and patriotic Japanese. Executives at the paper felt the defaced reef would stir a great deal of controversy. They were right, but not in the way they planned.

Unfortunately for the paper's editors, the photographer who brought the picture and the story to their attention had apparently defaced the reef himself—for reasons still obscure. The crime was detected by a local diver who wrote a letter to *Asahi Shimbun*'s editors accusing the photographer of lying. This led to an internal inquiry that ultimately resulted in the dismissal of the photographer and the demotion of two editors, including the photo editor. The repentant newspaper also printed two editorials apologizing for its behavior.

The incident damaged the paper's credibility with the public. But where it hurt the most was in *Asahi Shimbun*'s relations with right-wing politicians. The rightists surrounded *Asahi Shimbun*'s headquarters with thirty sound trucks, and for an entire day ridiculed the publication, denouncing it for hypocrisy and unethical behavior.

In the wake of these events the newspaper's president resigned, telling reporters the coral reef story involved "not merely false or excessive reporting, but an act to deceive our readers and society." In the past, the Japanese have been notably tolerant of dissembling from their institutions and elected officials. Government corruption and incidents like the coral-reef hoax have severely tested that tolerance. But perhaps the last word is that, the more things change, the more they stay the same. After the reef scandal, *Asahi Shimbun* continued its attacks on Takeshita, who ultimately stepped down in favor of Foreign Minister Sosuke Uno. Uno soon forced an unpopular tax hike through the legislature, and didn't last long either.

Iranian Prankster Leaves George Bush Hanging

So what if a prankster made George Bush look a little silly? At least Bush was willing to take a chance in order to free American hostages.

In March of 1990, a man claiming to be Iranian president Hashemi Rafsanjani called the White House. He said he wanted to talk with George Bush about the American hostages being held by pro-Iranian terrorists in southern Lebanon.

Some of these hostages had been in captivity for more than six years. Their presence in Lebanon was a lingering drain on the Bush presidency as well as on U.S. prestige around the world. Bush, aware that the United Nations was trying to free the hostages and conscious of the moral and political issues involved in the hostage situation, got on the horn and had a frank conversation with "Mr. Rafsanjani."

Unfortunately for Mr. Bush's dignity, the man on the phone was a prankster. The story made a brief splash in the papers and left the administration wiping egg off its collective face.

The real Rafsanjani had a great deal of fun with the situation. "Can it be," he said in his weekly speech, "that such a global power, with all its means, can talk to a person it cannot identify?" "America," he went on to say sarcastically, "is very much in need of talking to Iran, and praise be to God, is deprived of this. Iran is so important that the biggest power in the world, the biggest bully on earth, tries to contact its officials by telephone."

The White House, for its part, admitted the conversation between Bush and the man posing as Mr. Rafsanjani was "a little embarrassing." Spokesman Marlin Fitzwater explained that arrangements for the bogus phone call had all been made over the phone. "No one ever presented himself," Fitzwater told the press. "It was all done by phone. We did check it out a number of ways, including diplomatic. When the call came in, it was checked out appropriately, thoroughly, by all of our intelligence methods."

Though the entire sequence of events was bogus, Fitzwater claimed there were no regrets: "The president's feeling was: What if it's real? I want the American people to know and the families of the hostages to know that I am willing to check out every possibility."

As it turned out, the Iranian regime in cooperation with the United Nations was in the midst of orchestrating the release of the hostages. Within a year and a half, all the Americans and all the surviving English hostages would be free, and Rafsanjani would continue to straddle the line between fundamentalists who saw the West as devils and the Iranian economy's need for Western trade.

Third-World Rumor Mills: What's Up, Egypt?

Rumors spread quickly in illiterate and semiliterate societies. In Egypt, corruption, dizzying social change, religious hatred, and the threat of attacking enemies make even the most outrageous rumors seem possible. Despite having the freest press in the Arab world, the average Egyptian relies as much on word of mouth as he does on the often sensational reporting of the Cairo dailies.

In Egypt's poor southern province of El Minya, eighteen-year-old Ghada Ahmed Musa began telling a story about a lecherous Christian boy. According to the story, the boy blackmailed Muslim girls by luring them to an apartment where hidden video cameras filmed them in indecent postures. How the boy got the Muslim girls into his apartment and how he persuaded them to pose in indecent postures was not known.

The story was a complete fabrication by a good Muslim girl who had listened to too many episodes of a radio soap opera known as "Alarm Bells." Despite, or perhaps because of, its fantastic nature, the tale spread like wildfire. Sensing a story that would sell, the Egyptian press picked it up and average Egyptians, eager for clarity in a confusing world, began wondering how even a Christian could be so evil. Tensions between Muslims and Christians grew.

The rumor spilled from the realms of fantasy to fact in March of 1990, when a group of Muslim extremists, seeking revenge for the attack on Muslim womanhood, attacked property belonging to Coptic Christians, burning their churches, shops, and homes.

Ghada Ahmed Musa's tale of the evil Christian boy besetting the virtue of Muslim girls was only one of many sectarian rumors making the rounds in Egypt — another widely repeated story warned that Christians were using specially made American spray guns to mark Muslim clothing with indelible Christian crosses.

Among the darkest of rumors circulating through Cairo and the Egyptian countryside was a story that the Mossad, the Israeli intelligence agency, was smuggling prostitutes into the country to infect Egyptians with AIDS.

A comparatively innocuous rumor held that Egyptian President Hosni Mubarak, a man with a reputation for honesty, was enriching himself with a cut from every barrel of exported Egyptian oil. The rumor was ingeniously supported by attribution to a nonexistent report in the English newsweekly *The Economist*. Though flattering to *The Economist*, the rumor in a backhand way suggests why rumors run so rampant in Egypt: Citizens feel they can't trust Egypt's newspapers, and have to look elsewhere for the truth.

This Is a Test: The President's Dead

Teachers at Blalack Junior High School gave their students quite a shock one day in early October, 1991. Well-intentioned though their "experiment" was, the idea showed questionable judgment.

It all started in an eighth-grade class studying crowd manipulation and how people react to startling news. The example used was Orson Welles' 1939 radio play "War of the World's," which in breaking-news style told of Martians landing in New Jersey. At a time when the country was tiptoeing around in dread of marching into war with Germany, the broadcast sowed panic across the nation.

To further illustrate the lesson, teachers decided to stage their own crowd manipulation experiment and they took the idea to school principal Laura Folsom. The plan was to announce over the loudspeaker that President Bush had been assassinated. The rest of the faculty was alerted to expect something startling to happen that day.

The announcement was made, loud and clear. Four minutes later the students were told it was only a hoax.

But during those four minutes all hell broke loose throughout the school—dismay, bewilderment, tears, (some even laughed).

"I was shocked," student Chantelle Lindlief said. "I got tears in my eyes and everything. I couldn't believe it was happening." And neither could her mother, Boni Lindlief, who wanted to know why school officials would lie to their students while purporting to educate them.

Eighth-grader Shane Speakman said the announcement upset him so much "there were knots in my stomach." But while his parents, Larry and Becky Speakman, questioned the principal's judgment, Shane noticed some black humor in the incident. He said, "Some of them [his classmates] laughed and some were saying, 'Oh no, we're going to have Dan Quayle for president.'"

Her enthusiasm for the project quickly ebbing, Principal Folsom admitted that she had come up with the assassination idea. "I guess I'll have to take responsibility for that," she said. "Because of what the kids were doing, we wanted an announcement that would have a similar or same kind of reaction." Orson Welles must be proud.

$27 Million Bid for Lenin's Body Rejected

In Russian, his name was Vladimir Ilich Ulyanov. He was short, stocky, and bald at twenty-five. He had a large head, small, beady eyes, a high forehead, and a red beard.

Ulyanov loved to sharpen pencils. He loved to make long-distance phone calls and referred to the telephone as "she." He loved to ride bicycles. He hated newspaper photographs of himself.

He was one of the most written-about people in the world. During the last year of his life, Ulyanov spent most of his time picking mushrooms.

This is the man the world knew as Nikolai Lenin. Others of the seventy-five aliases he used during his lifetime included the initials "I," "L," and "S.T.A." He was born on May 4, 1870, and died on January 21, 1924, at the age of fifty-four. Lenin's body was embalmed and placed in Moscow's Red Square.

Sixty-seven years later, as the party he founded and the nation he led for five years was breaking up as a result of six decades of misguided leadership, a story appeared in "Forbes FYI," a supplement to *Forbes* magazine, that Soviet leaders wished to auction off the embalmed body for a minimum of $15 million. News organizations spread the story around the country and people with dead body hobbies lined up to snatch the prize.

After Peter Jennings reported the story on the "ABC Evening News," and the Soviet internal affairs minister promptly denounced it as a "brazen lie" and a "serious provocation," editor Christopher Buckley of "Forbes FYI" admitted to the press that the story was bogus. He just wanted, he said, to "test the limits of credulity" about events in the collapsing nation.

Peter Jennings of ABC apologized for being "gullible." The story was picked up by other news outlets too, including Tass and *USA Today*.

Andrei Chernenko, then head of the Russian Security Ministry's press office, shook his head in amazement as he told reporters that his office had received offers ranging from $1,000 to $27 million for the corpse of Vladimir Ilich Ulyanov.

"That type of joke has made several Western businessmen excited," Chernenko said. "But we would like to officially inform you that no government organization or institution have discussed the possibility of selling or moving Lenin."

Arabs Terrorize Romania

In Romania, rumors start and spread quickly across the hills and mountains to the 22 million Romanians who, until the ouster of the hated dictator Nicolae Ceausescu in December of 1989, hadn't enjoyed a free press in fifty years.

One rumor from the last months of his regime, that he had stashed away in a Swiss bank account $1 billion in cash and gold taken from the state treasury, seems likely to many observers. Another rumor, that snipers who terrorized the nation's major cities during Ceausescu's reign were hired terrorists from Libya, Iran, and the Palestine Liberation Organization, was believed to be true by Dr. Horia Georgescu of the Bucharest Emergency Hospital, who said his hospital held a dozen wounded terrorist suspects, all handcuffed to their beds.

As "proof" that the state security men were Arab terrorists, Dr. Georgescu said with a straight face, "Arab terrorists are known to wear a certain kind of black underwear. These men were wearing such underpants." During the anti-Ceausescu uprising, as is the norm in revolutionary upheavals, quite a few rumors were corroborated and acted upon with evidence just this compelling.

Another political rumor said that Elena Ceausescu, the dictator's wife, hung the corpse of a woman in the window of a Bucharest shop several years ago as a warning against abortion in a country that forbids abortion, in order to prop up birth rates in the exhausted population. No one had actually seen the corpse, but a friend or a distant relative was always said to have seen the gruesome sight.

Another rumor held that Ceausescu raised a specially trained army by touring Romania's orphanages and snatching young boys to be turned into robotic killers. Nobody in Romania was able to identify a single boy who was snatched from an orphanage, though the rumor persisted.

The rumor that sparked an explosion heard around the world surfaced in December 1989. It maintained that the dictator's secret police had killed more than four thousand antigovernment demonstrators in the town of Timisoara. This news led to a large demonstration four days later in Bucharest. Secret police fired on those demonstrators, an action that finally toppled Ceausescu the following day.

Western reporters who visited Timisoara several days after the demonstration found that a rather messy but not very large demonstration had occurred. A modicum of state-security violence had put down the demonstration handily. There was no evidence that four thousand people, or even forty—perhaps four—had been gunned down. But the rumor led directly to the huge Bucharest demonstrations that, just a few days later, toppled Ceausescu's regime.

Dukakis, Foe of Short Men

Massachusetts governor Michael S. Dukakis, the 1988 Democratic presidential candidate, is a short man, as presidential hopefuls go. At five-foot-eight, he stands about as high as the microphones he campaigned through.

So the nation had a laugh when the story was bruited through Republican circles that Dukakis had requested the U.S. Secret Service provide him with a broad spectrum of agents to protect him, including women, minorities, and "short men."

Robert Snow, a spokesman for the Secret Service, quickly scotched the demeaning rumor. He said a colleague had told him the same story, as a joke. Snow had been directly involved in meetings with the governor and his aides on the subject of protection, and he knew that no such request was made.

"He takes what he gets," Snow said sternly. "There is no selection . . . He requests protection. Period. [Protection] details are drawn from around the country. He gets what the mix of the crop is, and they get rotated every three weeks.

"His only request was that we respect as much as we can his private, personal time. We assured him we build our protection around lifestyle as much as we can . . . He wants to grow tomatoes, we'll try to be as accommodating as possible."

Dukakis' scheduler, Mindy Lubber, scoffed at the report. She said, "As for short men, I assume that's a joke . . .You know what Mike Dukakis would say if somebody recommended that to him? He'd think we were smoking something."

One Cuomo Rumor Shot Down

"Not me," said Jeremiah B. McKenna, veteran counsel to a Republican-controlled New York state senate committee, responding to charges that he supplied false information about Democratic Governor Mario Cuomo to a reporter. The charge was made by the reporter himself.

The flap occurred in December 1987, while Cuomo was being mentioned as a possible Democratic contender for the presidential nomination. The "false information" given to Nicholas Pileggi, who eventually wrote an article about it for *New York* magazine, was that Cuomo and his father-in-law had ties to the Mafia.

In the article, Pileggi gave as his source an unnamed "legislative aide." The *New York Post* later identified the aide as McKenna, and Pileggi confirmed that it was true.

Meanwhile, McKenna protested that he had only given Pileggi leads that turned out to be false. "He came to me," McKenna said, "looking for leads. I was not the source of the rumors. Someone else was," and McKenna was just innocently passing along scuttlebutt. He'd agreed to meet with Pileggi with the understanding that McKenna's committee was not to be mentioned, nor was he to be quoted without his permission.

Pileggi, a veteran investigative reporter, agreed to the deal. But when he found all the leads to be false he called McKenna and told him "none of the stuff is holding up. What are you going to do about it?"

"He just laughed," Pileggi said, "which struck me as not very responsible." Pileggi then wrote his article debunking the invidious rumors.

McKenna's boss, State Senator Christopher J. Mega, later wrote Cuomo a curious letter of quasi-apology, which McKenna blasted as "unnecessary."

Megas' letter, which apologized for nothing, said in part: "As one who shares your sense of outrage against any person or group that . . . spreads false rumors . . . I wish to join you in publicly condemning such tactics whenever and wherever they are practiced."

McCarthy Stages '50s Witch Hunts

One of the greatest rumor-mongers in American history scared congress, took on the army and the defense department, cowed Hollywood, and for four years conned the American public into believing his accusations. In those four years he never produced hard evidence that what he said was true.

His victims were legion. His triumphs were shallow, but left lifelong scars on the people he attacked and on the American soul. In the end, he lost a televised confrontation with a victim who wouldn't be intimidated, and he slipped into obscurity, then death at the age of forty-nine. The Wisconsin

Republican was described by Democrat Dean Acheson as "one of the most unlovely charactèrs in our history since Aaron Burr."

Joseph McCarthy's career as a Red-baiter started at a woman's Republican club meeting in Wheeling, West Virginia, when he waved some papers at the group while making a speech and said, "I have here in my hand a list of 205 — a list of names that were known to the Secretary of State as being members of the Communist Party and who nevertheless are still shaping the policies of the State Department." Within months, loyalty oaths were demanded of faculty at great universities, careers and lives were destroyed by whispers, and the twin scourges of paranoia and repression were unloosed across the nation.

McCarthy's wild attacks were finally exposed when he took on the army and defense department in five days of televised congressional hearings. His browbeating tactics, flimsy evidence, and perpetual sneer didn't hold up to scrutiny longer than a sound bite. The army's lawyer against McCarthy, a grandfatherly, pleasant man, shamed McCarthy's antics by simple contrast, and McCarthy's worshipful public quickly turned on him. Congress finally got the message and censured him in December of 1954.

Among McCarthy' misachievements: He was adept at scuttling the careers of political foes who opposed him, by accusing them of "protecting communists"; he effectively reversed the legal presumption of innocence with his insinuations and shouting; he snickered at President Eisenhower and smeared Adlai Stevenson; he played on the fear that gripped America when it was disclosed that Russia, too, now had the Bomb and that fear fueled the House Un-American Activities Committee during the years of hearings when blacklists were forged and the Puritan term "witch hunt" was resurrected.

"Joe wanted to win every battle," a survivor of the McCarthy era said, "and not six to nothing, but seventy-two to nothing."

He took his censure stoically, and promised to "get back to his real work of digging out communism in the U.S." Instead, he began drinking more and holding it less well. His health was failing, as was his heart for any more action. On May 2, 1957, he died of liver disease. His name lives on in the term McCarthyism, referring to his tactics of indiscriminate accusation and investigation, with no regard for truth going deeper than a headline.

Borneo Bogeyman Hunts Heads Too

In Borneo, the current Bogeyman has a local flavor all his own. A terrifying rumor recurrently sweeps the island, which resurrects the old, now disreputable custom of headhunting. But it gives the custom a contemporary twist.

The rumors center on the Sultan of Brunei, who reigns over a small, oil-rich enclave on the tip of Borneo, without great regard for the much poorer and larger nations of Malaysia and Indonesia that govern the rest of the island. It's been rumored lately that the Sultan fears his oil is running out, and on a fortune-teller's instruction, he's gathering the only talismans that will solve his problem: He needs human heads, according to the rumor, and lots of them.

The dull fact is that the Sultan has enough oil to pump for at least another generation. That might have quieted the rumors, at least for another season—if police hadn't found three decapitated bodies near the capital of Malaysian Borneo. Villagers began shuttering their houses at night, and pulling their children from school. The police, who said the headhunting rumors were ridiculous and that ordinary bandits had chopped off the heads to avert detection, were ignored.

So the chief of police got tough. He declared that rumormongers would be arrested under Malaysia's draconian Internal Security Act. He too was ignored. Soon, terrifying round objects were spotted floating in the seas off Borneo, and the terror continued even after the objects turned out to be coconuts. Finally, a police patrol came upon a roadblock in the jungle outside a town, where six men stood guard with homemade shotguns, blowguns, machetes, and a slingshot. The men explained that they were defending their village from a rumored fleet of Land Rovers, which supposedly were commissioned to collect hundreds of human heads for delivery to "a neighboring country." The men were arrested for rumor-mongering, and the public stopped ignoring the police.

But Borneo still had plenty of grist for the rumor-mill. Soon after the villagers were arrested, the Malaysian State Engineering Institution had to issue a statement to "reassure the general public that human heads have no bearing whatsoever on the strength of construction projects."

Tale of Two Sex Scandals

There's quite a difference between running for president and *being* president, as Bill Clinton will learn. Everyone knows that Clinton's presidential campaign was almost destroyed by a remarkably long-lived, breathless sex scandal revolving around a woman named Gennifer Flowers. But comparatively few followers of domestic affairs were aware that Clinton's opponent, then-President Bush, had also been dogged all through his years in and near the White House by a persistent, consistent rumor connecting him romantically to a woman named Jennifer Fitzgerald.

The Bush/Fitzgerald story broke out of the Washington gossip mill into print from time to time, but never into national media. In a book about a Washington lobbyist, *The Power House* by Susan B. Trento, an ambassador to the Geneva nuclear disarmament talks was quoted in a footnote as saying that he had arranged for Bush and Fitzgerald—who was a special protocol assistant in the State Department and frequently traveled abroad with the President's entourage—to stay together in a guest house when Bush visited the talks in 1984. At that time, Fitzgerald's duties included selecting appropriate gifts for Vice-President Bush to give the many dignitaries he met in the course of his duties.

In October of 1988 an alternative newspaper, *LA Weekly*, happened to titter in print about George's alleged Jennifer. Here is what happened next, as recapped by the London *Independent*: "Wall Street prices briefly plunged for fear that mainstream newspapers would pick up the story, destroy Mr. Bush's image as a family man, and dissolve his commanding lead . . . In the event, the story was reprinted abroad but ignored by the U.S. media services."

Bush, of course, went on to become president, and during the wind-up to his re-election campaign in 1992, he was asked directly by a CNN reporter about those persistent, long-standing rumors linking him with Jennifer Fitzgerald. "I'm not going to take any sleazy questions like that from CNN," Bush replied.

His press spokesman, Marlin Fitzwater, amplified the point. He shouted to the White House press corps that the CNN reporter "will never work around the White House again."

Any other questions?

Sununu Stung by Magazine

Spy magazine has a sharp sense of humor, and a perhaps correspondingly dull sense of ethics. But it's hard to concentrate on ethics while you're laughing, as all Washington did while reading *Spy*'s sting on John Sununu.

Sununu, George Bush's recently deposed chief of staff, was still in his office drawing a government salary for a time after he was effectively fired by the Bush administration, which was gearing up for Bush's re-election campaign. *Spy* publisher Gerald Taylor figured Sununu must be looking for work. The imaginary job he dangled in front of Sununu resulted in, not an offer, but an article entitled "John Sununu: What Color Is Your Parachute? An Exclusive Spy Prank on an Unemployed Despot."

Taylor posed as an executive headhunter for "a Fortune 200 company whose primary business is energy," and he got right to the brass tacks. "Now, I'm not negotiating here," Taylor said in *Spy*'s edited transcripts, "but the company anticipates offering a base salary in the high six figures with an incentive compensation package potentially equal to the base, so we're talking about low seven figures here as a total package. Does that sound competitive?"

Sununu replied, "Well, I can tell you that it enters the range. Most of what I've been putting together as packages start at three and a half million." As discussions continued, Taylor was understandably vague about the company he represented and its compensation package—he said he wouldn't name it "to protect the stock price." Sununu repeatedly protested against this coyness, saying "I really don't like negotiating in the abstract and talking in the abstract." He asked for confidentiality, and said he wouldn't like "people running around" suggesting "Sununu's looking for a job."

Then Sununu answered standard questions put to job applicants—which in this context got pretty hilarious: How would you rate your interpersonal skills? "Depends on how badly the other guy's screwing up," Sununu answered. Do you consider yourself a people person? "Yeah." How would you rate your organizational skills? "The federal government's been ticking quite well." What do your subordinates think of you as a boss? "Contrary to what the press has said, they'd say this is the smoothest-running White House they've ever had." Do you mind traveling? "No, no," Sununu replied, two weeks after he had been forced out of power for, most glaringly, using federal limousines and airplanes, and corporate jets, for personal business and pleasure.

Sununu cautioned that he wanted allowances for a six-month speaking tour that he said would earn him $2 million, but that otherwise he was ready to work. All in all, the *Spy* headhunting scam wasn't entirely a hoax: They got just the scalp they wanted.

Defense Secretary-Designate Disqualified by Innuendo

Senator John Tower of Texas didn't make many friends in the early 1980s, when he chaired the Armed Services Committee during Ronald Reagan's great defense build-up. Tower's high-handed ways came back to haunt him late in the decade. After an exceptionally nasty series of public hearings and document-leakings, the Senate narrowly rejected Tower's appointment as Defense Secretary under George Bush. As one senator said, Tower was "crippled beyond repair" by rumors of his drinking and womanizing.

The public, and no doubt many politicians, assumed that where there's smoke, there's fire. But in the several-thousand-page dossier compiled by FBI agents who assiduously solicited rumors and gossip about Tower, *not one charge* was substantiated. The FBI file was nonetheless leaked all over Capitol Hill, and from the Hill it passed straight into the pages of the daily press.

The newspapers neglected to explain the nature of the leaked FBI dossiers. Intelligence agencies collect *assertions*, not hard information. The former East German and Soviet peoples have learned to their horror what individual Americans, have confirmed through Freedom of Information Act perusal of CIA and FBI files: Informants for state security agencies can and do say anything about anybody, and whether or not the least jot or tittle is read, cared about, or confirmed, it goes into a file. But Tower's case was a little different. The FBI conducted its usual, thorough gossip sweep, and delivered its sweepings to the Capitol building's windowless, bug-proof, alarmed and guarded room S-407, which only senators can enter. From there, the leaks from the FBI report dribbled, then poured, through senators and their staffers, down upon the dizzy mass media, which was no doubt addled by all those fancy FBI seals and ribbons in which the muck was wrapped.

Even responsible media launched into an extended, exhilarating orgy of innuendo. The *Washington Post* alerted its readers that Tower might have endangered national security by carrying on "'a protracted relationship' with a Russian ballerina . . . The bureau has not yet confirmed any details." Indeed it didn't — ever contrary to the *Post's* standard practice.

Tower had many political and personal enemies — and rumors abounded about an angry ex-wife as well — so there was no end of muck to stir, and many personal as well as political motives for splattering the muck all over newspapers.

Ultimately, Senate Democrats found that confirming Tower would be too much of a risk. Citing his damaged reputation, they defeated his nomination fifty-three to forty-seven. The media, meanwhile, denounced the whispering campaign in editorial pieces, though it had itself helped spread the rumors in "news" columns.

Lincoln's Love Letters Prove
Too Good for This World

A far cry from the incisive words and the sonorous rhythms of the Gettysburg Address were these from Abraham Lincoln to

John Calhoun in 1848, about Ann Rutledge, his rumored sweetheart when both were in their early twenties: "Like a ray of sunshine and as brief—she flooded my life, and at times like today when I traverse past paths I see this picture before me—fever burning the light from her dear eyes, urging me to fight for the right."

Sounds like the last paragraph of a gothic novel, right?

In 1928 the normally reserved Boston magazine *Atlantic Monthly* published the first installment of a series of letters on "Lincoln the Lover," filled with such nineteenth-century goose grease as the specimen above. The editor who accepted these grotesque writings was Ellery Sedgwick, the Brahmin of Brahmins in the Boston literary world.

Sedgwick said he obtained the letters from Wilma Frances Minor, an attractive former actress and a columnist for the *San Diego Union*, who said she got them from her mother, who said she had gotten them from the attic.

Furthermore, Sedgwick said, experts had read the letters and found them "compelling." Lincoln's most famous biographer, Carl Sandburg, said "they seem entirely authentic—and precisely and wonderfully coordinate and chime with all else known of Lincoln." Muckraking journalist Ida M. Tarbell wrote Sedgwick," You have an amazing set of true Lincoln documents—the most extraordinary that have come to us in many, many years."

Sedgwick also cited the Reverend William E. Barton, who had written books on Lincoln, on the letters; he found them too pat to be credible. Then Barton met the attractive Minor and quickly wrote her a letter which should be in *his* collected letters some day. In it he invited her to visit him in Foxboro, Massachusetts, and "to come and sleep under the stars and see my Lincoln material and swim in my little lake. Tell your mother I made love to you and hope to do it again." His doubts about the correspondence vanished, and the *Atlantic* began publication.

A chorus of naysayers responded who definitely were no friends of Sedgwick's. One noted that the letters were signed "Abe" although he hated the nickname. Another pointed out that Lincoln, once a land surveyor, mentioned "Section 40" in a letter written before such sections were numbered higher than thirty-six. Still another said Lincoln referred to Kansas at a time when that region was commonly called "Indian country." The Reverend Barton nodded sadly. He wrote Minor while sitting under the stars by his little lake, "I have come to the conviction that the letters which you are sending to the *Atlantic* are not genuine. And, my dear, I am afraid you know it."

Minor did, sort of. She signed a statement saying her mother wrote the letters while in a trance. "The spirits of Ann and Abe," she explained, "were speaking through my mother to me, so that as a medium could hand in something worthwhile to the world." This unusual confession put an end to the matter, and the mother and daughter were not charged with any crime.

Psst! Did You Hear the One About President Jefferson?

People who found Bill Clinton's purported extramarital adventures to be of interest, and people who believed either that they were unproven, or that the stories weren't germane to his ability to govern need to realize that politicians have long clubbed their opponents with "character" issues.

Thomas Jefferson, the dashing red-headed author of the Declaration of Independence and the second president of the United States, took any number of hits that would have sunk a modern politician. As Ron Grossman of the *Chicago Tribune* summed it up: "Every school child learns that Thomas Jefferson was one our nation's Founding Fathers. His opponents attributed another fatherhood to Jefferson."

During Jefferson's campaign for a second term as president, opponents claimed that on returning to his plantation, Monticello, Jefferson sought refuge from the world's wearying ways in the arms of his house slave, Sally Hemmings.

The *Philadelphia Portfolio,* a leading newspaper of the day, turned the charge into a comical but damning mock-campaign song. Sung to the tune of "Yankee Doodle," the song's lyrics include this enthusiastic outburst:

> *When press'd by load of state affairs,*
>
> *I seek to sport and dally,*
>
> *The sweetest solace of my cares*
>
> *Is in the lap of Sally*

The *Portfolio*'s musical leap provoked a horde of imitations. Soon, what would be called an old-fashioned whispering campaign broke into a nationwide chorus of song.

Adultery wasn't the only rumor spread about Jefferson. During the campaign of 1800, his opposition combined two well-known observations about the man—his absence from public houses of worship and his familiarity with French literature and philosophy—and drew the "logical" conclusion that if elected he would repeat the excesses of the French Revolution.

This rumor was so successful that after Jefferson won his first term, pious women in Massachusetts hid their Bibles in wells, fearing that the new "infidel President" intended to confiscate the Good Book.

When the Jeffersonian reign of terror failed to materialize, opponents retwisted his fascination with things French into a charge of egg-headed intellectualism—similar to the charge leveled against Senator Adlai Stevenson when he ran for president in 1952 and 1956.

In his rendition of the *Philadelphia Portfolio*'s anti-Jefferson campaign song, thirteen-year-old William Cullen Bryant—who further distinguished himself as a leading American poet in years to come—combined the charges of adultery and eggheadism:

> *Go, scan, Philophist, thy Sally's charms*
> *And sink supinely in her sable arms;*
> *But quit to abler hands the helm of state . . .*

None of these attacks prevented Jefferson from reaching his political goals. Nevertheless, the tactic of spreading rumors about political opponents has remained a staple of our political system.

For what it's worth, books by the shelfload have been written on the nature of the clearly affectionate relationship between Jefferson and Hemmings—Jefferson gave Hemmings her freedom in his will. Later, one of their several reputed children gave a lengthy interview to an Ohio newspaper after the Civil War. While Jefferson's dalliances with Sally are accepted as fact by many historians, they are considered by others to be characteristically simple-minded political slanders.

Everything You Ever Wanted to Know About Marilyn, Somebody Knows

How did Marilyn Monroe really die? Why did she die? Over the past three decades since her death at thirty-six, the blond pop icon has stirred the imagination of conspiracy theorists the world over. Since her death on August 5, 1962, of a barbiturate overdose, more than fifty books have been written about her, dozens of documentaries have pieced her life together out of clips and sound bites, and countless newspaper and magazine articles have analyzed her mystique. The accounts of her demise, *Entertainment Weekly* observed in an article in 1992 titled "Some Like To Plot," rival "the most arabesque takes on the assassination of President Kennedy." The situation once prompted Johnny Carson to observe, "Next thing you know they'll be reporting Marilyn Monroe was the second gunman in Dallas." The particulars of Monroe's death offer a grab bag of conspiracy possibilities — a sort of cynics choice. Consider these theories:

(1) Marilyn, despondent over her fading movie career and failed marriages (to baseball Hall of Famer Joe Dimaggio and playwright Arthur Miller) killed herself on a fistful of barbiturates, according to Los Angeles County medical examiner Thomas Noguchi, county coroner Theodore J. Curphey and a suicide investigation team appointed by Curphey.

(2) To keep her from spilling some beans when she was dejected, Marilyn was somehow inadvertently overdosed, theorized Anthony Summers in his 1985 book, *Goddess: The Secret Lives of Marilyn Monroe*. To hush up her then-secret affairs with President Kennedy and his brother, a coverup followed involving Bobby Kennedy, his brother-in-law, actor Peter Lawford, and the FBI. All incriminating materials, including her diary, were taken from her home at the time of her supposed suicide.

(3) Fearing she would reveal their affair publicly, Bobby Kennedy, with the help of the "Communist Conspiracy," had Marilyn murdered. This according to *The Strange Death of Marilyn Monroe*, written in 1964 by ultra-right wing journalist Frank A. Capeli.

(4) To take revenge for exploding cigars, Mafia hoods, and other CIA assassination attempts against him, Fidel Castro had Marilyn murdered, hoping to pin it on Bobby Kennedy. This according to *Who Killed Marilyn*, written in 1976 by Tony Sciacca.

(5) The CIA and the Mob, with the help of Chicago boss Sam Giancana, who arranged for the hit men, had Marilyn murdered by inserting a lethal suppository into the already

drugged-out body of Monroe. This according to *Double Cross*, written in 1992 by the godson and brother of the elder Giancana, Sam and Chuck Giancana. The motive? Monroe was a CIA operative and had become a security risk, and the Mob wanted to frame then-Attorney General Bobby Kennedy in order to stop the Justice Department's attack on organized crime.

(6) Tormented by jealously, Marilyn's psychiatrist, Dr. Ralph Greenson, murdered her by a lethal injection administered to an already comatose Marilyn in the ambulance en route to the hospital. This according to *The Marilyn Files*, written in 1992 by Robert F. Slatzer. Greenson had died in 1979.

(7) After threatening to tell all, Marilyn was murdered by Bobby Kennedy and the FBI, according to *The Murder of Marilyn Monroe*, written in 1992 by a committee that included Leonore Canevari, Jeanette van Wyhe, Christian Dimas, and Rachel Dimas. How do they know? They interviewed Marilyn Monroe. Or, to be a little more precise, they interviewed her ghost. The authors claim to have talked to Marilyn, Peter Lawford, and others during seance sessions in 1990.

(8) Marilyn — after being kidnaped, drugged, and brainwashed by an Australian intelligence officer with the approval of JFK and RFK — is alive and living in Australia as the wife of a sheep rancher, according to a 1990 supermarket tabloid, the *Sun*.

Texas Widow Claims Husband Shot Kennedy

According to a story in the *Boston Globe*, anger, or perhaps greed for publishing rights, was motive enough for Texas housewife Geneva White Galle to blame John F. Kennedy's assassination on her dead spouse. In September of 1990 Galle hired private investigator Joe West and showed him a "diary" that implicated her late husband, former Dallas police officer Roscoe White, in the assassination of President Kennedy.

In the diary, Roscoe White supposedly confessed to participating in a Central Intelligence Agency plot to kill Kennedy, who was shot to death in Dallas on November 22, 1963. "They want me to kill the president," the diary read. "God help me. They say he's a threat to the United States."

The revelations contained in the White diary did not exactly make front-page news, since new hypotheses, if not explanations, for the Kennedy assassination turn up all the time. Moreover, the diary's believability was not helped by the fact that investigator West, who was dealing with the press, made public only parts of the diary. Meanwhile the former Mrs. White claimed she finally released the diary because she was dying and wanted "to use the few days she has left to let the truth be known."

Eventually, the family allowed former CIA agent John Stockwell — a man who has written extensively about the possibility that Kennedy was killed by a government-led conspiracy — to view the actual diary.

Stockwell was not impressed. "I believe," he told the *Globe*, "when analysis is done it will show this document is a fabrication — and one that's fairly easy to expose." Aside from the fact that most of the diary is written in felt tip pen, which was not available before 1971, the document also referred to the Watergate break-in almost a year before it happened.

Had the diary not been a hoax, it would have contained interesting revelations. It discussed White's relationship with Lee Harvey Oswald, whom he had purportedly known in the marines. It described a relationship with Oswald's murderer, Jack Ruby, and it disclosed a mafia gunman who, along with Oswald and Ruby, supposedly took part in the assassination.

While this particular diary was clearly a hoax, some doubts remain about the government's reaction to the diaries. In

August of 1990, a month before Joe West's news conference, White's son Ricky White held a press conference in Dallas where he told reporters his father's diary disclosed that he and another unnamed gunman, not Oswald, had shot Kennedy. The younger White went on to say that the diary mysteriously disappeared after a visit to his home by the FBI in 1988.

These news stories revived other conspiracy buffs, many of whom had fallen out of the convention and book-buying circuit by the end of the 1980s. A respected Cambridge, Massachusetts, writer, Carl Oglesby, author of *The Yankee and the Cowboy War*, was a founding member of the Assassination Information Bureau—which went belly-up with many other such organizations in the early 1990s—said, "When I first heard White's charges, I thought, great . . . His scenario fits with the body of the facts as we know them. But by the second day I'd decided that this was almost certainly a hoax."

Oglesby found implausible White's suggestion that the CIA's involvement in the assassination reached to the top and was not the work of a "rogue element" loose within the agency. Another problem he had with the story was Ricky's presentation of himself as a Texas good ol' boy, who was surely too dumb to have made the thing up.

On the other side, a group of seven Midland, Texas, businessmen are backing White. They have fronted him $100,000 to sell his story, from which they hope for a fat return from a book.

Hoaxer Tugs at Politicians' Heart Strings

In June of 1982, Secretary of Commerce Malcolm Baldrige, New York Senator Alfonse D'Amato, Delaware Governor Pierre Du Pont, South Carolina Senator Strom Thurmond, Georgia Representative Bo Ginn, and Secretary of Defense

Caspar Weinberger began receiving heartrending letters from, respectively, Malcolm Fox, Alfonse Fox, Pierre Fox, Strom Fox, Bo Fox, and Caspar Fox.

Young Master Fox, a nine-year-old San Franciscan, told of the traumas incurred by having the odd name he shared with the various pols he wrote to, and tugged harder at the politicians' heartstrings with mention of a recently deceased father. The boys asked for advice and earnestly begged for friendship from the busy political leaders.

Five of them sat down and wrote thoughtful personal responses. The sixth, New York Senator Alfonse D'Amato, went even further. He asked an aide to set up a phone call with Alfonse Fox. In the process of contacting the Fox family, the aide found there was no such boy — the letters were a hoax.

The leaders were not so much angry as they were disappointed and hurt at being fooled. One aide said, "Being hit in that soft spot kind of violates you." Defense Secretary Weinberger, whose letter to Caspar Fox had been printed in *People*, told that magazine, "I am very sorry to hear that there was no such small boy, but rather wish there were." Commerce Secretary Baldrige observed sincerely, "Nine or ninety, he sounded lonely and friendless."

Politicians are often characterized as people without feelings, but except for Weinberger (who allowed his letter to be printed by *People*), all of these men responded to the Fox letters in a private and sincere way. It is also noteworthy that the Fox "boy" was not a constituent or voter in any election that might have affected the careers of any of these figures. It's ironic that, in this instance where simple compassion motivated a politician's actions, the politician, and not his public, stood to be disillusioned by a cynical gesture.

The identity of the hoaxer has not been discovered.

Corruption from the Grave:
Marcos Is Dead, not Buried

Politics and rumors are ready bedfellows. After all, politicians are notorious both for shady dealings and mudslinging. The Philippines had a king-sized problem with rumors in 1987, after ousted president Ferdinand E. Marcos died.

Marcos died late in September, 1989, in exile in Hawaii. He had been exiled by Corazon Aquino, who displaced the corrupt leader. The issue was whether Marcos' body could be buried in his homeland. Aquino banned the entrance of the corpse into the country, because she felt that it had a "malignant power" that opponents to the existing government could exploit.

Followers of Marcos, however, were comparatively few, and many thought they posed little threat to the existing government. Filipinos began to call for Aquino to lift the ban since the corpse could not do any harm. They claimed it was wrong to deny him interment in his mother land. These sentiments sprouted rumors—a ninety-foot-high statue of Marcos was seen weeping, a huge black butterfly was seen above his old palace, and Marcos' body was said to have been shipped home disguised as cargo. All these phenomena pointed to the need for Aquino to lift the ban.

The Aquino party launched its own rumor of an intricate assassination plot by Marcos' followers. They said the assassins planned to use special mercury-tipped bullets that could kill merely by touching a victim. The gun could be hidden inside a briefcase for secrecy. Investigation of the plot showed that it was an unsubstantiated plot from months earlier.

How did Aquino decide to deal with the battle of the dead man? She decided to let the Supreme Court fight her deadly battles, after Marcos' lawyers petitioned to have the burial ban ended. At this writing, neither Marcos nor his exiled widow Imelda have been permitted to return home, though it looks more and more like just a matter of time. When Marcos' malign influence is satisfactorily dead and buried in the Philippines, he will be too.

Endangered Perks Worth Gossiping About

What images does the phrase "Capitol Hill" conjure up? Groups of hard working legislators and staff members ardently working to create the best America they possibly can? Or groups of treasure-seeking octopi snatching all the perquisites they can make off with? Although most Americans would prefer the former, evidence sometimes favors the latter. Bounced checks at the House bank, unpaid parking tickets, and scandal at the post office have not only offended the public, they have made the inhabitants of Capitol Hill downright paranoid about losing their precious perks.

The Senate store was a recent target of this sensitivity. It contains stationery items as well as luxury goods such as crystal vases and silver candlesticks. These items are sold at cost plus 5 percent, making the store a pleasant perk. Recently, rumors spread about the closing of the store. The closing was attributed to a cut down in perks in the wake of previous perk scandals.

Rumors of the closing of the Senate store sparked a flurry of activity of a magnitude seldom seen on Capitol Hill. Senate staff members stood in long lines at the store all day, grabbing luxury items with the fear that tomorrow would be too late. Shoppers searched the aisles for wedding gifts, birthday presents, joke gifts — anything to take advantage of the cut-rate prices. One senator, at the advice of his staffers, visited the store merely to watch the mania. He'd heard the scene described as "the last airlift out of Saigon."

The rumor, however, was unfounded. The store was not closing that day, or any other in the near future. The negative publicity about Congressional perks has been so strong that few doubt that the luxury items will soon be removed, and only necessary stationery items will remain. In the meantime, rumors suggesting the removal of such perks are bound to spark Capitol Hill into frenzied response.

Cabbage Address Too Wordy

In 1951, the *New England Homestead*, a provincial, semi-monthly Massachusetts farm journal, published an unsigned editorial criticizing the Office of Price Stabilization (OPS), a federal agency which then regulated the price and distribution of many key agricultural commodities. "The Gettysburg Address," the item read, "contains 266 words; the Ten Commandments, 297; the Declaration of Independence, 300. But a recent directive from the Office of Price Stabilization on the price of cabbage contains 26,911 words." Less than a month later, this wry observation surfaced again in the pages of the *New York Daily News*. These stories were remarkable on two counts. Not only was the reported wordage of the Declaration of Independence undercounted by more than 50 percent, but, more significantly, the word count for the OPS cabbage directive was incalculably flawed, in that no such document had ever existed.

Max Hall, the director of public information for the OPS, moved quickly to quell the rumor, reminding all and sundry that his organization was not, and had never been, in the cabbage pricing business; but the tall tale of bureaucratic puffery and overkill proved too amusing for most to discount. Within weeks, the item was picked up by the *Wall Street Journal*. From there, it made its way onto the NBC evening radio news. A few days later, Walter O'Keefe, the master of ceremonies of "Double or Nothing," a radio forerunner of "The $64,000 Question," incorporated the bogus data in a

"Grand Slam" question, paying $80 to the contestant who most closely guessed the length of the ghost edict.

Denunciations of the government's cabbage folly continued to appear regularly until 1960, despite the compelling fact that the OPS was dismantled in 1953. Even in this age of enlightened journalism, we may not be entirely clear of the specter: In 1977, inexplicably, the item appeared in an advertisement for the Mobil Corporation. It was promptly repeated by Walter Cronkite on the evening news.

Foley Smear Job Results in RNC Resignation

The summer of 1989 saw a rapid upsurge in talk about "ethics" on Capitol Hill, culminating in the resignation of Democratic speaker Jim Wright from the House of Representatives for alleged improprieties. His successor in the speaker's chair, Thomas Foley, however, subsequently became the subject of an insidious smear-job recalling the finest moments of the previous summer's high-minded presidential campaign — the one that made prison furloughs and flags the most important issues in the nation.

Shortly after Foley assumed the speakership, the Republican National Committee issued a memo titled "Tom Foley: Out of the Liberal Closet." The memo linked Foley's voting record to that of Massachusetts Representative Barney Frank, an admitted homosexual who had recently become embroiled in an ugly incident in which a male prostitute was accused of running a gay escort service out of Frank's Georgetown apartment.

The use of the phrase "out of the closet" and the comparison to Frank was seen widely in Washington as innuendo about Foley's sexual inclinations. Democrats, in an uproar, called for the resignation of Lee Atwater, Republican party chairman, saying they were tired of the "good cop/bad cop" routine wherein lower-level Republicans viciously attacked the Democrats, and President Bush chastised but did not stop them. Indeed, Bush termed the memo "disgusting," but stood by Atwater's claim that he had no prior knowledge of the memo. The RNC's communications director, Mark Goodin, did, however, resign over the flap.

In a strange twist, the *National Review* implied the real reason Goodin resigned was that Frank threatened to retaliate by exposing five Republican congressmen as homosexuals. In fact, the *Review* claimed, the rumor about Foley had been floating around Washington for several months and could be traced to Jim Wright's office around the time that Wright's speakership was in its final death throes.

INDEX

274

275